SECOND EDITION

The World Today

CURRENT PROBLEMS AND THEIR ORIGINS

Henry Brun
Principal (Ret.), John Jay High School
New York City

AMSCO SCHOOL PUBLICATIONS, INC.
315 Hudson Street / New York, N.Y. 10013

Revision by Norman Lunger

Cartoons by Randy Verougstraete
Maps by Ed Malsberg

When ordering this book, please specify:
either **R 631 P** or THE WORLD TODAY

ISBN 0-87720-897-2

Printed in the United States of America

2 3 4 5 6 7 8 9 10 00 99 98 97

PREFACE

This edition of *The World Today: Current Problems and Their Origins* provides information on issues, events, and topics not usually explored in standard textbooks. It will serve classroom needs by providing instructional material usually gleaned from a variety of periodicals. As a supplement to basal texts, it will facilitate enrichment of key topics by enabling students and teachers to examine these topics in the light of the most current information.

Rapid and dramatic changes have taken place in the world in the 1990s. This book deals with these changes, focusing upon their causes and immediate effects. Close attention is also given to historical background, providing a combination of readable, concise text and skill-building exercises.

The following features are included:

Comprehensive Coverage. Recent events and the world leaders associated with them are examined in several regions of the globe—Europe, Africa, Asia, the Middle East, and Latin America. A broad survey of global political developments is followed by analysis of the critical topics of international security, nuclear proliferation, and human rights. Significant attention is given to new patterns in world business and trade, including corporate enterprise and the ongoing technological revolution. Also examined are the innovations and trends which are propelling the world into the 21st century.

Unit and Chapter Overviews. Each unit and chapter begins with a brief overview that identifies the major developments to be treated.

Maps, Graphs, Charts, and Cartoons. Many maps appear in the text. They provide geographical references. Map exercises reinforce skills development, as do the graph and chart exercises. Students are given the opportunity to analyze and interpret data. Cartoons illustrate key developments and further stimulate critical thinking.

Exercises and Reviews. To enhance the usability of the book as an instructional tool, the text is supplemented by frequent, strategically placed questions and exercises. Additional reviews appear at the conclusion of each chapter and unit. These are designed to require a variety of response efforts—content and data search, reading for factual detail, and the skills of inference, critical thinking, and expository writing.

Reference Section. The index identifies topics of current importance.

Henry Brun

CONTENTS

MAPS AND GRAPHS

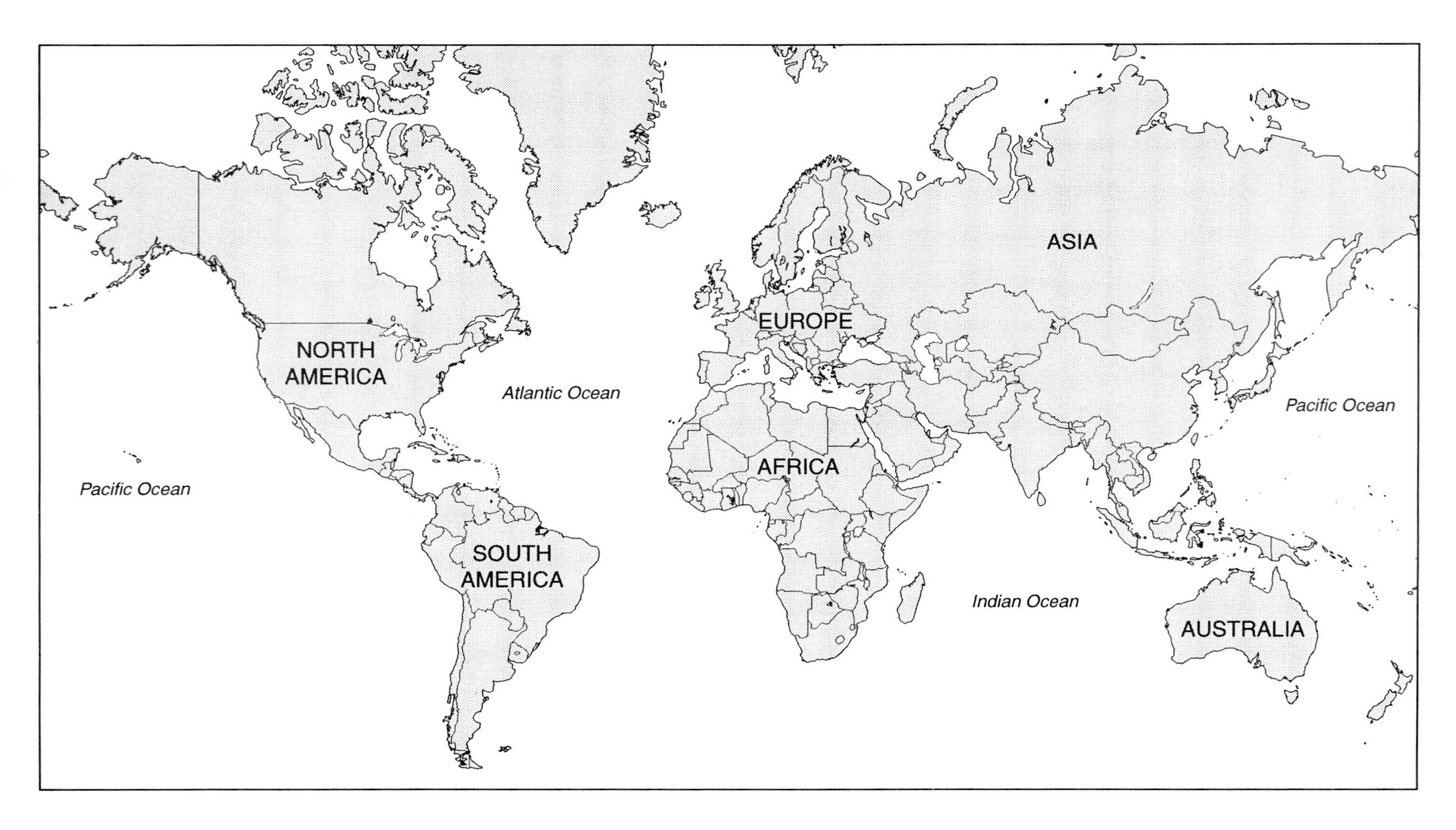
ASIA
EUROPE
NORTH AMERICA
Atlantic Ocean
Pacific Ocean
Pacific Ocean
AFRICA
SOUTH AMERICA
Indian Ocean
AUSTRALIA

UNIT I

GLOBAL POLITICAL SURVEY

The last decade of the 20th century is proving to be a period of political upheaval. The fall of communism in the Soviet Union and in Eastern Europe and the end of the cold war have not led to world peace. Although the threat of global thermonuclear war has lessened, national and ethnic rivalries have sparked regional conflicts in Europe, Africa, the Middle East, and Asia.

The early 1990s have been marked by wars and civil disorders. Racial conflicts have led to political repression and the movement of refugees across frontiers. International terrorism and drug trafficking remain as destructive forces. The struggle for human rights continues.

Chapter 1

The End of the Cold War

Created in 1922, the Soviet Union was the world's largest country. After World War II, it was also a military superpower able to compete with the United States for global supremacy. As the world's first Communist dictatorship, the Soviet Union (the Union of Soviet Socialist Republics, or U.S.S.R.) was distrusted by the capitalist nations of the West. During World War II (1939–45), the Soviet Union fought on the side of the United States and its Western allies against Nazi Germany, Fascist Italy, and the Japanese Empire. World War II ended with the nuclear bombing of Japan in August 1945. After the war, the Soviet Union made haste to develop nuclear weapons of its own. An *arms race* (a competition to achieve military superiority) developed between the United States and the Soviet Union.

- *Explain how tension developed between the Soviet Union and the West before and after World War II.*

The Rise of the Soviet Empire

During World War II, the nations of Eastern Europe were dominated by Nazi Germany. Toward the end of the war, advancing Soviet armies forced the Nazis to withdraw from the area. To provide the U.S.S.R. with a buffer zone between itself and the West, the Soviets remained in the countries they liberated and then influenced them to establish Communist

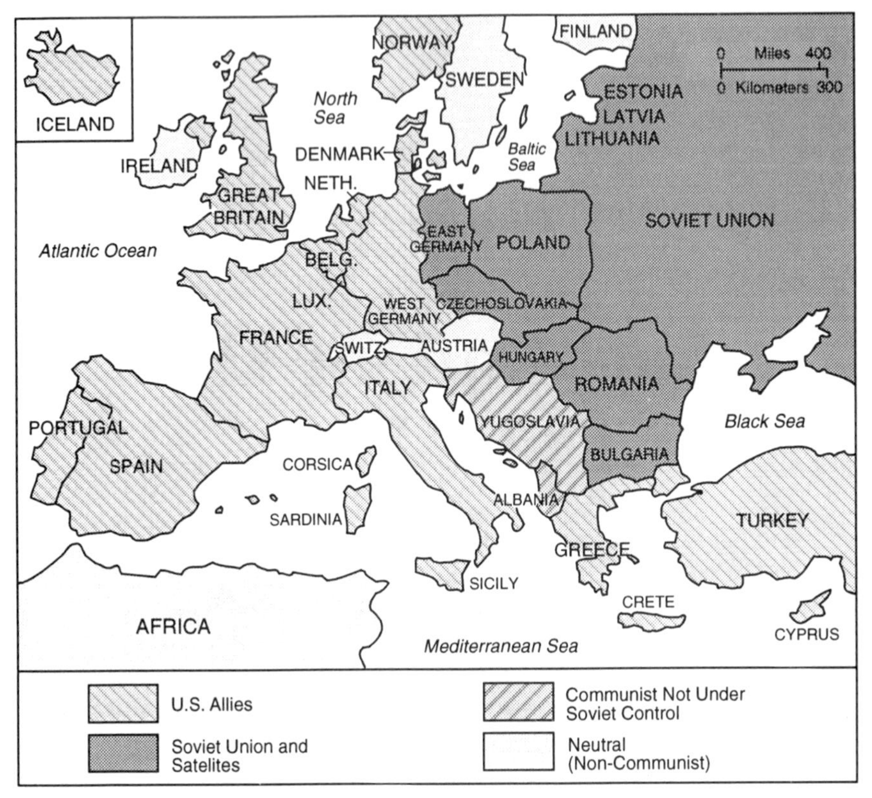

Figure 1.1 The Cold War—Antagonists and Neutrals

governments. Poland, Hungary, Romania, Bulgaria, Albania, and later, Czechoslovakia and East Germany became satellites of the Soviet Union. They depended on the Soviet Union for military and economic aid. It was said that these nations were behind an *iron curtain*. (Yugoslavia broke away from Soviet control in 1948, and so did Albania in 1968. Each followed an independent Communist course until 1990.)

A civil war began in Greece at the end of World War II. Communist guerrillas, aided by Soviet satellite nations, attempted to overthrow the Greek government. They wished to ally Greece with the Soviet Union. During the same period, the Soviets were pressuring Turkey to give up territory. The Soviet Union also wanted control of the Dardanelles, the passageway between the Black and Mediterranean seas. Turkey asked the United States for help.

♦ *Describe the growth of a Soviet "empire" in Eastern Europe.*

Cold War Opponents

The U.S. Resists Soviet Expansion

President Harry S. Truman responded in 1947 with a program to give military and economic aid to Greece and Turkey. The program was an outgrowth of the *Truman Doctrine,* a policy stating that the United States would support free peoples who resist being taken over by outside forces. The Truman Doctrine kept Greece and Turkey from becoming Communist.

The United States suspected that the Soviets would try to spread communism to Africa, Asia, and Latin America. So, in 1949, President Truman established the *Point Four Program* to give technical assistance to underdeveloped nations.

With the Truman Doctrine and the Point Four Program, the United States put into effect its containment policy toward the Soviet Union.

In the 1950s, the new policy created so much tension between the two superpowers that their hostile attitudes became known as the *cold war.* Each side took steps just short of a shooting war to advance its own interests. The cold war became a struggle between democracy and totalitarianism and between free market and command (state-directed) economic systems.

♦ *Define the following terms:*

a. cold war
b. totalitarianism
c. command economic system

The Superpowers in Conflict

In the four decades after World War II, the cold war moved beyond Europe to Asia, Africa, Latin America, and the Middle East. At times, it caused military conflicts. During the Korean War (1950–53) and the Vietnam War (1965–73), Asia was the scene of bloody struggles between anticommunist nations led by the United States and Communist countries supported by the Soviet Union and the People's Republic of China.

In 1948, the Soviets again tested the will of the United States and its allies to contain the spread of communism in Europe. The test came in Berlin.

After World War II, East Germany was controlled by the Soviet Union, and West Germany by the three Western allies. Although Berlin was located in East Germany, the Soviets occupied and governed only one section of it (East Berlin). Britain, France, and the United States held the rest of the city, called West Berlin.

In an effort to force the British, French, and Americans out of the city, the Soviets shut down all highways and railroad lines to West Berlin from West Germany, a trip that necessitated passage through East Germany. The blockaded city could not receive supplies by land. Instead of trying to break the blockade by sending in troops and possibly starting a war, the United States and its allies decided to airlift supplies to Berlin.

In spite of great difficulties, the *Berlin Airlift* kept the people of the city from starving. It brought in tons of food, fuel, and clothing every day. After 321 days, the Soviets ended the blockade and reopened the land routes across East Germany. The Berlin Airlift demonstrated Allied determination to oppose Soviet attempts to extend their influence or control.

Fear of Soviet aggression caused 12 Western nations to band

together in a mutual defense pact in 1949. The United States, Canada, Britain, France, Belgium, the Netherlands, Norway, Denmark, Italy, Luxembourg, Iceland, and Portugal formed the *North Atlantic Treaty Organization* (NATO). The members agreed that an attack on any one member was an attack on all. Later, Greece, Turkey, West Germany, and Spain joined. NATO's forces were stationed in Europe, especially in West Germany.

In 1955, in retaliation, the Soviet Union and the Communist nations of Eastern Europe organized their own military alliance. The purpose of the *Warsaw Pact* was to protect Eastern Europe from aggression by the NATO countries. The members of the pact were the Soviet Union, Albania, Bulgaria, Czechoslovakia, East Germany, Hungary, Poland, and Romania. Albania withdrew in 1968, when it became more closely allied with Communist China. Yugoslavia never joined. Marshal Tito (Josip Broz), the Yugoslav leader, preferred to remain independent of the Soviet Union.

The Warsaw Pact was dissolved in 1991, but NATO still exists. (See Chapter 8.) East Germany became part of NATO after it reunited with West Germany in 1990.

♦ *Describe the organization of alliance systems by the superpowers after World War II.*

Peaceful Coexistence and Détente

The post-World War II period was a time of economic devastation in Europe. To aid recovery and thus prevent the spread of communism, U.S. Secretary of State George Marshall announced, in June 1947, a program to assist Europe. Called the *Marshall Plan,* it resulted in the flow of $12 billion from the United States to 16 participating Western European nations between 1948 and 1952. Although the Communist countries of Eastern Europe could have participated in the Marshall Plan, they chose not to. Joseph Stalin, the Soviet dictator, accused the United States of using the plan to wage economic warfare on the Soviet Union.

Western Europe recovered and eventually achieved the greatest prosperity it had ever known. Despite the creation, in 1949, by the Soviets, of the *Council for Mutual Economic Assistance* (COMECON), to distribute financial aid to their satellite countries, Eastern Europe fell behind the West in economic development.

After the first crises of the cold war, American and Soviet leaders began to work out ways of easing tensions. In 1959, President Dwight D. Eisenhower invited Nikita Khrushchev to visit the United States. Through friendly talks, they reached some understandings. Hope for peaceful coexistence grew. Many people believed that the two powers could compete economically and politically without going to war.

Three international crises in the 1960s delayed progress toward better relations. In 1960, the Soviets shot down an American U-2 spy plane flying over the Soviet Union. It had been photographing Soviet military bases. Soviet anger resulted in the cancellation of meetings with American diplomats in Paris. A visit by Eisenhower to the Soviet Union was also canceled.

Relations between the superpowers became more tense in 1961. During the night of August 13, the East Germans constructed a barrier between East and West Berlin. Within days, a thick wall was built. East Berliners could no longer travel freely to West Berlin. The *Berlin Wall* remained as a symbol of repression until November 1989, when the borders of East Germany were once again opened, and portions of the Wall were torn down.

The Cuban Missile Crisis of 1962 brought the two powers to the edge of war. In the fall of 1962, the United States learned that the Soviet Union was placing long-range nuclear missiles in Cuba. This island, just 90 miles from Florida, was led by Fidel Castro. He had come to power in 1959 and made the country into a Communist ally of the Soviet Union. President John F. Kennedy demanded that the missiles be removed. After some hesitation, Khrushchev agreed to do so if the United States would promise not to invade Cuba.

In the 1970s, Soviet and U.S. leaders tried harder to lessen tensions. They pursued a policy called *détente,* meaning the relaxation of strained relations. In 1972, President Richard M. Nixon visited Moscow, the first U.S. president to do so. While in Moscow, he and the Soviet leader, Leonid Brezhnev, signed several agreements. They pledged to cooperate in science and technology, exploration of outer space, and trade relations. The most important agreement the two men signed arose from talks that took place between 1969 and 1972. The *Strategic Arms Limitation Talks* (SALT I) called for reducing the numbers of certain nuclear weapons, both offensive and defensive.

More meetings took place between 1973 and 1979. The result was a SALT II treaty to place limits on long-range

Berlin—The End of Communist Rule

bombers and missiles. When the Soviet Union invaded Afghanistan in late 1979, the U.S. Senate refused to approve SALT II and the treaty died. Relations cooled again. During most of the 1980s, the two countries kept economic, cultural, and diplomatic contacts to a minimum.

1. *Describe the events that caused tension among the superpowers.*
2. *Explain the policies of peaceful coexistence and détente.*

The Fall of the Soviet Empire

In addition to Cuba, the Asian nations of China, North Korea, Mongolia, and North Vietnam became Communist in the post-World War II era. As trade between the cold war antagonists was limited, the Soviet Union and other Communist nations became isolated from the economically advanced West. In the Soviet Union, efforts to compete with the West in the development of military technology and space exploration increasingly limited the availability of consumer goods and human services.

Also, the long and disastrous military involvement in Afghanistan (1979–89), whose purpose was to maintain a pro-Soviet government in that country, further drained Soviet resources and lowered public morale.

The arms race and the space race also constrained the

Soviets from giving economic aid to their faltering satellite nations and their allies. In fact, the Soviets depleted the resources of the satellite nations to maintain the military production levels of the Warsaw Pact.

In 1989, the failure of the Communist governments of Eastern Europe to provide consumer goods, social services, and more freedoms aroused demands for free elections. In East Germany, Hungary, Poland, Czechoslovakia, Albania, and Bulgaria, Communist rule ended peacefully. In Romania, however, the Communist dictator, President Nicolae Ceausescu, was forcibly overthrown.

- *Complete each of the following sentences:*

    a. The causes of Soviet economic problems were ____.
    b. Communism fell in Eastern Europe because ____.

Poland Breaks With Communism

Poland was the first country to free itself from communism. The Polish struggle was a long one. Soviet troops put down protests and strikes by Polish workers, students, and intellectuals in 1956, 1968, 1970, and 1976. But the Poles kept struggling. In 1980, workers took to the streets under the banner of *Solidarity,* a labor organization led by Lech Walesa. They demanded that trade unions be free of Communist control and called for changes in Poland's alliance with the Soviet Union.

At first, Poland's Communist government agreed to some changes, but the workers continued to make demands. Encouraged by the Soviets, Polish authorities outlawed Solidarity in 1981. They arrested Walesa and thousands of others and imposed military rule on Poland. After protests from around the world, Walesa was released in 1982, and martial law was lifted in 1983.

Solidarity won growing support as Poles struggled with rising prices and shortages of consumer goods. Finally, the Polish Communist Party allowed free elections, which Solidarity won in 1989. A Solidarity leader, Thaddeus Mazowiecki, formed the first noncommunist government in a satellite country. In 1990, the Poles elected Solidarity leader Lech Walesa to be the nation's president.

A unique feature of the Polish experience has been the immense influence of the Roman Catholic Church. Its opposition to communism gave the church great moral authority in Poland. The church continued to play a key role after 1990.

- *What was the role of Solidarity in Poland's transition from communism to capitalism?*

The Collapse of the Soviet Union

Mikhail Gorbachev, president of the Soviet Union (1985–91), abandoned the *Brezhnev Doctrine,* which stated the right of the Soviet Union to interfere in any satellite state. Therefore, the Soviet Union took no action to oppose the collapse of communism in Eastern Europe.

Severe economic and political problems had also developed in the Soviet Union. Shortages in food, clothing, consumer goods, and medical services made the Soviet people angry with their government and with the ruling Communist Party. In addition, protests and violence erupted among the Soviet Union's many ethnic groups. Georgians, Ukrainians, Lithuanians, and others demanded independence.

Through reform programs called *perestroika* (restructuring) and *glasnost* (openness), Gorbachev had attempted to make the Soviet economy more efficient and Soviet society more democratic. He also withdrew Soviet forces from Afghanistan in 1989 and discontinued economic and military aid to other Communist governments. To reduce cold war competition, Gorbachev negotiated an *Intermediate Nuclear Force* (INF) Treaty with the United States in 1987. It provided for the elimination of all medium- and short-range nuclear missiles in Europe. In 1991, the United States and the Soviet Union signed the *Strategic Arms Reduction Talks* (START) Treaty. It called for a 30 percent reduction in offensive nuclear weapons by both powers.

In August 1991, some Communist officials who were opposed to Gorbachev's reforms imprisoned him and seized power. President Boris Yeltsin of Russia and thousands of demonstrators opposed this coup. Unable to gain popular support, the coup leaders were forced to resign. Blaming the Communist Party for the coup attempt, Gorbachev withdrew from the party, and the Soviet Parliament suspended party activities. As a result, the Communist Party lost control of the government, the economy, and the military.

By the end of 1991, the 15 republics that made up the

Soviet Union declared their independence. The Soviet Union was no more. Mikhail Gorbachev resigned as president. Most of the republics formed a *Commonwealth of Independent States.* These events ended the cold war!

The fall of totalitarianism and command or government-directed economies in Eastern Europe stirred up demands in other parts of the world for increased democracy and private enterprise.

1. *Identify each of the following:*
   a. *Mikhail Gorbachev*
   b. *Boris Yeltsin*
   c. *Commonwealth of Independent States*
2. *Explain why the collapse of the Soviet Union ended the cold war.*

Chapter 1 Review

A. *Choose the item that best completes each sentence.*

1. *During World War II, the Soviet Union was a military ally of (a) Nazi Germany and Fascist Italy (b) the Japanese Empire (c) the United States.*
2. *After World War II, an arms race developed between the Soviet Union and (a) Britain (b) Japan (c) the United States.*
3. *The Soviet-dominated bloc of nations was in (a) Eastern Europe (b) Western Europe (c) Africa.*
4. *NATO was organized as a political and military alliance of (a) the United States and Western Europe (b) the Soviet Union and Eastern Europe (c) the Soviet Union and the United States.*
5. *The Warsaw Pact was a political and military alliance of (a) the Soviet Union and Western Europe (b) the Soviet Union and Eastern Europe (c) the Soviet Union and the United States.*
6. *The cold war was a struggle between (a) democracy and totalitarianism (b) private enterprise and command economies (c) both of these.*
7. *To assist the economic recovery of Europe after World War II, the United States developed the (a) COMECON (b) Marshall Plan (c) Warsaw Pact.*

8. *To prevent the expansion of the Soviet Union and the spread of communism, the United States created the (a) Truman Doctrine (b) Warsaw Pact (c) COMECON.*

9. *The financial resources of the Soviet Union were strained by competition with the West and by its military involvement in (a) Pakistan (b) Afghanistan (c) India.*

10. *The rule of the Communist governments of Eastern Europe ended in 1989 because of their failure to provide (a) consumer goods and services (b) freedom (c) both of these.*

B. *From the list below, select ONE person. Write a two-paragraph essay about that person by answering the following questions:*

HARRY TRUMAN
LECH WALESA
MIKHAIL GORBACHEV

1. *How did this person contribute to the ending of the cold war?*
2. *Why do you admire or not admire this person?*

C. *Explain why the ending of the cold war was a global victory for democracy and free enterprise.*

D. *Reread "The Collapse of the Soviet Union," on pages 11–12. Then do the following:*

1. *Explain how each contributed to the Soviet downfall:*

   economic problems
   nationalism among ethnic minorities
   glasnost and perestroika

2. *PROVE or DISPROVE:*

   a. *There is no difference between the Soviet Union and the Commonwealth of Independent States.*

   b. *The Communist Party played no part in the collapse of the Soviet Union.*

Chapter 2

The Rise of the New Europe

Crisis in Russia

By 1992, Russian President Boris Yeltsin had become the best-known political leader in the new Commonwealth of Independent States (CIS). Agreements reached by Yeltsin and the leaders of the other republics provided for establishing the commonwealth's headquarters in Minsk, the capital of Belarus. The leaders also decided to use the Soviet ruble as a standard currency, to work for nuclear disarmament, and to permit each republic to organize its own military forces. The CIS has remained a loose grouping of independent states with no strong central authority.

The United States and other nations quickly recognized the independence of the post-Soviet republics and opened diplomatic relations with them. Substantial economic and humanitarian aid came from the United States, Germany, France, and other industrialized nations. World leaders especially wanted to support Yeltsin's attempt to develop democracy and private enterprise in Russia, by far the largest of the republics.

Yeltsin's plan for Russia was to turn factories, farms, and other businesses over to private owners who would run them for a profit. This is called *privatization*. Many existing businesses were reorganized, with shares of stock being distributed to private individuals. Each Russian received a certificate, or voucher, that could be traded for stock. To win support for its reforms, the government gave managers and workers free shares of stock in the companies where they worked.

Figure 2.1 Europe and the Commonwealth of Independent States

Russians had mixed feelings about Yeltsin's policies. Many welcomed the introduction of private enterprise. Now they had new opportunities to make money. Others, however, resisted. People in high positions had done well under the old system. They were not eager to change. Ordinary workers—accustomed to being employed whether they were productive or not—feared losing their jobs. They did not welcome the thought of massive layoffs and cutbacks in social services.

The reforms did cause wrenching hardships. Production dropped sharply—more drastically than in the United States' Great Depression in the 1930s. Food and consumer goods became hard to get. Prices shot up. Millions lost their jobs. Crime rates rose as racketeers extorted protection money from small businesses, drug dealers found new customers, and armed gangs roamed the streets. What's more, day after day the press carried news of corrupt dealings in business and government.

Many Russians became convinced that democracy and private enterprise did not work. They doubted their president's ability to transform the defective economy.

1. *List the major problems facing President Yeltsin after the Soviet Union broke up.*
2. *State reasons for the support given to Yeltsin by Western nations.*

The Battle for Russia

By late 1992, a bitter power struggle was under way. On one side stood Boris Yeltsin. On the other stood his political enemies in the Russian parliament, elected before the breakup of the Soviet Union. Old-style bureaucrats, former Communist bosses, and supernationalists in parliament were determined to slow privatization and undermine Yeltsin's power.

In December 1992, the anti-Yeltsin deputies forced Yeltsin to replace his acting prime minister. That was a blow to Yeltsin's program of rapid economic reforms. The new prime minister, Viktor S. Chernomyrdin, proceeded more cautiously with economic reforms.

The anti-Yeltsin deputies kept up their attacks. They pointed to any and all signs of economic trouble as evidence that the reforms had failed. Demonstrations and counterdemonstrations broke out. Would the country collapse into civil war?

Yeltsin asked the deputies for constitutional changes that would give him greater control of the economy. But instead, parliament reduced his presidential powers.

In March 1993, Yeltsin announced that he was taking emergency powers and would govern Russia by issuing decrees. He scheduled a referendum for the following month. At that time, he said, Russian voters could resolve the power struggle between legislative and executive branches.

Those moves brought on a constitutional crisis. Communists and other parliamentary opponents of Yeltsin claimed the president had violated the constitution. They called for his impeachment and removal from office. Russia's top judicial body, the Constitutional Court, agreed that Yeltsin's moves had gone against the constitution. But the court did not try to remove him from office, and Yeltsin's opponents had too few votes in parliament to impeach him.

Finally, legislators accepted the idea of a referendum. Across Russia, 65 percent of the eligible voters turned out. They gave clear support to Yeltsin. In response to four questions, a majority indicated confidence in the president, support for his economic program, little desire for an early election for president, and considerable desire for early elections for parliament.

Immediately, Yeltsin proposed a new constitution that would strengthen the presidency and limit the parliament's powers. A constitutional conference met during June and July 1993. The constitutional conference drew up a draft constitution calling for a strong presidency, a new two-house parliament, and limits on each branch's powers.

Before the constitution could be accepted, however, the power struggle took a new and explosive turn. Yeltsin touched off the crisis by suspending his vice president, Aleksandr Rutskoi, with whom he had quarreled. Then Yeltsin announced that he was dissolving the parliament and calling new legislative elections. Parliament reacted angrily, claiming that Yeltsin's actions were illegal. Deputies voted to oust Yeltsin and make Vice President Rutskoi the new president. Yeltsin refused to yield.

With parliament holding round-the-clock sessions in its headquarters, known as the "white house," Yeltsin surrounded it with police and military forces. He threatened to arrest

Parliamentary Democracy

parliamentary leaders. After several days of standoff, civilians who supported the parliament charged the police with clubs and guns. That set off a bloody battle in the heart of Moscow on October 3, 1993. After 26 hours, heavily armed soldiers blasted their way into the parliament. They arrested Ruslan Khasbulatov, the parliament chairman; Vice President Rutskoi; and dozens of their supporters.

1. *Explain how 1993 was a year of crisis for Russia.*
2. *Name the person who fits each description:*
   a. *He led the parliamentary opposition to President Yeltsin.*
   b. *As prime minister, he slowed down Yeltsin's economic reform program.*
   c. *He was the man parliament tried unsuccessfully to make president of Russia.*
   d. *He was the best-known political leader in the CIS.*
3. *Describe the crisis of September and October 1993.*

Russia Struggles On

Despite President Yeltsin's victory, economic problems and crime continued to worsen. At elections in December 1993, Russian voters approved the proposed constitution. However, a large number of seats in the State Duma (the new lower house of Parliament) went to extreme nationalists and others opposed to Yeltsin's reforms. Clashes between the president and parliament continued.

Prices spiraled upward at a dizzying pace in 1994. Economic officials tried to ease people's hardship They slowed down privatization, printed more paper money, and sought ways to increase production. Some reformers feared that Russia might turn back to its old methods of rigid central control. But reforms limped along, and by 1995 Russia's economy was perking up. Inflation had begun to ease. Industrial output had stopped shrinking and begun to grow. And a flow of money from foreign investors further boosted the economy.

New problems cropped up in other areas, however. A rebellion in a small region of southern Russia flared into all-out warfare in December 1994. The Russian army poured into Chechnya, one of dozens of separate territories that make up the Russian federation. Like other small territories, Chechnya contains a largely non-Russian population with its own distinct culture and history. The Chechen people are mainly Muslim. They have been under Russian rule since the 1860s.

While other territories negotiated for more rights within Russia, Chechnya declared full independence. Russian leaders responded with overwhelming force. In an eight-month war, the Russian army destroyed the Chechen capital, Grozny, and wiped out much of the territory's industry. The war killed some 1,400 Russian soldiers and 20,000 civilians. A 1995 peace settlement provided for Chechnya to have its own government within the Russian federation. Russia promised Chechnya a large degree of self-rule—but not independence.

Although Western leaders expressed alarm at the bloody battles in Chechnya, they generally sided with Yeltsin in his domestic struggles. They praised Yeltsin for helping to liquidate the cold war. In January 1993, he signed a new arms-reduction treaty with U.S. President George Bush. *START II*, as the treaty was called, provided for the elimination of land-based missiles having more than one warhead. The START II agreement called for destroying two thirds of the nuclear warheads on each side by the year 2003.

Western leaders saw Yeltsin as a democrat. They believed he was preferable to most of his rivals, from the former Communists on the left to the nationalists on the right. An ultranationalist leader named Vladimir Zhirinovsky—feared by some as a budding Hitler—had won strong support in the 1993 parliamentary elections. His right-wing party campaigned under the slogan "Russia First." Among other things, Zhirinovsky called for a revival of Russia's empire and said he would end the "humiliation" of Russia by Western powers. His party won a large block of seats with nearly one fourth of the votes.

Seeking to cut into Zhirinovsky's support, Yeltsin began to take a tougher line on international issues. However, he still cooperated with Western nations on most matters.

Yeltsin and the reformers lost ground in the 1995 parliamentary elections—and Zhirinovsky's Party slipped even more. A revived Communist Party led by Gennady Zyuganov put in the best showing, winning nearly one third of the seats. With a presidential election slated for 1996, the reformers were hanging on by the skin of their teeth.

1. *Identify the following:*

   a. *Vladimir Zhirinovsky*
   b. *Chechnya*
   c. *START II*

2. *Explain why President Yeltsin began taking a tougher line on international issues.*

Beyond Russia: Nationalism and Economic Reform

Issues of nationalism and economic disarray also flared up in other republics of the Commonwealth of Independent States. Nations like Ukraine had troubles paralleling those that Russia experienced. In addition, leaders of the former Soviet republics cast a wary eye toward Russia, watching for signs of a revived Russian imperialism.

Ukraine. From czarist times right down to the collapse of the Soviet Union, Ukrainians resented Russian rule. During World War II, Ukrainian nationalists fought both the Germans and the Soviets. Ukraine's 52 million people finally broke away in 1991. In a national referendum, more than 90 percent of Ukrainian voters favored independence.

But it was a difficult break. For example, Ukraine and Russia quarreled over how to divide the fleet of ships that the Soviet navy had kept in the Black Sea. After long negotiations, they agreed to a formula. Russia would get the bulk of the fleet. In

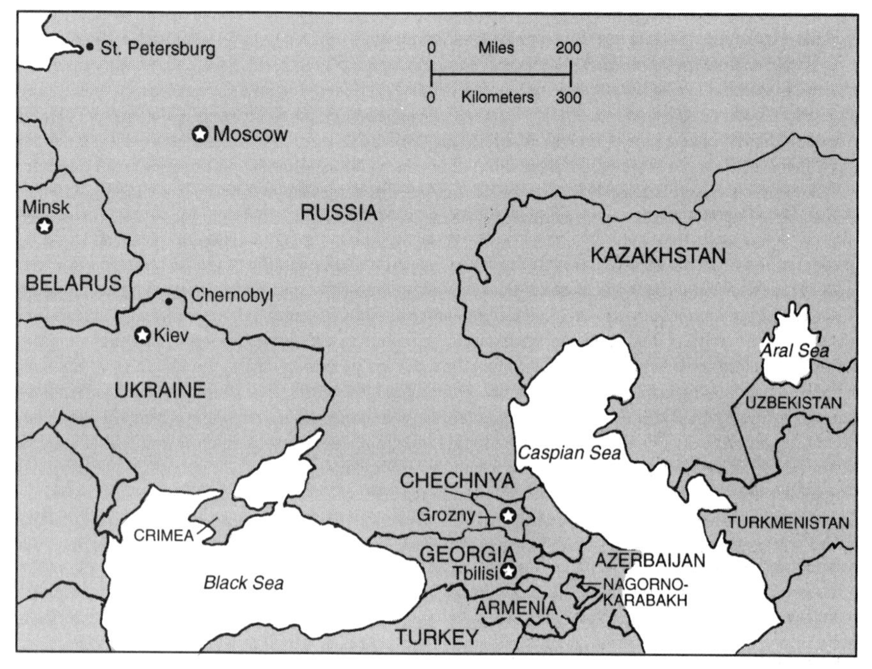

Figure 2.2 Russia and Neighboring C.I.S. Republics

return, it would write off part of Ukraine's debt for purchases of Russian natural gas.

The region called Crimea was another cause for dispute. Crimea is a peninsula on Ukraine's coast, jutting into the Black Sea. Crimea was traditionally part of Russia, and today two thirds of its 2.7 million people are Russians. However, in 1954 Soviet leader Nikita Khrushchev turned Crimea over to Ukraine as a gesture of friendship. After 1991, Russian nationalists in Crimea demanded that Ukraine give the region back to Russia—or at least allow self-rule. Nationalists in Russia's State Duma supported such demands. However, Russia's government adopted a hands-off policy.

Despite mutual distrust, Russia and Ukraine remained dependent on each other. Most of Ukraine's oil and gas came from Russia. Russia, in turn, got much of its food from Ukraine and needed the large Ukrainian market for its exports.

Some Ukrainians wanted to hold onto the nuclear missiles that the Soviet Union had stationed on Ukrainian territory. They believed the weapons would offer protection against any Russian bullying. In the end, however, Ukraine agreed to allow its nuclear weapons to be destroyed, as called for by the START I agreement. So did its neighbors, Belarus and Kazakhstan. That meant that, of all the former Soviet republics, only Russia would have nuclear weapons.

Under President Leonid Kuchma, elected in 1994, Ukraine launched its own free market reforms. Like Russia, Ukraine experienced sharp price rises and other economic shocks. Western nations supported Ukraine's reforms by offering large loans. They also offered to help Ukraine shut down the nuclear power plant at Chernobyl and build a safer plant in its place. Chernobyl was the site of the world's worst nuclear accident, in 1986, which spewed radiation across Europe.

♦ *Describe the relationship between Russia and Ukraine.*

Kazakhstan. Oil-rich Kazakhstan—a country four times the size of Texas—is one of the luckier states to have emerged from Soviet Central Asia. It has not only oil but also a modern space-launching facility, at Baikonur. Russia took out a 20-year lease on the facility, providing extra income for Kazakhstan.

Some 17 million people live in Kazakhstan, which borders on Russia and China. The country produces vast amounts of cotton and one third of the grain grown in the former Soviet Union. Its mineral resources go far beyond oil to include gas, iron, gold, silver, copper, and chrome.

The potential for economic growth has attracted Western investors and major American and European firms. Nursultan Nazarbayev, who became president before Kazakhstan claimed independence in 1991, focused on economic reforms rather than political change or democracy. His authoritarian rule won the seeming support of the people in a 1995 referendum extending his term to December 2000. Nazarbayev introduced a policy of gradual privatization, although some major economic enterprises were to remain state property.

Kazakhstan came under Russia's control in the 18th century. It has two main ethnic groups—Kazakhs (42 percent) and Russians (37 percent). Ethnic Kazakhs speak a Turkic language, follow the Sunni Muslim religion, and resemble Mongols in appearance. Ethnic Russians have dominated the industrial cities for more than 100 years. More than half of the people in Almaty, the capital, are Russians.

Independence brought a surge of Kazakh nationalism after 1991. More Kazakhs moved into major government posts. To avoid ethnic conflict, which would disrupt economic development, President Nazarbayev took steps to protect Russians' rights.

Kazakhstan's economy has remained closely tied to Russia's. Along with Belarus, Kazakhstan joined Russia in a customs union, or free trade zone. The three countries invited other members of the CIS to join them, but had no immediate takers.

- *Why is Kazakhstan considered to be one of the luckier states to have emerged from Soviet Central Asia?*

Azerbaijan and Armenia. The approaching collapse of the Soviet Union rekindled old quarrels between two former Soviet republics, Azerbaijan and Armenia. Violence erupted within Azerbaijan in 1988. The conflict brought turmoil to the eastern Caucasus Mountains, south of Russia.

Azerbaijan and Armenia are small countries. They are im portant because of their natural resources and their position at the southeastern tip of Europe. Turkey, Iran, and Russia have long competed for power and influence in the Caucasus region.

The people of Azerbaijan, known as Azeris, speak a language related to Turkish. They were under Turkish rule for the

Figure 2.3 C.I.S. Areas of Conflict

greater portion of their history. Therefore, their culture and their social institutions are largely Turkish. However, Azeris also were once under Persian (Iranian) rule. Like today's Iranians, most Azeris belong to the Shia sect of Islam, rather than the Sunni sect that is popular in Turkey.

Russia conquered Azerbaijan in 1813. The oil fields developed by czarist Russia near the capital city, Baku, were among the first in the world. Oil has brought wealth, but also pollution, to the region. As a result of the oil economy, Azerbaijan was the only part of the Soviet Muslim world where the Communist effort to create an urban working class succeeded.

In contrast to the Azeris, the Armenians are mainly Christians. In the 19th century, they looked to Christian Russia for protection against the Turks and Persians. The traditional territory of Armenia was split in two, with half ruled by Turkey and half by Russia.

Armenians recall with horror Turkey's deliberate and systematic effort to destroy the Armenian people in 1915. At the time, World War I was raging, and Turkey looked on the Armenians as pro-Russian enemies. As a result of the genocidal actions of the Turks, more than one million Armenians died.

Both Armenia and Azerbaijan came under Soviet rule after the Russian Revolution of 1917. Turkey kept control over part of ancient Armenia. Large numbers of Armenians found themselves within the borders of Azerbaijan, in a region known as Nagorno-Karabakh.

It was in Nagorno-Karabakh that trouble erupted in 1988, before the breakup of the Soviet Union. The mainly Armenian people of the province resented Azeri rule and wanted Nagorno-Karabakh to become part of Armenia. Armenia's government shared that goal. Mass demonstrations by Armenians demanding political change touched off riots between ethnic Armenians and Azeris in Azerbaijan. Soon ethnic Armenians from all over Azerbaijan were fleeing to Nagorno-Karabakh or to Armenia.

Outright warfare erupted as ethnic Armenians in Nagorno-Karabakh organized an army and the Azeri government sent troops to quell the revolt. At times Armenia's army joined the fighting. In 1991, when the Soviet Union collapsed, both Armenia and Azerbaijan became independent, but fighting continued. By June 1993, the Armenians had won major victories, pushing Azeri forces out of Nagorno-Karabakh. This resulted in a mutiny in the Azeri army. Rebellious officers, dissatisfied with the conduct of the war, overthrew the Azeri government, and a new leader took power. He was Heydar Aliyev, chairperson of Azerbaijan's parliament, leader of Azerbaijan's Communist Party, and a former general in the Soviet secret police.

The war over Nagorno-Karabakh redrew the lines of influence in the southern Caucasus. Armenia turned more and more toward Russia. Azerbaijan forged links to Turkey. Using its great oil and gas wealth as leverage, Azerbaijan cut off fuel shipments to Armenia and began an economic blockade. That torpedoed the Armenian economy, shutting down factories and forcing people to bundle up during winter weather as homes went unheated. Militarily, however, the Armenians had the upper hand.

By 1994, the war had taken at least 20,000 lives and caused more than a million people to flee their homes. Late in the year, Russian mediators helped to arrange a cease-fire, and peace negotiations began. However, they made no immediate progress; both sides kept their guns ready for more fighting.

1. *Identify each of the following:*

   a. *Heydar Aliyev*
   b. *Armenia*
   c. *Azerbaijan*
   d. *Nagorno-Karabakh*

2. *Complete the following sentences:*

   a. *War broke out between Azeris and Armenians because ____.*
   b. *The president of Azerbaijan was ousted when ____.*

Latvia. Latvia is a small republic on the Baltic Sea. Latvians harbor great resentment against Russia, because the Soviet Union invaded Latvia in 1939–40 and annexed it. During the 1980s, Latvia was a leader among Soviet republics demanding independence. In 1988, voters elected a proindependence People's Front government. Formal independence was declared in May 1990.

Ethnic divisions are a source of strife in Latvia. Only 53 percent of the population of 2½ million are ethnic Latvians. Some 33 percent are Russians. Most others came from other parts of the former Soviet Union. Large numbers had been sent to Latvia to aid industrialization after World War II.

Since the collapse of the Soviet Union, the ethnic Latvians

Figure 2.4 Baltic Republics and Eastern Europe

have moved toward radical nationalism. The Russian-speaking minority was shocked to learn that the nationalist majority in parliament would not grant them Latvian citizenship. Automatic citizenship went only to those whose families were in Latvia before 1940. Others became "noncitizens." They were not permitted to vote in national elections held in 1993 and 1995. A Latvian law adopted in 1994 promised that most "noncitizens" born in Latvia could become citizens by 2000. Only then could those born outside Latvia begin to become citizens.

Latvian nationalists have revived an armed militia called the Aizsaigi. Some of its members are veterans of the Nazi S.S. of the World War II era. The nationalists and their militia hope to make conditions so uncomfortable for the 1¼ million "noncitizens" that they leave the country. Denial of voting and property rights to these "Soviet colonists" has become acceptable to many ethnic Latvians.

Two neighboring Baltic republics, Estonia and Lithuania, have experienced similar strains of anti-Russian nationalism. They too were annexed by the Soviet Union during World War II.

1. *Match the description in Column B with the country in Column A.*

Column A	Column B
1. *Ukraine*	a. *Oilfields near Baku bring wealth to the nation.*
2. *Kazakhstan*	b. *Nationalists have denied rights to "noncitizens."*
3. *Azerbaijan*	c. *Suffered under an oil and gas cutoff and a trade embargo.*
4. *Armenia*	d. *Oil and gas reserves are expected to make it rich.*
5. *Latvia*	e. *Quarreled with Russia over the Black Sea fleet.*

2. *PROVE or DISPROVE: Nationalism has influenced the actions of the former Soviet republics in the post-cold war era.*

Conflict and Change in Eastern Europe

Since the fall of communism, the former Soviet satellite nations have struggled to develop democracy and free market economies. They have also attempted to negotiate closer relations with the economically stronger nations of Western Europe.

In Czechoslovakia, an agreement between political leaders led to a peaceful division of the country. In January, 1993, Czechoslovakia split into two independent nations, known as the Czech Republic and Slovakia.

Czech Republic and Slovakia. Created in 1918 by the uniting of Czech and Slovak lands, Czechoslovakia was occupied and dissolved by the Nazis during World War II. When Soviet armies drove out the Nazis, an elected Czechoslovak government took office in 1946. Communists seized power in 1948 and installed a harsh regime. All dissent was repressed.

In 1968, an invasion of Soviet troops supported by Polish, East German, Hungarian, and Bulgarian forces crushed a movement for democracy. Repressive policies remained in force. Czechoslovak demands for more human rights led to another crackdown in 1977.

In 1989, tens of thousands of people took to the streets of

Prague, Czechoslovakia's capital, to demand free elections. Millions went on strike. The Communist Party leadership resigned. Vaclav Havel, a Czech playwright and human rights advocate, was elected president of a noncommunist government.

The Slovaks had been independent during World War II. Their demands for a separate state, in 1992, were opposed unsuccessfully by President Havel, who failed to win reelection as a result. Following separation, the Czech parliament elected Havel to the presidency of the new Czech Republic.

Traditionally, the Czechs have been oriented toward the West while the Slovaks have looked to Hungary and Russia for trade and support.

- *State an event in the history of Czechoslovakia for each date: 1918, 1948, 1968, 1989, 1993*

Yugoslavia. Located in the Balkan mountain region of southeastern Europe, Yugoslavia also splintered when communism fell. Yugoslavia's breakup brought war and vast suffering.

Yugoslavia was created in 1918. It was a federation of six republics in which a hodgepodge of ethnic groups lived side by side. The ethnic groups had a long history of bitter quarrels. As long as strong Communist leaders held them together, the people managed to get along. But the crumbling of communism in the early 1990s sparked a wave of nationalist feelings, and old hatreds bubbled to the surface.

Four of the six Yugoslav republics—Croatia, Slovenia, Bosnia-Herzegovina (Bosnia for short), and Macedonia—declared independence in 1991 and 1992. War quickly broke out in Croatia and Bosnia, where ethnic mixing was most pronounced. Fighting involved three main groups: Serbs (mostly Eastern Orthodox Christians), Croats (mostly Roman Catholics), and Muslims. Before the fighting, the Serbs, Croats, and Muslims lived together, often intermarrying or becoming friends. But as nationalist passions grew, old hatreds revived. Each group became suspicious of the others. The Serbs (in Croatia and Bosnia) and the Croats (in Bosnia) formed armies to fight for separate homelands. They aimed to create "ethnically pure" areas for themselves by driving out other groups.

Serbia, the largest and most powerful of Yugoslavia's six republics, had opposed the breakup of the federation. Now Yugoslavia was reduced to two republics—Serbia and Montenegro. Serbia controlled the Yugoslav army, and used it to support Croatian Serbs fighting against the Croatian army. Serbia also aided Bosnian Serbs who fought the Muslim-dominated government of Bosnia. By 1994, the governments of Croatia and Bosnia had formed an uneasy alliance against the Serb armies in Croatia and Bosnia. The Yugoslav army under Serbia's control had withdrawn to the sidelines.

Atrocities committed in the pursuit of *ethnic cleansing* (expulsion of people of different religion or national origin), especially by Serbs, caused worldwide outrage. The United Nations put an embargo on trade with Serbia and banned arms sales to all parts of the former Yugoslavia. The arms ban stirred controversy, with many arguing that the ban favored the well-armed Serbs while unfairly preventing the Bosnian and Croatian governments from getting needed weapons.

The United Nations and the European Union sponsored peace talks and arranged a series of cease-fires. The U.N. sent peacekeeping troops to patrol cease-fire lines and to ensure the delivery of desperately needed food to suffering civilians. Meanwhile, the United States and other NATO nations agreed to enforce a U.N.-declared no-fly zone over Bosnia in order to protect the war-ravaged population against Bosnian Serb air attacks.

In 1994, the Croats and Muslims of Bosnia accepted a Western peace plan. They agreed to stop fighting and live together in a federated state, with separate areas for Serbs,

Figure 2.5 Former Yugoslavia

Ethnic Cleansing

Croats, and Muslims. Just under half of all territory was to be under Serb control. The Bosnian Serbs, however, refused to lay down their arms. They balked at giving up territory they had won in battle. The Bosnian Serbs were led by Radovan Karadzic, with off-and-on support from Serbian President Slobodan Milosevic. The Bosnian government's main leader was President Alija Izetbegovic. Croatia's leader was Franjo Tudjman.

The crisis in the former Yugoslavia became the bloodiest conflict in Europe since World War II. By mid-1995 an estimated 200,000 people had been killed. Many U.N. peacekeepers lost their lives. Britain and France, which sent troops for the peacekeeping force, tried to limit the force's role in order to minimize danger to their soldiers. The United States had no ground troops in the war zone. U.S. leaders favored a more assertive role for NATO's planes, such as bombing Serb targets when the Serbs violated U.N. rules. Republicans in Congress pushed for the U.S. to stop enforcing the arms embargo, so that Bosnia's government could build up its armed forces.

In August 1995, a lightning offensive by the Croatian army drove Croatian Serb forces out of western Croatia. A wave of Croatian Serb refugees fled across Bosnia into Serbia. The

Croatian and Bosnian Serbs, who had been on the offensive, were suddenly on the run. Fearing a deadly clash between Croatia and Serbia, world leaders stepped up their peacemaking efforts. They urgently wanted to keep the Balkan war from spreading. At a conference in Dayton, Ohio, in December 1995, the presidents of Bosnia, Serbia, and Croatia signed a peace agreement. Bosnia was divided into a Bosnian Croat federation and a Bosnian Serb republic, both under a central government in Sarajevo.

- *What role did the United Nations play in the crisis in the former Yugoslavia?*

Poland. Although Poland welcomed democracy with enthusiasm, it faced immense economic problems. Poland tried what was called "shock therapy." That meant introducing free market capitalism all at once, rather than step by step as in some other countries of Eastern Europe.

"Shock therapy" (an economic stimulus) brought a rush of Western consumer goods and a sharp rise in foreign trade. However, Polish businesses found it hard to withstand the international competition. At first, industrial production fell, wages dropped, and unemployment soared. Many Poles were alarmed and angry to find their standard of living threatened. Opinion polls showed a sharp drop in the popularity of President Lech Walesa, who spearheaded the changes.

In 1993, public dissatisfaction led to the election of former Communists to the largest block of seats in the Polish parliament. Former Communists were able to assemble a majority and elect a new prime minister. Under Poland's system of parliamentary democracy, President Walesa had to share power with the new government, although he sharply criticized it. In the presidential election of 1995, Polish voters replaced Walesa with a former Communist, Aleksander Kwasniewsky.

Despite the pain, Poland's "shock therapy" has begun to pay off. From 1992 to 1995, Poland led the former Communist nations of Eastern Europe in economic growth. By 1995, private enterprise accounted for more than half of Poland's output. But inflation and unemployment remained high.

Poland was the first nation to free itself from communism. Its methods of pursuing a free market economy helped to guide some of the other nations of Eastern Europe.

1. *Write the term that best completes each sentence.*
   a. *The Czech Republic has been traditionally oriented toward the ____ for trade.*
   b. *In the former Yugoslavia, the policy of ____ was aimed at creating areas in which only one ethnic group remained.*
   c. *In Poland, the sudden introduction of free market capitalism was known as ____.*
2. *Complete the following sentence: Events in the former Yugoslavia in the early 1990s attracted worldwide attention because ____.*

Conflict and Change in Western Europe

Germany. Germany's economic strength and political stability have allowed it to take a leading role in European affairs. Recently, however, Germany has been troubled by problems arising from the nation's reunification in 1990.

At the end of World War II, Nazi Germany surrendered to the Western allies and the Soviet Union. Early in the cold war, Germany split into two nations. East Germany became a Communist satellite of the Soviet Union; West Germany became a

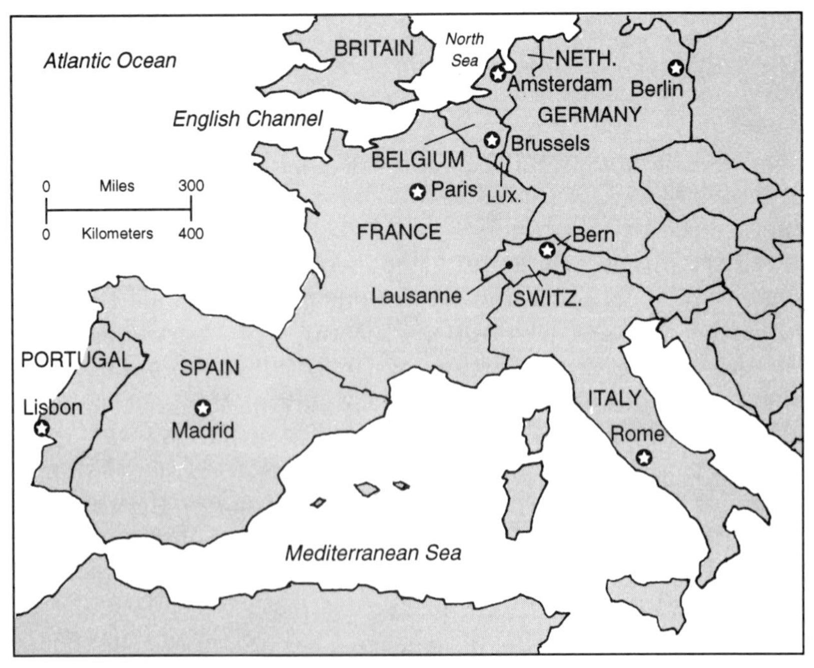

Figure 2.6 Western Europe

democratic, noncommunist ally of the United States. The former German capital, Berlin, was also divided. In 1961, the Communists built a wall across Berlin to prevent East Germans from escaping to a better life in prosperous West Germany.

The fall of communism in Eastern Europe brought down the East German government and the Berlin Wall. In October 1990, the two Germanys reunited. Berlin once more became the capital of a unified Germany.

Reunification brought new problems and tensions. Eastern Germany was far less developed economically than the western portion of Germany. Its markets in the former Soviet Union were gone, and East Europeans were no longer interested in buying eastern Germany's heavy machinery. To overcome eastern Germany's widespread poverty and unemployment, the German government, led by Chancellor Helmut Kohl, offered far-reaching economic assistance, ranging from business subsidies to welfare payments for families. By 1995, such assistance had cost $600 billion. It was expected to continue for many years.

Germany had to raise taxes to help finance the aid to eastern Germans. Both western and eastern Germans found much to criticize. Some western Germans thought eastern Germans were "freeloaders." Many eastern Germans resented what they saw as the "high-and-mighty" attitude of the richer westerners. These tensions were made worse by a 1992–93 recession—the worst to hit Germany since World War II.

The economic slowdown helped to spark a flare-up of violence against foreigners. During the 1970s and 1980s, West Germany's expanding industries had hired large numbers of "guest workers" from Turkey and other countries. At the same time, crises in the Middle East and elsewhere sent large numbers of refugees flooding into Germany to escape war and hunger. With unemployment rising, resentment of foreigners grew. One result was a surge in activity by *neo-Nazis*—people who seek to bring back the "Germany-for-Germans" policies of Hitler's time. For a few years, attacks on foreigners and other hate crimes occurred almost daily. In response, thousands of Germans held demonstrations against crimes of hate. The turmoil stirred fearful memories of the Holocaust of 1939–45, when the Nazis murdered more than 6 million people.

Chancellor Kohl's government introduced law enforcement measures to curb extremist violence. Also, Germany's parliament voted to limit the number of economic refugees permitted to enter Germany. Human rights groups criticized that action, saying it seemed to reward the extremists who had resorted to violence.

- *PROVE or DISPROVE: The reunification of Germany in 1990 led to severe problems.*

France. Significant political change came to France in the 1990s. In 1993, voters swept the Socialist Party of President François Mitterrand out of power in the National Assembly. Conservatives took control of the lawmaking body, and a conservative prime minister took office. Thus, France entered a period of divided rule, with a conservative prime minister and a Socialist president.

Two years later, divided rule ended when conservatives captured the presidency too. Seriously ill, Mitterrand stepped down after 14 years in office. Jacques Chirac, the conservative mayor of Paris, defeated a Socialist candidate by 52 percent to 48 percent and became president.

Although France was one of the victors in World War II, postwar political and economic instability made recovery difficult. Problems were made worse by costly colonial wars, from 1946 to 1958, in Southeast Asia and Algeria.

General Charles de Gaulle became prime minister, and then president, in 1958. Under a new constitution, de Gaulle had greatly expanded powers as president. He encouraged economic and technological advances and supported European unity, with the idea of placing France in a leadership role. De Gaulle resigned from office in 1969 after losing a national referendum on changes to the constitution—changes that would have further strengthened presidential powers.

Under de Gaulle, France experienced economic growth and urbanization. Cities were rebuilt. Consumer goods became more widely available. More students went to universities. Such changes had been under way before 1958, but Gaullist economic reforms helped them along. Also, de Gaulle turned France away from colonialism in Asia and Africa, negotiating independence for Algeria in 1962. Instead of colonialism, increased trade with Europe became France's priority.

De Gaulle was succeeded as president by Georges Pompidou (1969–74) and Valéry Giscard d'Estaing (1974–81). Both were conservatives and supporters of Gaullist policies. But in

1981, economic problems resulting from a global oil crisis brought a Socialist victory. François Mitterrand became president with backing from French Communists. A Socialist prime minister served with him.

For a time, the Socialists increased government control of the economy. They added more public services and utilities to France's nationalized sector. They gave workers and unions more power in the workplace and increased social welfare benefits. However, in the face of high inflation and rising unemployment, the Socialists switched gears in 1984. They cut taxes sharply and reduced government spending.

When economic conditions remained poor, voters turned to conservative parties. The conservatives had called for privatization of industry and deregulation of the economy. Growing resentment of foreign workers, especially those coming from the former French colonies in North Africa, also strengthened the conservatives. In 1986 elections, the conservative parties won control of the National Assembly. Jacques Chirac, a Gaullist, became prime minister. For two years France experienced divided rule. However, after voters reelected Mitterrand in 1988, the Socialists won new legislative elections, and a Socialist became prime minister.

By now, the Socialists had moved from the political left toward the center and right. They focused on strengthening France's ability to compete economically in world markets and on building European unity. However, they were unable to stave off new economic problems, and suffered a crushing defeat in 1993 legislative elections. Conservative parties won 460 of the 577 National Assembly seats. The assembly came under the control of two conservative parties: Chirac's Rally for the Republic (RPR) and Giscard d'Estaing's Union for French Democracy (UDF).

Chirac turned down a new chance to be prime minister, and that post went to Chirac's friend Édouard Balladur of the RPR. Later, however, the two had a falling out. In 1995, Balladur ran against Chirac in the presidential elections, placing third in the first round. Chirac won the election by promising to create new jobs to bring down France's high unemployment rate. He also promised to give French voters the final say in a referendum on any new steps toward European union.

Before the end of 1995, however, Chirac and his prime minister, Alain Juppé, faced a storm of public discontent. Widespread strikes brought public transportation grinding to a halt. Hundreds of thousands of citizens marched through the streets of Paris and other cities. They were protesting against a government plan to raise taxes and slash spending. Government officials saw the moves as necessary to wipe out a large budget deficit and prepare for closer European union. But many French citizens saw them as gutting social welfare programs and undermining the French standard of living. Observers said the unrest was the worst to hit France in a decade.

1. *Identify each of the following:*
   a. *Charles de Gaulle*
   b. *François Mitterrand*
   c. *Jacques Chirac*
   d. *Édouard Balladur*
2. *List the factors that caused French Socialists to lose power in the 1990s.*

Political Parties. Socialist and social democratic movements were in trouble throughout Europe in the 1990s. Responding to voter pressure, Socialists in many countries were following the French Socialists in moving rightward. They were reexamining the idea that government should run major industries and calling for cutbacks in spending to help balance national budgets.

In Britain, the Labor Party had not won a national election since 1979. Despite a long economic recession that hurt Prime Minister John Major and his Conservative Party, British voters rejected Labor in a 1992 election. Admitting that its policies had cost many votes, Labor in 1995 abandoned its longtime support for nationalization of industry.

Germany's Social Democratic Party last controlled government in 1982. Italy's Socialists were involved in financial scandals that forced the resignation of their chairman and the imprisonment of many of their leaders. Only in Sweden, Spain, and Portugal did Socialists win major national elections between 1990 and 1995.

The drop in voter support for socialist parties had three causes. First, the goals of socialism—labor unionism, social security systems, social welfare programs, high minimum wages, equality of opportunity in the workplace—had largely been achieved. Second, the collapse of the Communist governments of Eastern Europe undermined faith in socialism,

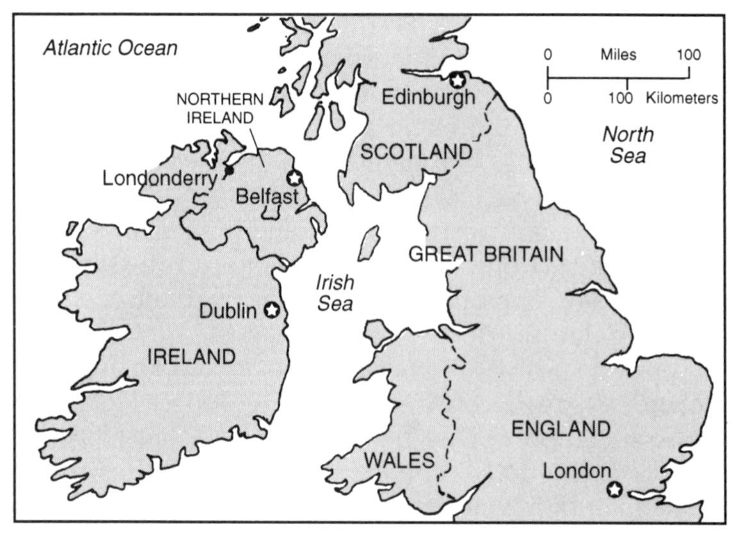

Figure 2.7 Great Britain and Ireland

which shared communism's emphasis on state control of economic resources and facilities (even though socialism has distinct differences from communism). Third, the post-cold war revival of nationalism and ethnic rivalries throughout Europe raised new issues and problems unrelated to social democracy.

In the new Europe of the 1990s, new political parties arose, reflecting new concerns. In Germany, France, Italy, and Spain, such political groupings as environmentalists ("greens"), nationalists, and supernationalists made striking gains. In March 1994, nationalist and neo-Fascist parties won the Italian elections. Silvio Berlusconi formed a new right-wing government. Although Berlusconi lost his parliamentary majority and left office at the end of the year, rightists remained a powerful force in Italy.

- *Explain why voter support for socialism declined in Europe in the 1990s.*

Northern Ireland. British-ruled Northern Ireland has been troubled by internal conflicts for many decades. In 1921, the rest of Ireland became a self-governing dominion of the British Commonwealth of Nations. Six of the nine counties of Ulster province, in the north of Ireland, chose to remain part of the United Kingdom. In 1948, Ireland declared itself a republic and withdrew from the commonwealth.

While Roman Catholics are in a majority in the Irish republic, Protestants outnumber them two to one in Northern Ireland. Tensions in Northern Ireland have often boiled over. Catholics accuse the Protestants there of discriminating against them in voting rights, employment, and housing.

Violent troubles began in Northern Ireland in 1969. Catholic groups staged demonstrations demanding an end to property qualifications for voting in local elections. Protestant extremists attacked the demonstrators. Soon rival terrorist groups were carrying out murderous attacks. On the Catholic side, the Irish Republican Army (IRA) battled to unite Northern Ireland with Ireland. On the Protestant side, a group called the Ulster Defense Association (UDA) bombed Catholic targets and carried out assassinations. The Protestants were loyalists who wanted to maintain ties with Britain.

Bombings and murders brought danger to Northern Ireland's chief cities, Belfast and Londonderry. In an attempt to influence public opinion, IRA terrorists also carried out bombings in England, often killing innocent bystanders. Britain sent troops to Northern Ireland to try to restore order. It suspended the parliament of Northern Ireland and imposed direct British rule.

The British put IRA terrorists and suspected terrorists in prison. "Imprisoned nationalists," as they called themselves, used hunger strikes to dramatize their plight. In 1981, ten such protesters starved themselves to death in an attempt to force the British to treat them as political prisoners.

Human rights groups criticized the British government for its raids on civilian homes and harsh treatment of IRA suspects. They accused British courts in Northern Ireland of being more concerned with convictions than with justice.

The government of the Irish republic denounced the violence in Northern Ireland. Irish police acted to block IRA gun-running and other activities. Ireland's leaders said Irish unity could not be achieved through violence.

In 1985, Britain and the Irish republic concluded a pact known as the Anglo-Irish Agreement. The agreement gave the republic of Ireland a limited say in decisions about Northern Ireland. Protestant loyalists condemned the agreement as a betrayal of their cause. Catholic extremists rejected it as an empty gesture. However, some moderates welcomed the agreement as a step forward.

During the 1990s, the search for a settlement began to make headway. In 1992, Northern Ireland's four moderate political parties began talks about the future of the province. Their main concern was *devolution*, or the transfer of political power from Britain to Northern Ireland. Soon after, moderate Catholic leaders made overtures to the IRA's political wing, known as Sinn Fein. Behind the scenes, the British began secret contacts with IRA agents.

A breakthrough came in August 1994, when the IRA declared a cease-fire. Militant Protestant groups responded with a cease-fire of their own. For the first time in 25 years, people felt safe in the streets of Belfast and Londonderry. From 1969 to 1994, more than 3,100 people had died in "the troubles."

Efforts to reach a lasting settlement began in earnest. In March 1995, Britain and the Irish republic proposed direct peace talks between Protestant loyalists and their Catholic opponents. They also suggested creating a new political body in which representatives from Northern Ireland and the Irish republic could work together to resolve disputes. However, many stumbling blocks remained.

In early 1996, the British and Irish governments agreed to begin negotiations among all sides on the future of Northern Ireland. This decision was made after a series of bombings in London shattered the 17-month-old truce. Restoration of the cease-fire by the IRA was made a condition for the participation of Sinn Fein in the talks.

1. *List the causes of violence in Northern Ireland.*
2. *Describe efforts to bring peace to the province.*

Fragile Peace

Immigration. Immigration has become a major factor in shaping the new Europe. Western Europe, especially, has become home to millions of non-Europeans classified as immigrants, guest workers, or asylum seekers. The leading host nations are Germany, France, Italy, and Switzerland. The non-Europeans provide unskilled labor at low wages and thus keep production costs down. However, increased exposure to the cultures of Asia, Africa, the Middle East, and the Caribbean has presented Europeans with new social stresses. An economic recession in the early 1990s boosted resentment of foreigners. Rising unemployment was accompanied by violence against non-Europeans in Britain, France, Germany, and elsewhere.

The future of Europe will depend on the development of nonviolent approaches to building more multicultural societies, as much as upon the growth of democracy and free market economies.

1. *Select and describe ONE problem that has threatened the peace of Western Europe in the 1990s.*
2. *Write a sentence of your own to define or identify each of the following.*
   a. *German neo-Nazis*
   b. *Rally for the Republic (RPR)*
   c. *Socialists*
   d. *Irish Republican Army (IRA)*
   e. *Guest workers*

Chapter 2 Review

A. *Choose the item that best completes each sentence.*

1. *Russia was a nation in crisis in the 1990s because (a) President Boris Yeltsin wanted to restore the power of the Communist Party (b) conflict developed between President Yeltsin and members of parliament (c) President Yeltsin was unable to gain the support of Western leaders.*
2. *A major problem of Ukraine in the 1990s was (a) rising inflation (b) its refusal to admit Western investors (c) a lack of government direction of the economy.*
3. *Among the most important resources of Kazakhstan are*

(a) rubber and bamboo (b) oil and gas (c) timber and manganese.

4. *Two former Communist nations that divided into smaller republics in the 1990s were (a) Hungary and Poland (b) Bulgaria and Romania (c) Czechoslovakia and Yugoslavia.*

5. *A struggle for territory among Muslims, Serbs, and Croatians developed during the 1990s in (a) Bosnia-Herzegovina (b) Moldova (c) Latvia.*

6. *Solidarity played a major role in the political development of (a) Romania (b) Hungary (c) Poland.*

7. *A major problem facing the German government in the 1990s was (a) Soviet aggression (b) the economic cost of reuniting east and west Germany (c) emigration of Germans to other countries.*

8. *In 1993 and 1995, Socialist defeats in legislative and presidential elections caused significant political change in (a) France (b) Germany (c) Italy.*

9. *The Catholic minority of Northern Ireland has protested against (a) lack of opportunity due to the control of the government and economy by the Protestant majority (b) a British plan to withdraw military forces from Northern Ireland (c) an invasion by the forces of the republic of Ireland.*

10. *A major factor in shaping the new Europe of the 1990s has been (a) immigration of non-Europeans (b) emigration of Europeans to other areas (c) declining population.*

B. *Reread ''Conflict and Change in Western Europe,'' on pages 32–40, and examine the maps of that region. Which of the following are correct statements? How can the incorrect statement be corrected?*

1. *Germany has one of the strongest economies in Europe.*

2. *Socialist political leaders remained in power in both France and Spain in the second half of the 1990s.*

3. *Politically, six counties of Ulster are part of Britain. Geographically, they are part of Ireland.*

4. *Voter support for Socialist parties and candidates declined in Western Europe in the 1990s.*

5. *Immigrants have experienced hostility in Britain, France, Germany, and elsewhere in Western Europe.*

C. *Review the maps in Chapter 2 and complete the following:*

1. *The largest republics of the former Soviet Union are ____, ____, and ____.*
2. *Kiev is the capital of ____.*
3. *____ is the capital of Armenia.*
4. *In the 1990s, ____ and ____ fought over Nagorno-Karabakh.*
5. *Three former Soviet republics bordering the Baltic Sea are ____, ____, and ____.*
6. *Prior to January 1993, the Czech Republic and Slovakia were united as ____.*
7. *Sarajevo is the capital of ____ and ____.*
8. *The large country on Poland's western border is ____.*
9. *From the 1940s to 1990, Berlin was in the Communist nation of ____.*
10. *Luxembourg is a tiny nation bordered by ____, ____, and ____.*

Chapter 3

Africa in Crisis

Africa is a continent in crisis. It faces not one but many challenges. Perhaps foremost is the struggle for democracy, which rages in many parts of the continent. Often, the end of colonialism brought dictatorship and one-party rule. People in many African nations have been struggling to build democracy. A second major problem is ethnic violence. Vicious ethnic wars have devastated Rwanda, Burundi, the Sudan, and Liberia in recent years. Thirdly, many parts of Africa have suffered from a severe and prolonged water shortage, or *drought,* brought on by insufficient rainfall. The continent's deserts have expanded and its food-growing areas have shrunk. Almost one fifth of the African population has faced sustained hunger in recent years. Additional problems confronting Africa's 61 countries are political instability, global recession, and rapid population growth.

The Struggle for Democracy: Zaire

Sewage flowed in open ditches through the streets of Zaire's capital, Kinshasa. In the countryside, highways were so full of potholes that trucks moved only at a creep. Hospitals lacked medicines. The government barely functioned.

In the first half of the 1990s, Zaire became a case study in disintegration. Billionaire President Mobutu Sese Seko was widely denounced as a grasping dictator. Observers blamed his repressive policies for military mutinies, destructive riots, and economic ruination. At a time when other African nations were struggling to turn dictatorships into democracies, Zaire seemed lost in a time warp.

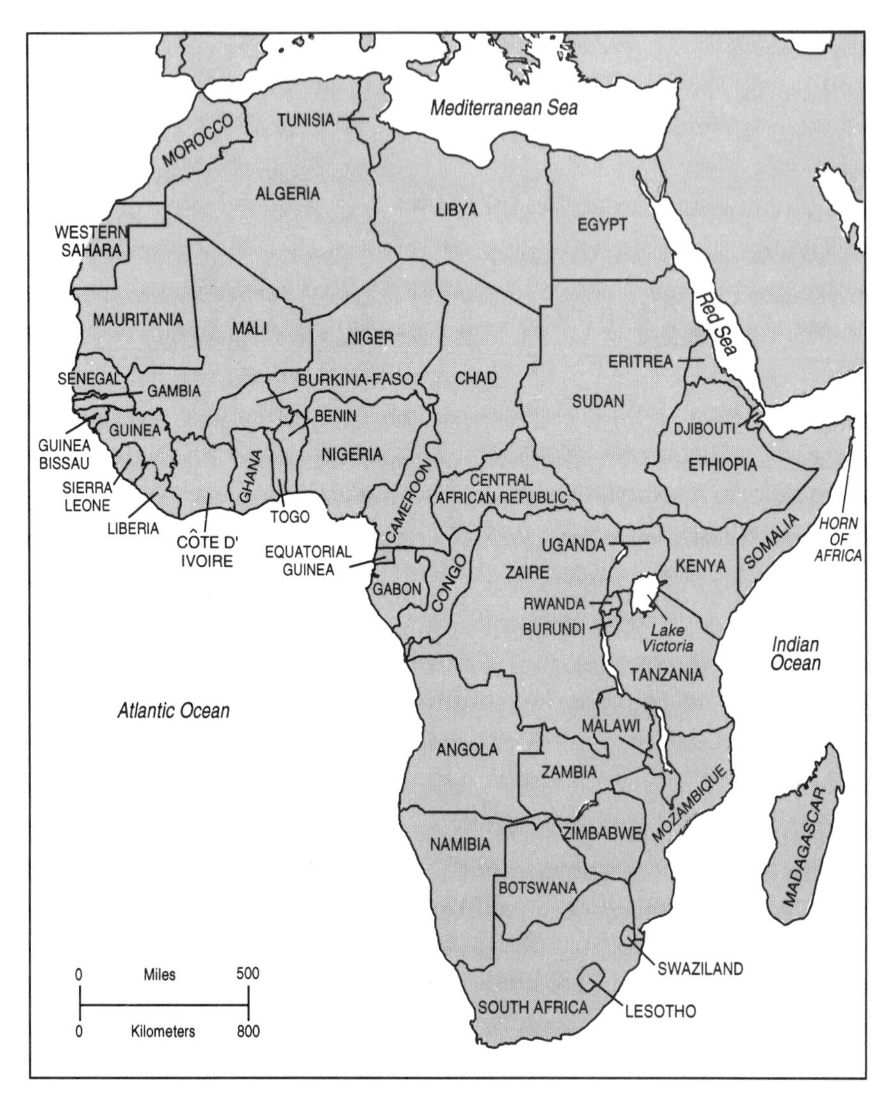

Figure 3.1 Africa

Zaire has known many hardships over the past century. Under Belgian control from 1885 to 1960, the country was known as the Belgian Congo. The Belgian authorities did little to prepare the country's people to govern themselves. As a result, when Belgium granted independence in 1960, the new nation (called Congo-Kinshasa) plunged into political chaos.

Almost at once, the mineral-rich province of Katanga (now called Shaba) attempted to secede. The Congo-Kinshasa government asked the United Nations to help it keep the country united. When the U.N. sent troops to help end the provincial rebellion, fighting broke out between U.N. forces and the Katangan army. Not until 1963 did Katanga come under the control of the Congolese central government. (It tried unsuccessfully to break away again in the 1970s.)

♦ *Identify each of the following:*

a. Kinshasa
b. Congo-Kinshasa
c. Katanga

While the civil war was raging, political rivalries resulted in the imprisonment and murder of the prime minister, Patrice Lumumba. Although a new government was formed in 1964,

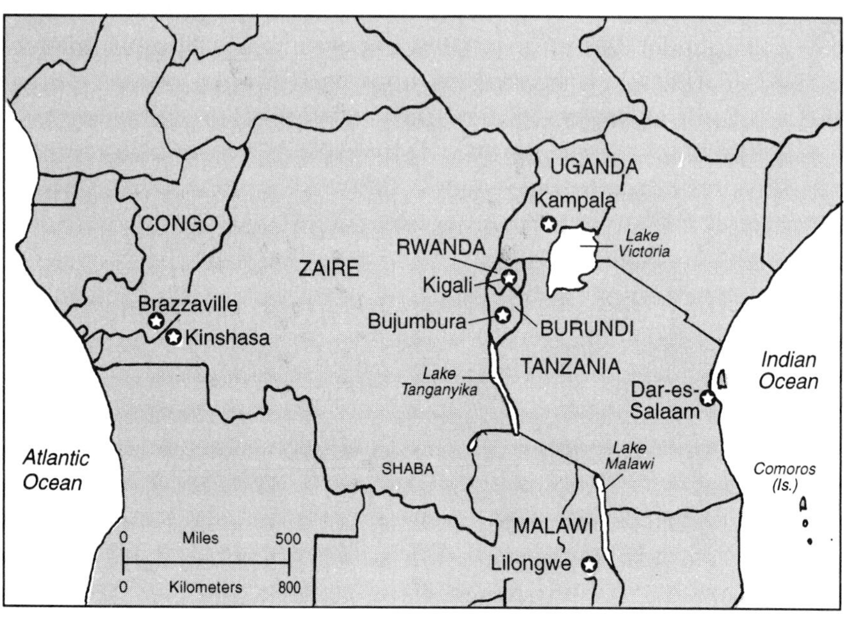

Figure 3.2 Central Africa

continuing civil strife made this country one of Africa's bloodiest battlegrounds. Taking advantage of the disorder, an ambitious young army general named Joseph Mobutu seized power in 1965. He later Africanized his name to Mobutu Sese Seko. Mobutu changed the country's name to Zaire in 1971. He has ruled ever since.

Zaire has been one of the world's major producers of diamonds, copper, and cobalt. It has rainfall and farming conditions suitable for growing a variety of crops, as well as potential for the development of logging and hydroelectric power. However, much of Zaire's modern industry was destroyed by politically motivated arson and looting, in 1991 and 1993. Zairean exports dropped drastically. Prices rose 5000 percent in just one year. As a result, the people became increasingly poor. Corrupt and inefficient government also contributed to the decline in the nation's standard of living.

Mobutu's personal wealth is legendary. His opponents say control of the state-owned diamond, copper, and cobalt mines enabled Mobutu to divert billions of dollars for his own use. During the 1970s and 1980s, the outside world did not seem to mind. The United States, France, and other Western nations found Mobutu a useful tool in the cold war politics of Africa. But as the cold war drew to an end, the Western nations began pressing for economic reforms and democratization.

In response, Mobutu in 1990 allowed new political parties to be created in opposition to his own Popular Movement of the Revolution. Dozens of new parties popped up. They formed a coalition and chose Étienne Tshisekedi, once a political ally of the dictator, to be their leader. At a national political conference in 1991, delegates elected Tshisekedi to be prime minister. He began trying to wrest control of Zaire's government away from Mobutu.

However, Mobutu still held the main power centers. In particular, he controlled the army and other security forces. They were composed mainly of people from Mobutu's native province. The president was able to use the security forces to keep troubles brewing among Zaire's major ethnic groups, in a policy of "divide and rule."

In the years that followed, Mobutu managed to stay in power. He dismissed Tshisekedi in 1993 and named another prime minister. Mobutu negotiated with the opposition over plans for elections. However, the talks kept stumbling over issues such as how to register voters and whether to hold the elections before or after adoption of a new constitution. It did not help that the opposition was deeply divided.

Mobutu's supporters claimed he was bound to be reelected as president. While Mobutu was unpopular in the capital, he had supporters in other areas. Tshisekedi, who insisted that his dismissal was illegal and that he was still prime minister, seemed popular in Kinshasa. But no one knew how far outside the capital his support extended. Until Zaire managed to hold free and fair elections, political and economic disorder seemed likely to continue.

1. *List three natural resources that could be sources of wealth for Zaire.*
2. *Explain why many Zaireans were opposed to the rule of President Mobutu Sese Seko.*

The Struggle for Democracy: South Africa

In the Republic of South Africa, white-minority rule, supported by the rigid *apartheid* system of racial separation, prevailed after 1948. This outgrowth of European colonialism made South Africa unique. In the 1990s, however, significant change took place.

The white population of South Africa consists of two major groups. The Afrikaaners are the descendants of Dutch, French, and German settlers who began arriving in the 17th century. Their language, Afrikaans, contains elements of these European tongues. In order to acquire the rich farmlands of the veld, or plains, the Afrikaaners fought long wars against the Zulus and other black Africans who were the original inhabitants. In the process, they developed a strong feeling of enmity toward the blacks and a determination to regard them as inferior people.

The Afrikaaners also conflicted with the English, who began arriving in the 19th century. Attracted by the diamond and gold deposits of the country, powerful empire builders such as Cecil Rhodes wanted to strengthen British control over the colony. Differences in culture and lifestyle resulted in the Boer War of 1899–1902. The Afrikaaners failed in their attempt to break away from British rule. But their resentment of the English persisted, and they vowed to run South Africa in their own way.

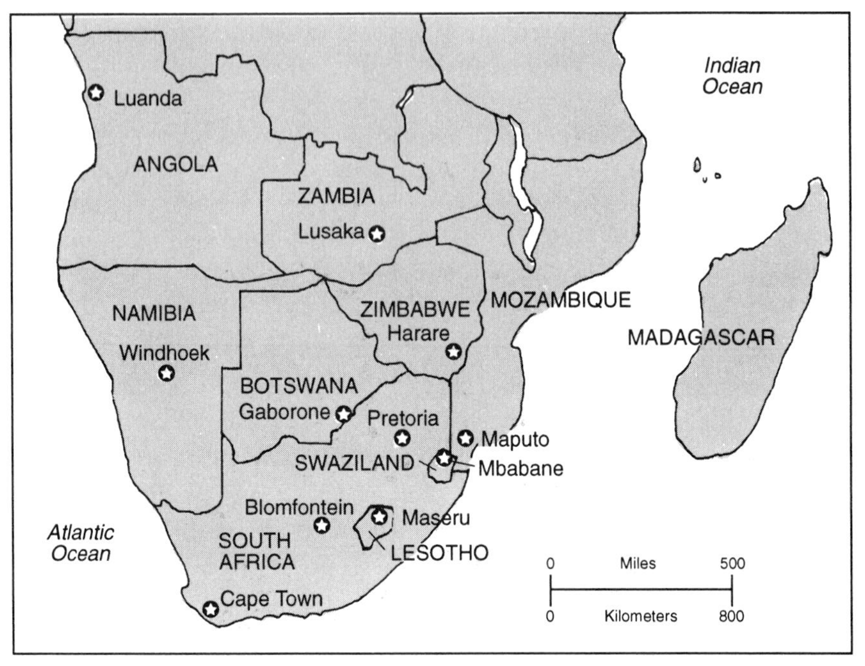

Figure 3.3 Southern Africa

Despite the challenges to colonialism that were emerging elsewhere, South Africa's whites instituted a policy of apartheid after World War II. It was designed to ensure the continued rule of the country by a white minority comprising only 13 percent of the population. Apartheid was introduced by the National Party, led by Daniel F. Malan. It was a system of rigid separation of the races and denial to blacks of political rights, education, and economic opportunity. It also involved the creation of ten black "homelands," in which blacks could live and develop separately, but under despotic governments and without any economic resources or capabilities. From 1953 to 1989, the National Party held power in ten consecutive parliamentary elections. In response to British criticism of South Africa's racial policies, the National Party withdrew the country from the British Commonwealth of Nations in 1960.

Blacks and some whites organized resistance to apartheid. The largest mainly black group fighting to end white minority rule was the African National Congress (ANC), which set up an underground army. ANC leader Nelson Mandela became an international symbol of resistance during the 27 years he spent in South Africa's prisons.

The white government put a new constitution into effect in 1984. It allowed some representation for "coloreds" (people of mixed racial descent) and Asians. Blacks, however, were still denied political rights.

The ANC's war against the white-dominated government kept South Africa in a continuous state of violence. To express disapproval of apartheid and the disorder it bred, the Western nations agreed, in 1986, to impose limited economic sanctions on South Africa. (*Sanctions* are laws forbidding a nation's businesses from buying or selling goods to a country that violates international law.) The economic consequences, and a desire to end internal violence, led some white South Africans to demand change and reconciliation with blacks.

The pace of change picked up in 1990. F. W. De Klerk had become president of South Africa and leader of the National Party. Under his leadership, the government took a series of steps designed to ease tensions and create a new future for the country. These included lifting a ban on the ANC and freeing Nelson Mandela. De Klerk and Mandela began talks to plan a process of political change.

In 1991, De Klerk announced his intention to end all apartheid laws. For blacks, the most hated law was one that required South Africans to register with the government by race. That law was repealed, to widespread praise from the international community. However, ANC leaders criticized De Klerk for moving too slowly. Guerrilla warfare between blacks and South African security forces continued.

Conflict between the ANC and the Inkatha Freedom Party became another source of violence in 1992 and 1993. Led by Mangosuthu Buthelezi, Inkatha gained power in rural areas by promoting Zulu tradition and by making allies of Zulu tribal leaders. The Zulus were the largest ethnic group in South Africa. Unlike Buthelezi, the African National Congress rejected tribal authority. It regarded leadership by chiefs and elders as undemocratic. Nelson Mandela and the ANC called for the election of a national government by South Africans of all backgrounds under the principle "one person, one vote."

After a series of shootings that left 20 dead in March 1993, the ANC and the opposing Inkatha Freedom Party called upon their followers to end the violence. In the same month, a conference of 26 political party delegations began meeting in Johannesburg to discuss the political future of South Africa.

The broadly based conference was made possible by an agreement between the government and the ANC on a plan to hold national elections by April 1994, under universal suffrage. Although Chief Buthelezi did not approve the details of this plan, he committed his Inkatha Freedom Party to participation in the long-range discussions to form a multiracial government.

In April 1994, the eyes of the world were on South African voters of all races as they went to the polls together for the first time. They elected a new legislature. Sixty percent of the votes went to Mandela's ANC, 20 percent went to De Klerk's National Party, and 10 percent to Buthelezi's group.

At the same time, a new constitution took effect. It attempted to balance majority rule with safeguards to reassure whites and other minorities. A bill of rights promised freedom of speech and other liberties that in the past were reserved mainly for whites. The constitution abolished such remnants of apartheid as the ten self-governing black homelands.

With his strong backing in parliament, Mandela became president in May 1994. A multiracial "unity government" set to work to convert South Africa into a truly democratic nation.

Now the Work Begins

Under the rules of the balloting, parties winning 5 percent or more of the legislative vote were to be entitled to seats in the cabinet for five years. Buthelezi took a cabinet seat. De Klerk became one of two vice presidents.

Since 1994, Mandela's government has tried to improve the lives of black South Africans while keeping the support of other races. It has promised to preserve South Africa's system of free enterprise. As economic sanctions ended, trade with other African nations boomed. South Africa's economy—the strongest in Africa—began to bounce back.

Yet immense problems lay ahead. More than one third of black South Africans had no jobs, and one person in four lived in squalid and inadequate housing. A year after Mandela's election, a reporter asked a slum resident in Port Elizabeth if her life had improved. She shrugged, "We struggled before the election. We are still struggling even now." Observers wondered how long voters would support Mandela if they failed to see improvements in their day-to-day lives.

1. *What were the most important changes that came to the Republic of South Africa in the 1990s?*
2. *Write one or two sentences to identify each of the following:*
    a. *Daniel F. Malan*
    b. *F.W. De Klerk*
    c. *Nelson Mandela*
    d. *Mangosuthu Buthelezi*

The Struggle for Democracy: Angola

In the 1970s, the United States competed with the Soviet Union for influence in Africa. Intervention by the superpowers in the affairs of African nations became common. In military conflicts, governments supported by the Soviet Union were offered the assistance of troops from Communist Cuba. A civil war that broke out in Angola as it prepared to receive independence from Portugal in 1975 evolved into the worst cold war confrontation in Africa.

Agostinho Neto, leader of the Popular Front for the Liberation of Angola (MPLA), was able to take control of most of the country with Soviet aid and the direct support of Cuban troops. Neto was opposed by Jonas Savimbi, leader of the National Union for the Total Independence of Angola (UNITA).

Savimbi received aid from the United States and troops from South Africa.

Originally, UNITA and the MPLA had fought side by side to end Portugal's rule of Angola. After Portugal agreed to independence, they turned on each other. Cold war rivalry resulted in the involvement of the two superpowers, as well as Cuba and South Africa. The result was one of the longest and bloodiest of Africa's wars. Between 1975 and 1994, at least 500,000 people were killed. In addition, 3 million Angolans, in a population of 10 million, became refugees. The war also threatened the operation of Angola's oil industry. The country depended on oil for 95 percent of its export earnings, which were used to purchase weapons and food. As the country's agriculture was ruined, most food had to be imported.

In December 1988, Angola, South Africa, and Cuba agreed on a timetable for the withdrawal of Cuban troops. The withdrawal was linked to the independence of Namibia, a former German colony controlled by South Africa and located on Angola's southern border. Namibia became independent in 1990. The Cuban forces departed by 1991.

That same year, UNITA signed a peace agreement with the MPLA government, now led by Jose Eduardo Dos Santos. The following year, national elections were held under United Nations supervision. Dos Santos won, but Savimbi refused to accept the results. Once again, he and his 40,000 guerrillas took up arms. As before, violence spread across the country.

For a time, Savimbi's troops managed to outmaneuver the government's forces. UNITA launched a campaign that gave it control of nearly two thirds of Angola by April 1993. Capture of the country's diamond and oil-producing regions provided UNITA with substantial financial resources. In addition, it was able to acquire large stores of weapons, including tanks, artillery, and antiaircraft guns.

This time, however, Savimbi had lost the support of his main backers, the United States and South Africa. In 1993, the United States officially granted diplomatic recognition to Dos Santos' government. By 1994, Savimbi's troops had lost their headquarters town of Huambo and were on the defensive. The U.N. arranged a new cease-fire in November 1994. At a speech to a UNITA party conference, Savimbi referred to the problems he faced. "The boat is taking on water," he said. "If I said it wasn't, I'd be lying."

Would the cease-fire finally bring peace to Angola? That

remained to be seen. After several false starts, Dos Santos and Savimbi met in Zambia in May 1995. They shook hands and embraced but settled nothing. Three months later they held a second meeting in Gabon. Angolans were enjoying a shaky peace, but Savimbi's guerrillas remained in readiness for more fighting if the peace talks failed to reach a full settlement. Meanwhile, the United Nations sent the first of a planned 7,000 peacekeeping troops to the troubled country.

1. *Explain why the civil war in Angola was regarded as a cold war conflict.*
2. *State two actions taken by the United Nations to restore peace in Angola.*

The Struggle for Democracy: Kenya

A country of 25 million people, Kenya is an agrarian nation. Its leading exports are coffee and tea. Tourism is a major industry. Kenya has been one of Africa's most stable and prosperous countries. It has been under authoritarian rule

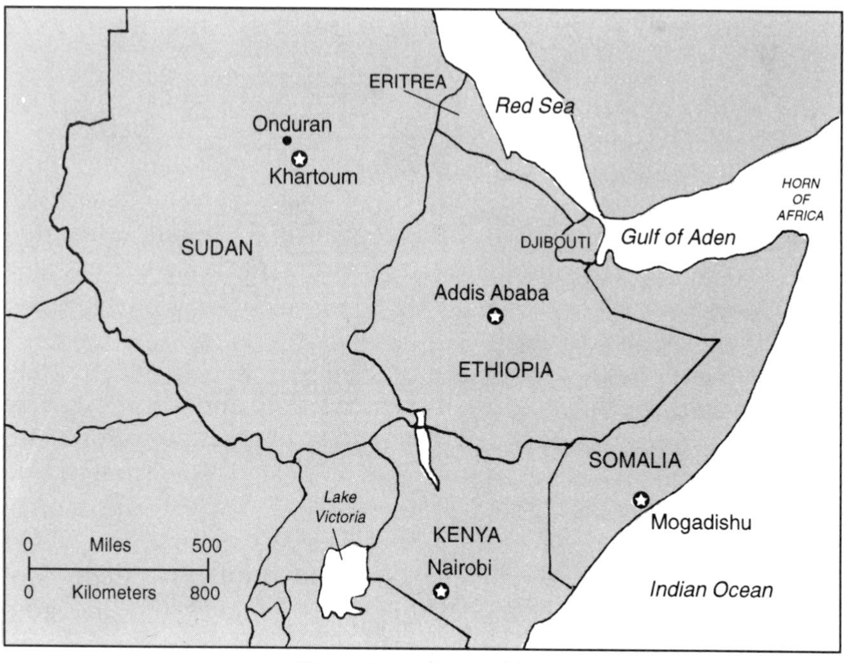

Figure 3.4 East Africa

since 1964, when the Kenya African National Union (KANU) became its sole political party. Until 1978, KANU was headed by Jomo Kenyatta, who had led the struggle for independence from Britain. Kenyatta was prime minister and then president. Upon his death in 1978, Daniel arap Moi became KANU leader and president of Kenya.

As is the case in many African countries, tribalism has played a major role in Kenyan politics. Mr. Moi is a member of the Kalenjin, a minority tribe. In May 1992, members of the larger Kikuyu tribe demanded democracy and multiparty elections. The Kikuyu had governed Kenya during the presidency of Jomo Kenyatta. A Democratic Party was organized by Mwai Kibaki, a former vice president and a Kikuyu. Other tribes, the Luo and the Luyha, supported the demand for free elections. Another political party, the Forum for the Restoration of Democracy (FORD), also demanded political change. It was led by Oginga Odinga, a Luo. Eventually, FORD split, forming a second branch under Luyha and Kikuyu leadership.

Kenya owed money to Western nations, and pressure from those nations forced President Moi to agree to hold elections in December 1992. However, officials of his government encouraged armed bands of Kalenjin to attack Kikuyu homes and farms. The attackers told people to support KANU and to remain quiet. In the violence that resulted, hundreds were killed. Many were made homeless.

Although Daniel arap Moi was reelected to the presidency, the opposition parties captured many seats in parliament. After the election, they pledged themselves to the unity necessary to make a multiparty democracy work. They also charged President Moi with fraudulent practices and demanded new elections. The president suspended parliament one day after it opened in January 1993.

A major figure in Kenya's struggle toward democracy was United States Ambassador Smith Hempstone. Mr. Hempstone was an outspoken critic of the corruption and repression of President Moi's regime. His demands for human rights and multiparty elections infuriated the KANU-led government. He also encouraged the United States and other Western nations, which have provided nearly half of Kenya's annual budget, to freeze economic assistance to Kenya until President Moi stopped the persecution of dissidents. As a result, the government was forced, in 1991, to repeal its constitutional amendment outlawing opposition parties.

During the 1970s and 1980s, Kenya's pro-Western political orientation, and its strategic location on the Indian Ocean, resulted in large amounts of Western aid. The economic pressure placed on President Moi in the 1990s reflected a post-cold war change in policy. Anticommunist dictators would no longer be supported by the West.

1. *PROVE or DISPROVE: Tribalism has played a major role in the political life of Kenya.*
2. *Which of the following statements are true and which are false?*
   a. *Jomo Kenyatta led Kenya to independence from Britain.*
   b. *The Kikuyu are the smallest tribe in Kenya.*
   c. *KANU was the only political party allowed by law until 1991.*
   d. *FORD split into two smaller parties.*
   e. *The Western nations have had little influence on the decisions of the Kenyan government.*

The Struggle for Democracy: Ghana

A former British colony, Ghana gained its independence in 1957. Kwame Nkrumah, who led the struggle for independence and was Ghana's first president, wanted to make the country a model African state. A socialist, Nkrumah used government funds to build roads, schools, hospitals, factories, and homes. He established an airline, improved railroads, and encouraged foreign investment.

Nkrumah did not, however, develop democracy. He kept political power firmly in his own hands, harshly repressing all opposition.

In 1966, elements of the army and police led a revolt against Nkrumah's regime. A National Liberation Council was established to govern the country, and a general became head of state. Kwame Nkrumah was banished from Ghana. He died in exile in 1972.

A military government ruled Ghana until 1979. Then a new constitution was introduced and an elected civilian government assumed office. At the end of 1981, however, Jerry Rawlings, a young military officer, took over the government. He ruled as chief of a military junta called the Provisional National Defense Council.

Still another new constitution to provide for civilian government took effect in 1992. In the election of November 1992,

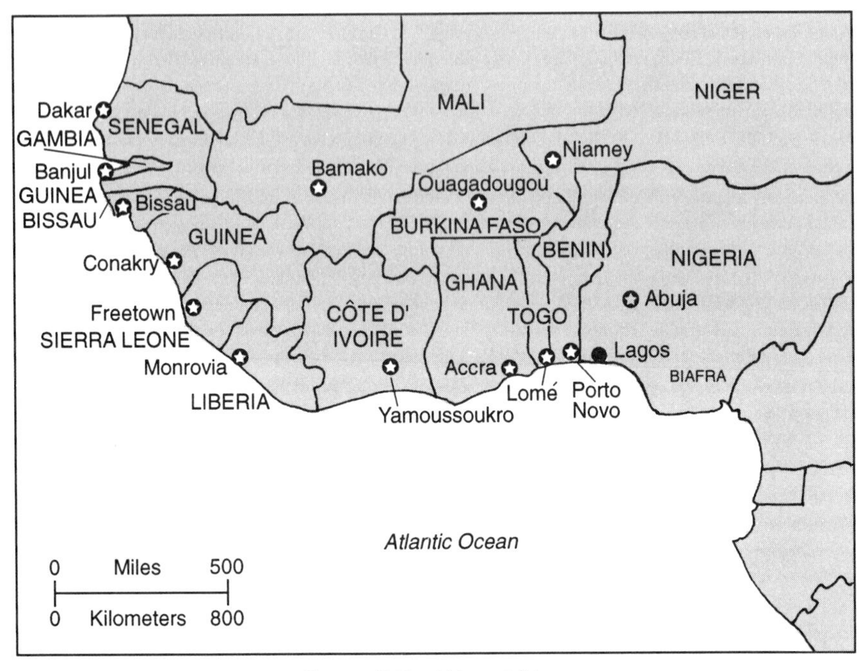

Figure 3.5 West Africa

Rawlings' National Democratic Congress (NDC) defeated three political parties loyal to the socialist policies of Kwame Nkrumah, as well as the New Political Party, a free enterprise group. He captured 58 percent of the vote and was elected president. Despite opposition claims of pressure placed on voters by agents of the ruling military junta, Rawlings' election was judged to be fair by foreign observers. As a result, Ghana was recognized as a democracy. In the 1990s, such recognition has become an essential requirement for the support of Western moneylending nations.

Most of Ghana's 16 million people are subsistence farmers. Cacao is the primary cash crop, bringing in half of the country's income from exports. Also, rich deposits of bauxite, coupled with cheap hydroelectric power provided by the Volta River Project, have enabled aluminum production to be Ghana's largest industry.

Despite these assets, Ghana has had severe economic problems. Inflation reached 100 percent in the 1980s. Rawlings' military junta imposed an economic recovery program that reduced inflation to under 15 percent in 1991. Public resentment of certain economic measures may be tempered, in the future, by the fact that the government has been democratically elected.

♦ *Explain why Jerry Rawlings, like other African dictators in the 1990s, agreed to allow multiparty elections.*

Genocide in Rwanda

In 1994, Rwanda was the scene of one of Africa's most vicious civil wars. At least 500,000 people lost their lives in massacres sparked by animosities between two rival ethnic groups, Hutus and Tutsis. The killing occurred on such a large scale that it was referred to as genocide. (*Genocide* is the killing of a group of people because of their race or religion.)

The Tutsis are an aristocratic minority (one seventh of the population) in Rwanda and neighboring Burundi. Under Belgian rule before 1959, a Tutsi king and his nobles ruled over a Hutu majority. Then Belgian colonial authorities supported a Hutu revolt. In doing so, the Belgians hoped to gain greater control over the Tutsis, who demanded independence. During the uprising, Hutu peasants killed hundreds of thousands of Tutsis. Surviving Tutsis fled to neighboring countries.

After Rwanda became independent in 1962, Tutsi exiles staged guerrilla attacks into Rwanda. Finally, in 1990, an exile army known as the Rwandan Patriotic Front (RPF) managed to get a foothold on Rwandan soil. It waged a guerrilla war against the Hutu-dominated government of President Juvénal Habyarimana. He was a dictator who came to power in a military coup in 1973. Rwanda was the most densely populated nation in Africa, with 94 percent of its arable land under cultivation. President Habyarimana argued that there was no room in Rwanda for the exiles.

Nonetheless, his government signed a cease-fire with the rebels in 1993. United Nations peacekeeping troops arrived. But in April 1994, a missile blew up a plane carrying President Habyarimana and the president of neighboring Burundi. Had extremist Hutus killed Habyarimana to block his plans for peace with the Tutsis? That was a common belief—seemingly confirmed when Rwandan government soldiers and Hutu militia immediately began slaughtering Tutsis and moderate Hutus.

As the killing spread, swarms of refugees fled to neighboring countries. In one 24-hour period, 250,000 people poured into

What Now?

Tanzania. More than a million fled to Zaire, where tens of thousands died in epidemics of cholera. In Rwanda, U.N. peacekeepers found scenes of carnage—headless bodies, rotting corpses, mainly of Tutsis. Even though most of the killing had been carried out by Hutus, the refugees were mostly Hutus.

Amidst the chaos, the RPF took control of Rwanda's capital, Kigali. It established a new government that included both Tutsis and Hutus. Major General Paul Kagame, a Tutsi who had led the rebels, became vice president. In 1995, the government asked U.N. troops to leave. The Rwandan army, now mainly Tutsi, prepared to defend itself against expected attacks by Hutu soldiers who had reorganized outside Rwanda. It seemed that Rwanda's nightmare was not over yet.

- *Explain why you agree or disagree with the following statement:*

  The civil war in Rwanda differs from other African conflicts of the 1990s.

The Americo-Liberians

Like other African nations, Liberia was colonized by Westerners in the 19th century. In Liberia's case, however, the colonists were freed black slaves and their freeborn children and grandchildren from the United States. Later called Americo-Liberians, these American colonists began arriving in the area in 1822. They bought land from native chiefs and settled on the coast. They built Monrovia, the capital, and other coastal cities.

Cultural differences soon caused tension between the American colonists and the original inhabitants. The native Africans were treated badly, forced into the interior, and, at times, enslaved. Eventually, an American form of government was established.

The Americo-Liberians are Western in culture, English speaking, and Christian. The rest of Liberia's population of 2.8 million are traditionally African in language, culture, and religion. Some are Muslim. Despite the fact that the Americo-Liberians are less than one fourth of the population, they controlled the country's government and economy until 1980.

Charging the government with corruption, soldiers from the interior, mainly enlisted men, staged a bloody coup and took control of the government in April 1980. Sergeant Samuel Doe became head of state. Later, he was elected president.

In 1989, when a guerrilla army tried to overthrow President Doe, several tribally based militias formed and battled for power. A destructive civil war quickly spread across the country. In September 1990, rebels captured President Samuel Doe and executed him. But the fighting went on. Famine and war made refugees of more than half the population. Desperate Liberians sought shelter in Monrovia, which was itself largely destroyed by the fighting. Neighboring African countries formed a multinational military force to help restore order.

After many failed truces, the Liberian militias stopped the war in August 1995. By then, more than 150,000 Liberians—6 percent of the population—had died. The three main warlords took seats on a six-person council of state. Its job was to govern Liberia until free elections could be held in 1996.

- *Complete the following sentence:*

  Control of Liberia's government and economy by Americo-Liberians ended in 1980 because ____.

Morocco: A Saharan Kingdom

The North African nation of Morocco is a constitutional monarchy. Its king is head of state. He exercises authority over the government, which is led by a prime minister appointed by the king. The one-house national legislature has 333 members, of whom two thirds are elected directly by the people and one third are chosen by an electoral college. The king may dissolve

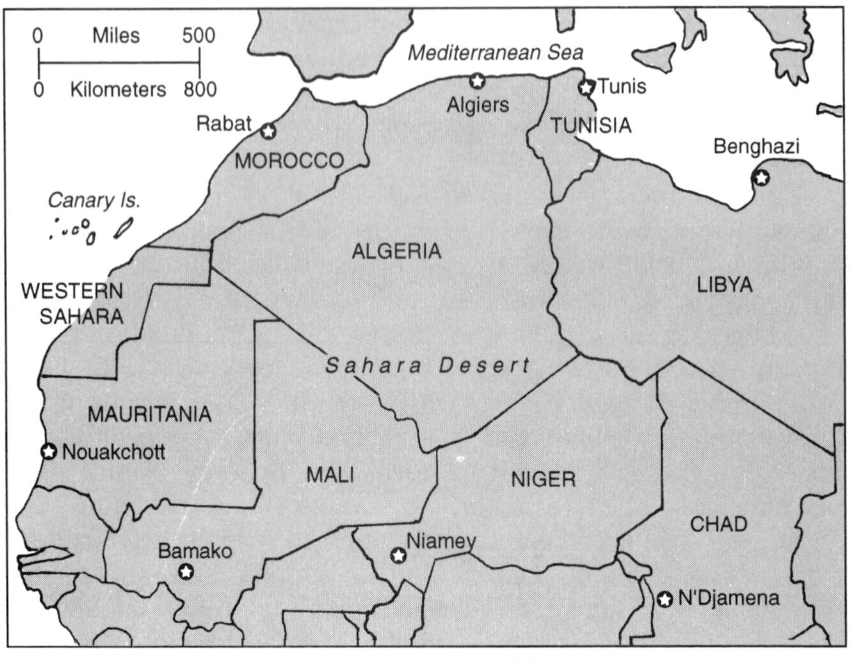

Figure 3.6 North Africa

the legislature at will. In 1995, King Hassan II proposed a new, two-house legislative system.

French and Spanish colonialism strongly affected the northwestern portion of Africa. Morocco gained independence from France in 1956 after a long struggle by nationalists. At the same time, Spain let Morocco annex its colony of Spanish Morocco. Morocco also received the internationalized seaport of Tangier and some additional Spanish-held land.

Until 1976, Spain also controlled Western Sahara, an area to the south of Morocco along Africa's Atlantic coast. Morocco took control of two thirds of this territory in 1976 and occupied the rest in 1980. Moroccan rule was challenged by a nationalist organization called the Polisario Front, which demanded the independence of Western Sahara.

Other African nations supported the Polisario claim. The resulting dispute caused Morocco to withdraw from the Organization of African Unity (OAU) in 1984. (The OAU is a coalition of African states that seeks to coordinate the economic, political, and cultural policies of its members; fight colonialism; and guard against threats to its members' independence.)

Western Sahara is a sparsely populated area with no agriculture and little developed industry. Its value to Morocco lies in its rich coastal fisheries and its valuable phosphate deposits, which the Moroccans have developed. Morocco has built a fortified defense wall around most of Western Sahara, enclosing almost all its people, its fisheries, and its mineral resources.

The people of Western Sahara are called Sahrawis. Traditionally, they were nomadic Arabs and Berbers raising cattle, camels, sheep, and goats. Drought has forced many of them to abandon their nomadic lifestyle and join the Europeans and Moroccans living in the cities.

The United Nations had planned to hold a referendum on independence for Western Sahara in mid-1992, but the vote was postponed. Therefore, the fate of this portion of Saharan Africa remains one of the continent's unsolved territorial disputes.

1. *Why has Morocco wished to retain control of Western Sahara?*
2. *From the list that follows, select the term that best completes each sentence.*

   Sahrawis nomads drought Morocco
   Berbers Polisario independence

   The ____ have been ____ raising cattle and sheep. Most are Arabs or ____. Many were forced to live in cities after a long ____ as a result of reduced rainfall. The ___ Front, a nationalist movement, demanded the ___ of Western Sahara from ____.

War and Famine: Sudan

After independence in 1956, war and famine struck Sudan, in northeast Africa. The country is deeply split between Arab northerners, who are mostly Muslims, and black African southerners, who tend to be Christians or animists (those who believe in the spirits of animals, vegetation, or natural forces).

By the early 1990s, decades of warfare between the Muslim north and the Christian south had driven hundreds of thousands of mostly nomadic southern Sudanese to the brink of starvation. More than 500,000 people were refugees outside the country. Thousands more were encamped just inside Sudan's borders, and 1.5 million displaced people were in and around Khartoum, the capital city.

Sudan has the largest area of any country in Africa. Its population is more than 27 million. Much of the country is desert or receives limited rainfall. Cotton and livestock have been Sudan's chief exports.

Until 1956, Sudan was administered by Britain and Egypt. Following independence, a parliamentary coalition government ruled. A military coup deposed the government in 1958. All political parties were banned. A Supreme Council of the Armed Forces ruled the country until riots in 1964 forced a change. A brief period of civilian rule ended in another military coup in 1968.

Jaafar Mohammed al Nemery, leader of a ten-person Revolutionary Council, won election as president in 1971. Nemery was reelected in 1977 and 1983. Each time, he ran without opposition.

Despite the granting of autonomy to the southern Sudan, a civil war broke out in 1983. Tensions between the Muslim north and the Christian south had been intensified by Nemery's decision to impose Islamic law on civil courts throughout the country. In addition, the country's severe economic problems were compounded by a great drought that affected much of Africa, and by an influx of refugees fleeing from wars in Chad and Ethiopia.

Still another military coup ousted Nemery in 1985. An elected civilian government took office in 1986. Unable to stop the fighting in the south, it was overthrown by a military coup in 1989.

During the 1990s, the government stepped up its campaign against the southern rebels. It also sought to reduce Khartoum's population of southern refugees. Government bulldozers roared through shantytowns, crushing the refugees' shacks and forcing them into desolate resettlement camps called "peace villages."

Haunted by war and famine, thousands of Sudanese in the south had come to depend daily on food relief provided by the United Nations and private relief groups. Chances of a return to stability appeared dim. Rebel southern groups often fought one another as well as the government. The death toll in the civil war had already passed the one million mark, with no end in sight.

- *Which statement is correct?*
  - a. *The Sudanese have been the victims of both natural and political disasters.*
  - b. *The Sudanese government was able to negotiate a peace with rebel leaders in the 1990s.*
  - c. *Military dictators have played no role in Sudanese political history.*

War and Famine: Somalia

World attention focused on Somalia in the early 1990s. There, too, human suffering was extreme.

Located on the Indian Ocean, in the mainly desert area known as the Horn of Africa, British Somaliland was given its independence in 1960. Shortly after, it joined with the Italian-held portion of Somaliland to form the larger nation of Somalia.

In the 1970s and 1980s, the United States and the Soviet Union competed for influence in the Horn of Africa region. When Somalia laid claim to Ogaden, a section of neighboring Ethiopia largely inhabited by Somalis, the Soviet Union sent Cuban troops to assist the Ethiopian government. During the long war that followed (1977–88), Somali forces were defeated by the Soviet-equipped Cubans. The weapons and military equipment left by the Cubans, and those given by the United States to the Somalis, were later used by rival Somali leaders to equip their personal forces.

These local leaders, or warlords, battled one another and the Somali government. By late 1992, Somalia had almost ceased to exist as a nation. All government had been destroyed. Drought and famine further increased the misery and led to the deaths of several hundred thousand people.

Humanitarian organizations, such as the International Committee of the Red Cross, worked with the United Nations to bring supplies of food, fuel, and medicine to Somalia. However, distribution of these supplies was disrupted by the rival militias, which attacked the relief workers and looted their convoys and warehouses.

In December 1992, the United Nations approved a plan to send United States and other military forces to Somalia to protect relief workers and ensure the distribution of food. By early 1993, large numbers of troops from the United States, France, Britain, and Italy had arrived in Somalia. The effort to use those troops to ensure the distribution of relief aid and to stop factional fighting was led by U.S. envoy Robert B. Oakley and General Robert Johnston, the American military commander in Somalia.

To stabilize the country, Oakley and Johnston concentrated on disarming the warlords and persuading them to shift from military to political competition. Oakley persuaded 14 major faction leaders to attend a national reconciliation conference in March 1993. It resulted in a pact among the rival groups to disarm, to establish a transitional government, and to hold national elections in two years. At the same time, plans were made for an expanded United Nations military force to eventually assume responsibility for bringing peace to Somalia.

The strongest Somali warlord, General Muhammad Farah Aydid, opposed the U.N. role. U.S. and U.N. forces carried out attacks against his supporters and attempted to capture him. However, the U.N. intervention began to go awry in October 1993, when 18 U.S. soldiers died in a fight with Aydid's forces. Under pressure from Americans who wondered why U.S. soldiers were dying in Somalia, the United States withdrew all its forces by March 1994.

Several nations were troubled that U.N. troops had fought against one Somali faction, rather than acting as a neutral peacekeeper. Consequently, in March 1995, the U.N. pulled out its troops. The Somali factions fought on, with no end to the war in sight.

1. *Compare the role played by the United States in Somalia during the 1970s and 1980s with its actions in the 1990s.*
2. *Complete the following sentence:*

   The United Nations withdrew its troops from Somalia because ___.

Poverty and Military Repression: Nigeria

In the early 1980s, Nigeria's economy boomed. Oil wealth poured into the nation's coffers. Skyscrapers rose over the port city of Lagos, and jobs were easy to find. But when oil prices crashed, so did Nigeria's economy. In the 1990s, Nigeria's basic public services almost ceased to function. Telephones went dead. Lights blinked off in routine electrical blackouts. Lagos and other big cities turned into filthy, crowded places, with dirt roads, open sewers, and piles of rubbish rotting in the heat.

While the nation's poorest dressed in rags, however, the soldiers and police were clothed, comfortably housed, and well fed, for the military ran the government. Since 1960, when Nigeria gained independence from Britain, the armed forces have run the country for all but nine years.

Nigeria is Africa's most populous nation, with 98 million people. The first military government seized power there in

1966. The next year the eastern region seceded, calling itself the Republic of Biafra. That plunged the country into a bloody civil war. An estimated one million casualties resulted before the secessionists surrendered in 1970.

Military rule lasted until 1979, when General Olusegun Obasanjo turned power over to an elected civilian government. But democracy did not last long. Military rule returned after a coup in 1983, and in 1985 yet another coup made General Ibrahim Babangida the military dictator of Nigeria.

Over the next several years, Nigeria experienced a sharp drop in living standards. This was due in part to a worldwide fall in the price of oil, Nigeria's most valuable export. Critics also alleged high-level corruption. They said General Babangida let his closest associates, mostly military men, grab hundreds of millions of dollars from the country's oil revenues. Babangida himself became quite wealthy.

Finally, responding to widespread criticism, Babangida promised to restore civilian government. He allowed two political parties to form. After many fits and starts, Nigerians went to the polls in June 1993, to elect a civilian government. A businessman named Moshood Abiola seemed to have won

Revolving Door Government

by a landslide. But Abiola never took office. Babangida tossed out the election results and stayed in power. Then, in August 1993, Babangida resigned, appointing a hand-picked civilian to head the government.

Civilian government lasted just 82 days. A coup in November 1993 brought to power a new military dictator, General Sani Abacha. He dissolved the National Assembly and the elected governments and assemblies of all 30 states of the Nigerian federation. General Abacha also banned the two political parties permitted by Babangida.

General Abacha established what was called the most repressive military government since Nigeria's independence. It jailed prominent Nigerians (including Obasanjo and Abiola), closed newspapers, and shut down labor unions. General Abacha promised to restore civilian rule—but he seemed in no hurry to do so.

1. *Describe the evolution of military dictatorship in Nigeria.*
2. *General Babangida was sometimes called "Nigeria's Mobutu." Explain why.*

Africa: General Observations

In addition to civil wars and dictatorships, Africans today must overcome many instances of political corruption and economic mismanagement. Their situation has been made more difficult by an AIDS epidemic that has reduced the middle class in numerous countries. Africa today has the highest infant mortality rate, the lowest literacy rate, and the highest rate of population growth of the developing world. Fewer than half the people living south of the Sahara have basic health care. Nearly two thirds lack safe drinking water. African life expectancy is 52 years compared to the world average of 63 years.

Nevertheless, progress is being made. The number of Africans immunized against serious diseases increased from less than 20 percent in the 1980s to 60 percent in the 1990s. Average life expectancy has risen, as has primary school enrollment. Of great importance is Africa's richness in human and natural resources. As the struggle for democracy goes on, better leadership and increased economic efficiency may make possible a better future.

Chapter 3 Review

A. *Which item best completes the sentence?*

1. *Arson and looting, in 1991 and 1993, caused widespread destruction of industries in (a) Ghana (b) Rwanda (c) Zaire.*
2. *In the Republic of South Africa, a long struggle succeeded in (a) ending apartheid (b) establishing a multiracial government (c) both of these.*
3. *Civil war in Angola resumed in 1992 because the results of a national election were not accepted by (a) MPLA (b) UNITA (c) RPF.*
4. *The Kikuyu and Luo peoples are important groups in (a) Kenya (b) Ghana (c) Morocco.*
5. *The genocide in Rwanda in 1994 was committed mainly by (a) Hutus against Tutsis (b) Zulus against Hutus and Tutsis (c) whites against blacks.*
6. *One country that replaced a ruling military junta with an elected civilian government in the 1990s was (a) Zaire (b) Kenya (c) Ghana.*
7. *Control of Liberia's government and economy by the descendants of American colonists was ended in 1980 by (a) religious dissidents (b) minority tribes (c) military rebels.*
8. *Morocco's conflict with the Polisario Front was over the question of (a) independence for Western Sahara (b) control of Tangier (c) voting rights for Spanish residents.*
9. *Fighting between the Muslim-dominated north and the mainly Christian south caused economic collapse and a huge refugee problem in (a) Zaire (b) Sudan (c) Angola.*
10. *Widespread starvation and continuing violence in Somalia in the 1990s was caused by (a) the breakdown of all government (b) a border war with Ethiopia (c) an influx of refugees from Sudan.*

B. *Compose a brief essay on Contemporary African Problems by writing one or two paragraphs in response to each of the following questions:*

1. *What difficulties have Africans encountered in attempting to establish democratic governments?*
2. *Why has famine become so critical a problem in certain African nations?*

C. *Complete the table.*

Leader	Nation	Major Problem
Mobutu Sese Seko		
Nelson Mandela		
Eduardo Dos Santos		
Daniel arap Moi		
Paul Kagame		
Samuel Doe		
Sani Abacha		

D. *Examine the maps of Africa in Chapter 3 and indicate whether each of the following statements is true or false.*

1. *Zaire and Shaba are separate countries.*
2. *Pretoria is the capital of the Republic of South Africa.*
3. *Angola and Namibia have Atlantic Ocean coastlines.*
4. *Lake Victoria is located in Somalia.*
5. *Ghana is one of the nations of East Africa.*
6. *Forces opposing the government of Rwanda can cross that nation's border from Zaire.*
7. *Liberia and Sierra Leone border the Indian Ocean.*
8. *Conflict in Western Sahara can affect both Morocco and Algeria.*
9. *Refugees from the civil war in Sudan might seek refuge in Egypt and Uganda.*
10. *The easternmost part of Somalia is called the Horn of Africa.*

Chapter 4

War and Peace in the Middle East

Often called "the crossroads of the world," the Middle East has historically been an arena of conflict. Nations, empires, and superpowers have struggled for primacy in religious, ethnic, and territorial disputes. In the 20th century, Middle Eastern oil reserves have increased the importance of the region to the rest of the world. The era of colonialism has ended, but outside nations continue to attempt to exercise influence within the Middle East.

Poverty, overpopulation, inadequate housing, and government corruption have contributed to the spread of radicalism and unrest in the Middle East. The growth of Islamic fundamentalism has added a new element to the volatile mix. Islamic fundamentalists reject many elements of modern life as disruptive of family and society. They seek to "purify" Middle Eastern societies by enforcing a strict interpretation of Muslim law and tradition.

The Sword of Islam

In 1979, Muslim fundamentalists led a successful rebellion against the United States-backed Shah of Iran and took control of that country. Since then, Islamic fundamentalism has grown as a political and religious force. It has spread from the Middle East to North Africa, the Muslim republics of the former Soviet Union, and elsewhere.

Many Muslim fundamentalists focus on trying to live up to the ideals of Islam in their daily lives. They live peacefully

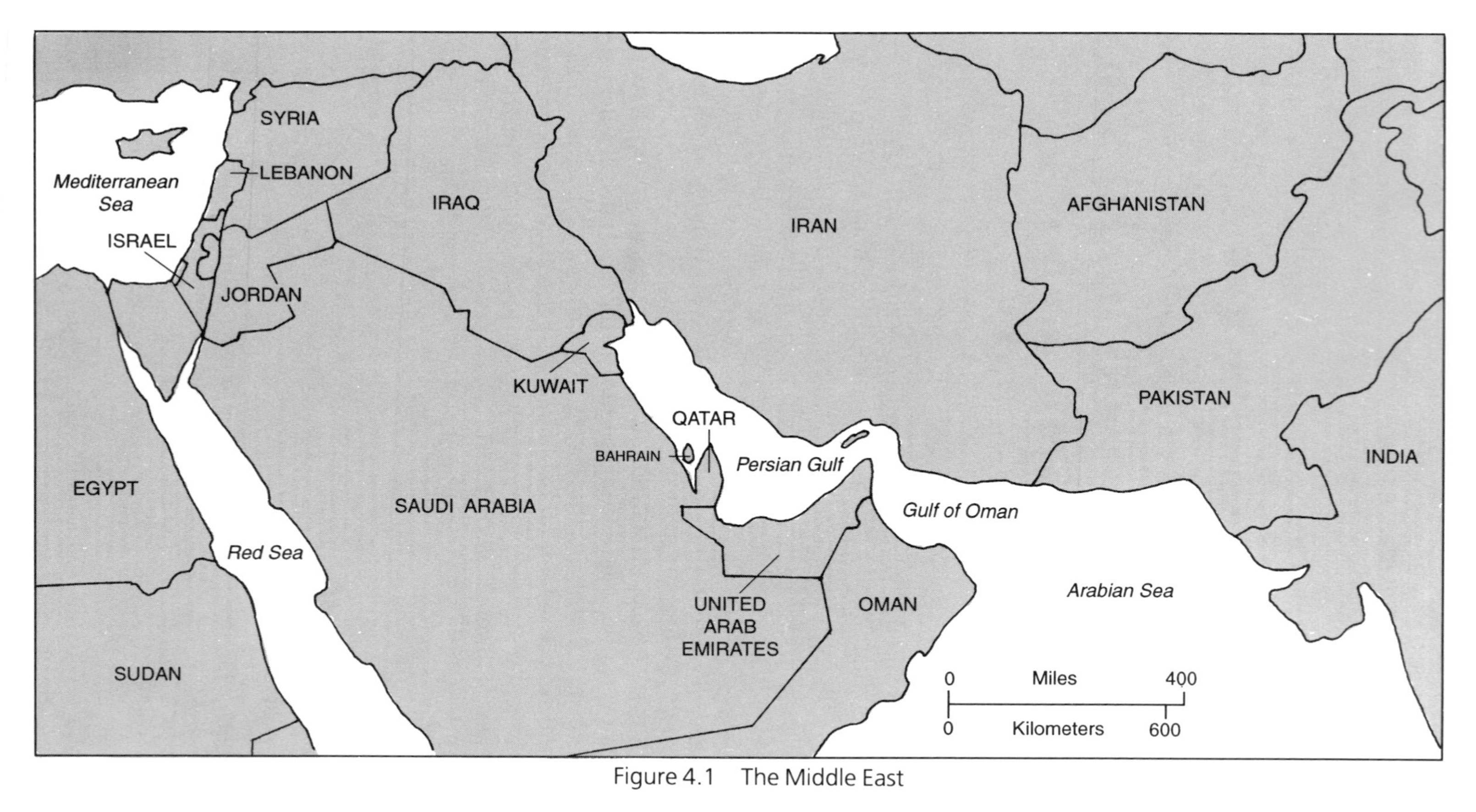

Figure 4.1 The Middle East

with their neighbors. Other fundamentalists have resorted to violence. They seek to overthrow existing governments and impose their ideal of Islamic society by any means necessary.

The most militant fundamentalists, or *Islamists*, reject Western culture and political ideas as remnants of imperialism. They seek to establish Islamic regimes run according to the rules of the Prophet Muhammad, the founder of Islam, and his immediate successors. They also preach the destruction of Israel and the replacement of the Jewish state by an Islamic Palestine. Many Islamists consider the United States a special enemy because of its close ties to Israel and its support for Arab governments that try to crush fundamentalist movements.

Militant Islamists have made their presence felt in many ways. They have seized Western hostages. They have committed terrorist acts. A British Muslim and writer, Salman Rushdie, lives in England under threat of murder. The leaders of Iran declared one of Rushdie's books offensive to Islam and passed a sentence of death on him. Also, Islamists were convicted of exploding a car bomb at the World Trade Center in New York City in February 1993.

How to respond to militant fundamentalists has become a challenge to the West and to moderate Muslims. One reason Islamists turned to violence in the first place is that most Middle Eastern governments repress peaceful opposition and refuse to allow free elections. In 1991, Algeria tried a different tack. Hoping to defuse tensions, the government permitted elections. But when Islamic militants won the first round, Algeria's government canceled a second round. Islamists responded by launching a guerrilla war, using terrorist attacks against government supporters, moderates, and foreigners.

Islamic militants have also participated in efforts to overthrow the governments of Egypt, Aden, Yemen, Tunisia, Jordan, Pakistan, and Turkey. Many of the militants are veterans of the long war in Afghanistan (1979-92). They have used Afghanistan and Pakistan as bases from which to attack other Middle Eastern nations.

Pakistan. Pakistan, which borders Afghanistan, has had close ties to the United States. During the Afghan war, Pakistan's military helped the United States to channel weapons to the Afghan rebels fighting the Soviet occupiers of their country. Also, Pakistanis trained some 25,000 guerrilla volunteers to

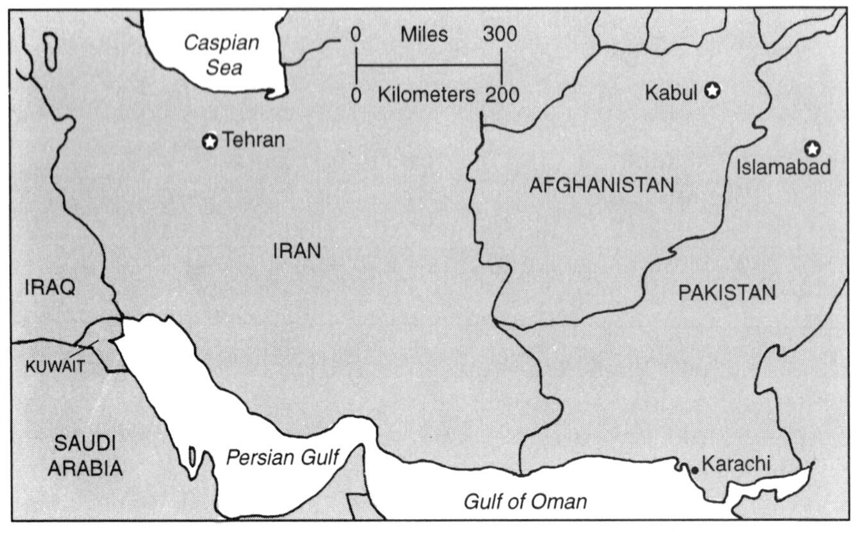

Figure 4.2 Eastern Islamic Nations

be sent to Afghanistan. In 1993, however, Pakistan's government expelled many Afghan war veterans in order to stop them from using the country as a base from which to attack other governments.

- *Explain how militant fundamentalists benefited from the war in Afghanistan.*

Egypt. President Hosni Mubarak of Egypt has been a special target of the Islamic Group, a fundamentalist organization that has been active in Egypt in the 1990s. The Islamists have many reasons for despising Mubarak: (1) Egypt has maintained a separate peace with Israel, a nation hated by the Islamists. (2) Mubarak works closely with the United States, and thus Islamists consider him a puppet of "imperialism." (3) Mubarak mantains a semblance of democracy but allows no real opposition. (4) Corruption is widespread within government circles.

The Islamic Group launched a campaign of violence in 1992. Terrorists set off bombs in cities along the Nile River, with the intention of intimidating tourists, foreign residents, and Egyptian Christians. Islamist gunmen took control of portions of Cairo, the capital city. By 1995, the death toll in the Islamist campaign has passed 800.

In June 1995, the Islamic Group tried to assassinate Mubarak as he arrived in Ethiopia for an international conference.

Mubarak was unhurt, although a number of people were killed in an attack on his motorcade.

The objective of the fundamentalists is to overthrow President Mubarak and establish a purely Islamic government. A major figure in the Islamic Group is Sheik Omar Abdel Rahman, an Egyptian cleric who has preached against the Mubarak government from mosques in the United States. In 1995, a federal court jury in New York convicted the sheik and nine other Islamists of conspiring to carry out terrorist bombings and assassinations in the New York area.

Egyptian security forces raided the areas controlled by the Islamists and arrested thousands. President Mubarak accused the radical regimes of Iran and Sudan of aiding the Islamic Group. Government officials said Egyptian volunteers who had fought in the Afghan war had committed much of the violence.

Western advisers counseled the Mubarak administration to supplement police action with political and economic reforms. They said widespread poverty and government repression helped to build support for radicalism in Egypt. Mubarak's supporters wanted him to find ways to keep the fundamentalists from convincing Egyptians that life under an Islamic government would be better.

The struggle between fundamentalism and secularism in Egypt, a nation whose 53 million people comprise one third of the Arab world's population, has worried the United States government. Egypt's support of U.S. interests and its peace with Israel are considered critical to the success of American policies in the Middle East. The U.S. Embassy in Cairo has been a vital center for intelligence-gathering in the region and for maintaining contact with a number of organizations. A fundamentalist victory in Egypt would curtail U.S. activities and could change the balance of power in the Middle East.

1. *Define the term "Islamic fundamentalism."*
2. *Explain why militant fundamentalism has been a problem for governments in the Middle East and elsewhere.*
3. *Identify each of the following:*
   a. *Salman Rushdie*
   b. *Hosni Mubarak*
   c. *Islamic Group*
   d. *Omar Abdel Rahman*

Israel and the Arabs

A state of war has existed between Israel and almost all its Arab neighbors since 1948, when Israel became a nation. Refusing to accept the Jewish state in their midst, the Muslim Arab nations went to war with Israel in 1948, 1956, 1967, and 1973. Before the 1990s, only Egypt had signed a peace treaty with Israel (1979).

Palestine is regarded by the Jews as their Biblical homeland. After the defeat of the Ottoman Empire in World War I, Britain administered Palestine as a League of Nations mandate. With Hitler's rise to power in Germany, Jews seeking a haven from persecution in Europe returned to their ancestral land in large numbers. Palestinian Arabs resented the influx of new settlers and feared that the newcomers would displace them. Relations between Arabs and Jews became increasingly hostile, with riots and acts of terrorism. Unable to stop the violence, Britain decided to surrender its mandate and turn over the problem to the United Nations.

In a historic 1947 vote, the U.N. partitioned Palestine into separate Jewish and Arab states. The Palestinian Jews accepted the U.N. decision and proclaimed the independent state

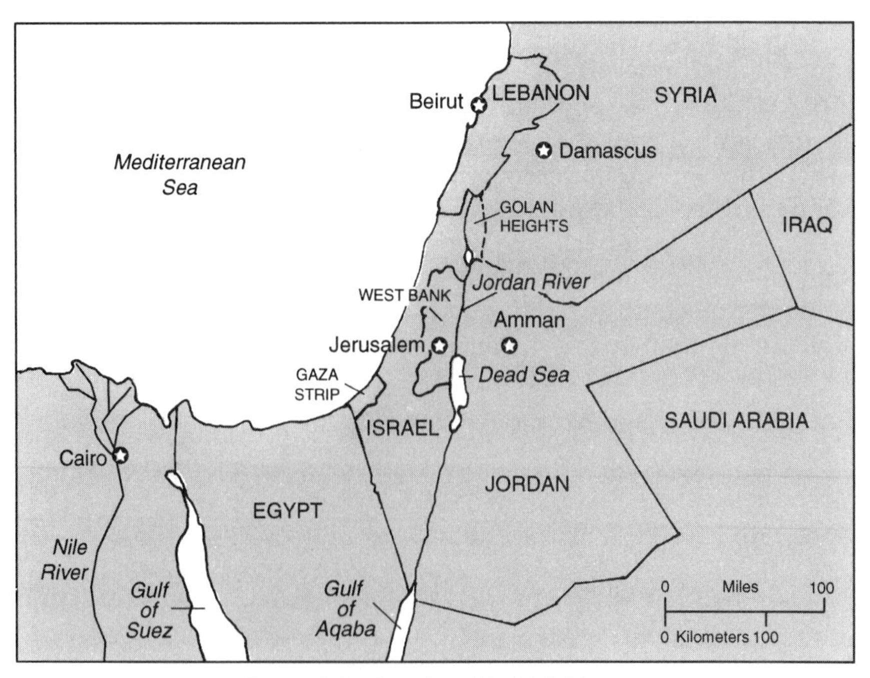

Figure 4.3 Israel and Its Neighbors

of Israel in May, 1948. The Palestinian Arabs, however, rejected the plan. So did the neighboring Arab countries. Seeking to destroy the new Jewish state, they launched a joint attack against Israel. The Israelis fought off the invading armies.

The 1948 war led to a massive flight of Palestinian Arabs to neighboring countries. To escape the fighting, about 75 percent of the Arab population of Israel abandoned their homes. They expected to return after the war, but were unable to do so. Although the host countries permitted the Palestinians to remain, they kept them apart from their own people. The Palestinians settled in refugee camps and had little opportunity to obtain jobs, provide for their families, or lead normal lives. For their survival, Palestinian refugees had to depend on aid provided by international agencies and charities.

For decades, the refugees' condition was a major obstacle to peace in the Middle East. Another obstacle was disagreement over arrangements for the West Bank and Gaza. Those territories, inhabited by Arabs, were occupied by the Israeli army in 1967, when the Jewish state defeated Egypt, Syria, and Jordan in the Six-Day War. In 1987, the Palestinians of the West Bank began street protests and riots against Israeli authority. They called their actions an *intifada,* or uprising.

♦ *Describe the growth of the Palestinian refugee crisis.*

Efforts to negotiate a peace settlement were complicated by disagreements within Israel itself. The two leading political parties took sharply contrasting stands. The rightist Likud Party favored a hard-line policy against concessions to the Palestinians. The leftist Labor Party was more open to peace talks and bargaining. The two parties took turns controlling the government through shaky coalitions.

Under a coalition led by Likud leader Yitzhak Shamir, Israel's government in the early 1990s encouraged Jewish settlements in the occupied territories. The Shamir government also announced its intention to annex those territories, making them a permanent part of Israel. Shamir's policies infuriated the Arab inhabitants of the conquered territories, who stepped up their *intifada.* Violent clashes broke out with Israeli police and military forces.

Palestinian demands for independence and the fate of Gaza and the West Bank were among the emotional issues that figured in an elaborate peace process arranged by the United

States, beginning in 1991. Peace talks involved delegations from Israel, Syria, Lebanon, and Jordan, as well as Palestinian representatives.

♦ *State the main cause of the* intifada.

A 1992 election brought to power a new Israeli coalition, with Labor Party leader Yitzhak Rabin as prime minister. One of Rabin's first moves was to commit his government to cut back Jewish settlements in the occupied territories. That policy drew strong opposition from many Israelis. But it brought a positive response from the leading Palestinian group, the Palestine Liberation Organization (PLO).

For years, Israeli leaders had depicted the PLO as a terrorist group dedicated to the destruction of Israel. Yasir Arafat, the PLO leader, was widely hated by Israelis. Since the late 1980s, however, the PLO had moderated its stance. Arafat had renounced terrorism and accepted the partition of Palestine. By 1993, a growing number of Israelis were ready for their government to engage in direct talks with the PLO.

Israel and the PLO held secret talks in Norway. The PLO agreed that Israel had a "right to exist in peace and security." Israeli negotiators accepted the PLO as "the representative of the Palestinian people." In September 1993, Israel and the PLO signed a historic accord. At a public ceremony in Washington, Rabin and Arafat shook hands as flashguns blinked and video cameras recorded the event.

The agreement was called a Declaration of Principles. It provided for Palestinian self-government in two places to be turned over by Israelis—Gaza, a strip of land along the Mediterranean coast, and Jericho, a town in the West Bank. Later, the Israelis would turn over more of the West Bank. The PLO would be in charge of a new Palestinian Authority that would act as an interim government until elections could be held. Most of the details were left to be worked out in later negotiations over a five-year period.

World leaders hailed the Israeli-PLO pact as a major step toward peace, as did many Israelis and Palestinians. However, a large number of Palestinians and Israelis criticized the accord. Palestinian militants said it created an empty facade that would leave Israelis in control of most of the West Bank for many years. Israeli critics said the pact would undermine the security of Israeli settlements in the West Bank and expose more Israelis to terrorist attacks.

As the two sides began to implement the accord, serious problems emerged. In February 1994, an Israeli settler murdered 29 Muslims at prayer in a mosque at the West Bank town of Hebron. In the months that followed, Palestinian extremists staged a number of suicide bombings. Dozens of Israelis were killed or maimed as they rode to work on buses or passed along busy streets. A militant Islamist group called Hamas claimed responsibility for the bombing campaign. Hamas said it would continue the war against Israel with the goal of creating a fully independent and powerful Palestinian state.

Reaching Out

Both the Israeli government and Arafat's Palestinian Authority struggled to keep the peace process on track. Arafat took up residence in Gaza and cracked down on Hamas and its terrorists. Israel and the PLO missed a 1994 deadline for agreeing on further steps. However, during 1995 they reached a series of agreements and began arranging for an extension of Palestinian control to more parts of the West Bank. The deadline for establishing Palestinian self-rule was set as May 1999.

The bitterness caused by the developing peace process erupted anew in November 1995, however. A Jewish extremist shot and killed Rabin as the prime minister left a peace rally. Police immediately seized a 25-year-old Israeli student, who seemed to believe the killing had been a religious duty. He called Rabin a traitor to Jews and Israel. Rabin's successor, Shimon Peres, vowed to continue the peace process.

In an extension of the peace process, Israel and Jordan signed a peace treaty in 1994. Jordan held sovereignty over the West Bank at the time the Israelis occupied it in 1967. It was the second Arab government to accept the existence of Israel.

A third Arab country, Syria, also entered into peace talks with Israel. Syria wanted Israel to return the Golan Heights, a territory that had been under Israeli occupation since 1967.

1. *Explain why you AGREE or DISAGREE with the following statement: Between 1992 and 1995, prospects for peace between Israel and its Arab neighbors increased.*
2. *Indicate whether each of the following statements is true or false:*
   a. *Israel took control of the West Bank and Gaza in 1967.*
   b. *The* intifada *began as a pro-Israel demonstration by Palestinians.*
   c. *Prime Minister Yitzhak Rabin led the Labor Party to victory in Israel's 1992 elections.*
   d. *Israel reached a peace agreement with the PLO in 1993.*
   e. *Israeli settlers in the West Bank have supported the government's steps toward peace.*
   f. *The Golan Heights are part of Syria.*

The Persian Gulf War

In August 1990, Iraq invaded its tiny neighbor Kuwait and annexed it. The Iraqi dictator, Saddam Hussein, wanted Kuwait for its rich oil fields and as a seaport on the Persian Gulf. Hussein then moved his forces to the border of Saudi Arabia. He seemed poised for an invasion of that oil-rich nation also.

U.S. President George Bush led worldwide opposition to the Iraqi aggression. He sent troops to Saudi Arabia, a pro-Western nation and an ally of the United States, to protect it. The United Nations demanded Iraq's withdrawal from Kuwait.

Operation Desert Storm began on January 17, 1991. A U.N. coalition of 28 nations used overwhelming military power (mostly that of the United States) to drive Iraq out of Kuwait. U.S. General H. Norman Schwarzkopf commanded the coalition forces. The victory, however, neither ended Saddam Hussein's control of Iraq nor brought peace to the region. U.N. forces

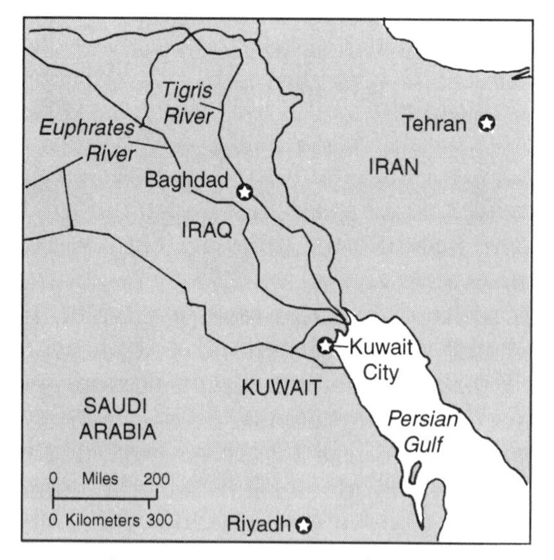

Figure 4.4 Persian Gulf States

stayed to protect the Kurds, a minority group within Iraq, from Hussein's troops. And U.N. inspection teams made periodic visits to ensure that Iraq was dismantling its nuclear, chemical, and biological weapons factories.

- *Identify each of the following:*

  a. Saddam Hussein
  b. H. Norman Schwarzkopf

Significant changes occurred in the Middle East as a result of the Persian Gulf War. The Arab nations that had been part of the U.N. coalition demonstrated a greater willingness to engage in U.S.-sponsored peace talks with Israel. That helped lead to direct peace talks between Israeli and Syrian diplomats. (See the previous section.)

A continuing U.S. military presence in the Persian Gulf region was another result of the war. To block future aggression by Hussein and to keep him from seizing control of the region's oil resources, the Gulf nations agreed to permit the United States to store military equipment in the area and to engage in joint military exercises with them. In the postwar period, U.S. planes helped to enforce a "no-fly" zone in southern Iraq, from which all Iraqi planes and missiles were excluded.

The Gulf states that had joined the U.S.-led coalition experienced postwar problems of their own. After its restoration to power, the ruling al Sabah family of Kuwait failed to honor its promise to develop democratic government. Also, human rights organizations accused the government of Kuwait of mistreating the country's Palestinian minority. Hundreds of thousands of Palestinians who had worked in Kuwait before the war were not permitted to return after the war. They were perceived as Iraqi sympathizers.

Two thirds of Kuwait's cash reserves, which had been $100 billion before the war, were wiped out. Kuwait spent huge sums to repair its badly damaged oil fields and equipment and to buy new weapons for defense.

Economic damage to Iraq was even greater. Destroyed were its industries, roads, bridges, and telecommunications. After the war, the United Nations maintained the wall of sanctions it had erected around Iraq's economy. Iraq could not sell its oil on the world's markets and thus had little income with which to buy food and other necessities. The sanctions were intended to force Hussein to comply fully with the terms of the cease-fire and to give U.N. inspectors full freedom to examine Iraq's weapons facilities.

Desert Storm

The U.N. sanctions caused immense suffering among the Iraqi people. Government food rations were inadequate to meet basic needs. People who tried to buy extra food often found they could not afford it. Middle-class people sold their furniture and even the bricks of their houses in order to buy food. Poor nutrition contributed to diseases that hit children and old people especially. Although U.N. sanctions were designed to allow humanitarian aid to reach Iraq, aid workers said there was too little aid to meet the people's needs.

U.S. and other Western leaders encouraged Iraqis to blame Hussein and his government for their hardships. They hoped to provoke a popular uprising or military coup that would oust Hussein and install a more moderate government.

- *On your answer paper, prepare a table as shown below and enter the required information.*

PERSIAN GULF WAR

Dates	*Cause(s)*	*Leaders*	*Major Results*

Mediterranean Neighbors

In the 1990s, Syria experienced some economic progress. Although a major power in the Middle East, this nation was not previously noted for its prosperity. Neighboring Lebanon, nearly destroyed by 16 years of civil war, began to rebuild.

Syria. Syria was once the center of a Muslim empire. Under French rule after World War I, it regained its independence in 1946. Syria participated in the Arab attempt to destroy Israel in 1948 and remained at war with the Jewish state.

Syria and Egypt became partners in the United Arab Republic in 1958. The arrangement ended in 1961, when Syria withdrew. In 1963, a combination of military officers and political leaders of the Socialist Baath Party, an organization dedicated to pan-Arab unity, seized power. The Baath became the only legal party. Its leaders, members of the minority sect of Alawite Muslims, control the Syrian government. President Hafez al-Assad, in office since 1971, is an Alawite.

During the Six-Day War of 1967, Syria tried once again to

defeat Israel but failed. A result of the war was Syria's loss of the Golan Heights, a high point of land from which Syria often shelled settlements in Israel. Syria's loss was Israel's gain, as Israeli settlers moved into the area. In 1973, Syria joined Egypt in still another attack on Israel, but gained nothing from its participation in the Yom Kippur War. The following year, several oil-rich Arab nations agreed to provide Syria with funds to continue its anti-Israel activities. In addition, Syria received billions of dollars in military aid from the Soviet Union during the cold war. The aid helped the Syrians build one of the most powerful armies in the Middle East.

♦ *Describe how Syria became a major power in the Middle East.*

Its military power enabled Syria to dominate Lebanon after civil war broke out there in 1975. The war involved numerous Muslim and Christian factions, as well as the Palestine Liberation Organization. Most government functions collapsed and the once-prosperous Lebanese economy crumbled.

Eager to limit the power of Lebanese-based Palestinian guerrillas who operated near its border, Syria sent troops into Lebanon in 1976 as part of an Arab peacekeeping force. Syria's troops battled Muslim forces and Christian militias, and even took on the Israeli army, which invaded Lebanon in 1982. Syrian troops eventually helped to restore order in Lebanon in 1991.

During the Persian Gulf War, Syria's President Assad condemned Iraq for its aggression in Kuwait and sent troops to join the U.S.-led coalition. In gratitude, Kuwait rewarded Syria by contributing to a development fund. Assad then instituted a program of limited economic reform. It was designed to lure investors to Syria without dramatically changing Syria's system of state-run factories. Despite this effort, Syrian industry showed little improvement in the 1990s. Although oil revenues rose sharply, Western investors and Arab businesspeople from the Gulf states were cautious about investing substantial sums in a police state where government policy might change overnight. However, Syria's food production boomed, and the importation of consumer goods increased significantly.

Syrian security forces brutally suppressed an attempted rebellion by local Muslim extremists in the early 1980s. In the 1990s, Assad, recognizing the growing power of Islamic fundamentalism, became a patron of religious revival. He promoted weekly Islamic lectures on state-owned television and permitted the building of large new mosques throughout the country. Despite Syrians' rising interest in Islam, however, Assad's efficient security forces prevented any Islamic political party from forming.

Syria opened talks with Israel in 1991 as part of a U.S.-sponsored "peace process." By 1995, the two nations had agreed on the need for a demilitarized zone around the Golan Heights. But a full peace treaty still eluded negotiators.

♦ *Explain how Syria benefited from the Gulf War.*

Lebanon. Prime Minister Rafiq al-Hariri of Lebanon, whose government took office in early 1993, began the process of reestablishing the authority of the state. Power to govern had been shattered by years of civil war.

After receiving independence from France in 1943, Lebanon prospered. Beirut, the capital, became the banking and intellectual center of the Middle East. Lebanon was a showcase of free enterprise in a region largely dominated by socialism.

Under the terms of the National Covenant of 1943, government offices were divided among the religious communities. At first, the Christians were in the majority. In the 1970s, Muslims became the majority and demanded a larger political and economic role. Tensions increased when the Palestine Liberation Organization decided to make Lebanon its base of operations, after being expelled from Jordan because of Jordanian distrust of the PLO's political ambitions.

Lebanon's problems exploded into a full-scale civil war in 1975, with widespread destruction. Under a mandate from the Arab League, Syria sent a peacekeeping force that assumed control of much of the country. Meanwhile, Israel established a "security zone" in southern Lebanon to protect its northern settlements from terrorists. Syria helped to broker the peace accord that ended the Lebanese civil war in 1991. Its troops remained in Lebanon to enforce the peace.

Upon taking office, Prime Minister Hariri began working to restore Lebanon's economy. He raised the value of the Lebanese pound against the U.S. dollar. He took steps to reorganize the civil service and to restore law and order. The army raided criminal havens in several parts of the country. Quantities of drugs, weapons, and stolen vehicles were seized. The prime minister also dispatched troops into areas controlled for years by terrorists who had been responsible for taking Westerners hostage during the 1980s. These steps were made possible with Syria's support.

An estimated 250,000 Palestinian refugees remained in Lebanon in the 1990s. They had fled from what is now Israel at the time of the 1948 war, or had been born in refugee camps after 1948. Many of the refugees bitterly opposed the PLO-Israeli peace accords, because they made no provision for the return of refugees who came from Israel itself.

1. *Identify each of the following:*
    a. *Socialist Baath Party*
    b. *Hafez Assad*
    c. *Rafiq al-Hariri*
2. *Complete the following sentences:*
    a. *Syria and Lebanon have been strongly linked because ____.*
    b. *After the Persian Gulf War, Syrian economic progress was stimulated by ____.*
    c. *Islamic fundamentalism did not cause political upheavals in Syria because ____.*
    d. *A major problem facing the Lebanese government after the civil war was ____.*

The Hashemite Kingdom of Jordan

Putting an end to 46 years of hostility, the prime ministers of Jordan and Israel met at a desert outpost on the two nations' border and signed a treaty of peace in October 1994. Jordan thus became the third Arab entity, after Egypt and the Palestine Liberation Organization, to make peace with the Jewish state.

Jordan is a latecomer among Arab states. The British carved it out of Palestine in 1921, to reward the Hashemite family for its aid to Britain against the Ottoman Turks during World War I. Jordan received its independence in 1946. It first king was Abdullah. Since 1952, Abdullah's grandson has reigned over Jordan as King Hussein.

Jordan participated in the Arab nations' attack on Israel in 1948. The Arab Legion, Jordan's British-trained and British-led army, was one of the best in the Middle East at that time. In the 1948 war, Jordan gained control of the old city of Jerusalem and the West Bank of the Jordan River. However, it lost those territories to Israel in the Six-Day War of 1967 and has since transferred its rights over them to the PLO.

During the Arab-Israeli wars, Palestinian refugees flooded into Jordan. Following Iraq's invasion of Kuwait in August 1990, approximately 700,000 more Palestinians from Kuwait fled to Jordan. The Jordanian economy was already deteriorating, with unemployment between 20 and 25 percent. The Persian Gulf War brought Jordan's economic life to a standstill. After the war, hundreds of thousands of the new refugees remained in Jordan, unable to return to Kuwait and the jobs they had held there. Palestinians now make up about half of Jordan's population of 4.2 million.

The refugee problem strained transportation and communication systems, health and education services, and water supplies. Consequently, the government had to revise its economic development program, changing its focus from growth and prosperity to maintenance of minimal living standards. Jordan's problems were compounded by the loss of foreign aid from countries embittered by Jordan's support for Iraq in the Persian Gulf War.

Jordan's assistance to Iraq took the form of shipments of food and other goods. Maintaining good relations with its larger, more powerful neighbor, and its dictator, Saddam Hussein, was considered a wise policy by Jordan's King Hussein. His grandfather had been murdered by Islamic militants in the 1940s for his moderate views toward Israel.

Although Jordan is a constitutional monarchy, King Hussein has broad powers. Democracy has made little progress in this mainly desert country.

- *How did the Arab-Israeli conflict and the Persian Gulf War affect Jordan?*

The Kingdom of Saudi Arabia

The mission of the U.S.-led coalition during the Persian Gulf War was not only to liberate Kuwait but also to protect Saudi Arabia. With an estimated one fourth of the world's oil reserves, the Saudi kingdom has been a vital source of energy for the world. Saudi Arabia is a long-time ally of the United States and has received much military and technical assistance. In return, the Saudis often use their influence to encourage moderation among other Arab nations and oil producers.

After liberation from Turkey at the time of World War I,

much of the Arabian peninsula was united by a desert warrior named Abdul Aziz Ibn Saud. Ibn Saud became Saudi Arabia's first king and the founder of its ruling family. Although Saudi Arabia covers a large area, only 2 percent of its land is arable. The discovery of oil transformed the Saudi economy in the 1930s. Oil provided the kingdom with a source of enormous wealth, and gave it global importance.

Since 1982, Saudi Arabia has been ruled by King Fahd. He is both the head of state and the head of the government. The Islamic religious code is the law of the land. Traditionally, the use of alcohol and Western forms of public entertainment are banned or severely limited. Women have an inferior legal status. The two holy cities of Islam—Mecca, the birthplace of the Prophet Muhammad, and Medina, which contains his tomb—are located in Saudi Arabia. Hundreds of thousands of pilgrims visit those centers of Muslim worship each year.

Saudi Arabia has opposed Israel since 1948, sending troops to fight against the Jewish state in that year and in 1973. The Saudis extended aid to the PLO and other militant groups, as well as to Egypt, Syria, Jordan, and other Muslim countries. In an attempt to force the United States and other Western nations to abandon their support of Israel, the Saudi government participated in an oil embargo in 1973. The withholding of oil from the West produced severe fuel shortages and high prices but failed to achieve its political objective. Saudi Arabia joined most of the other Arab nations in condemning Egypt in 1979 when it negotiated a peace treaty with Israel.

Using its vast oil wealth, Saudi Arabia created what has been called "the world's most extravagant welfare state." The government offered Saudi citizens free health care, free college education, interest-free home loans, and subsidized gasoline (21 cents a gallon in 1994). Since those programs were financed from oil revenues, Saudis paid almost no taxes.

However, the boom times began to go sour in the 1990s. Oil prices, after peaking in the early 1980s, went into decline, thus reducing the state's income. Meanwhile, expenses soared. During the Gulf War, for example, Saudi Arabia paid $55 billion to finance the anti-Iraq coalition, thereby easing the burden on the United States and its partners. Alarmed at its rapidly dwindling bank accounts, the Saudi government announced sharp spending cutbacks after the war.

Saudi Arabia's tough times brought rising political tensions. Although the government repeatedly stressed its Islamic goals,

The New Poor

militant Muslims accused it of obeying the wishes of the United States and betraying the principles of the Qur'an. In 1994, the government cracked down on Islamist movements, arresting two prominent religious leaders. It was hard for observers to know just how broad the discontent might be, since Saudi Arabia allowed no political parties and had no legislature.

1. *Explain the importance of Saudi Arabia to the West.*
2. *What role did Saudi Arabia play during the Persian Gulf War?*
3. *Why has Saudi Arabia experienced economic difficulties in recent years?*

The Tragedy of the Kurds

Another post-Gulf War problem was the ongoing plight of the Kurds. For centuries, the Kurdish peoples of Turkey, Iraq, Syria, and Iran have struggled to establish a nation of their own. Hostile governments and rivalries among Kurdish factions have prevented the creation of an independent Kurdistan.

The Kurds are an ancient people, known for their military nature and for so often being subjected to others. They have rarely been independent. Now numbering 20 million, the Kurds are the largest ethnic group in the Middle East without their own government.

World attention turned to the Kurds in 1991. Encouraged by the Gulf War victory of the United States-led coalition, Iraqi Kurds revolted against Saddam Hussein. Iraqi troops quickly crushed the uprising and drove thousands of Kurdish rebels and civilians to the borders of Iran and Turkey. Many refugees died of starvation and exposure in the snowbound mountains.

The military forces of the United States and its allies responded by establishing safe havens for the Kurds. Operation Provide Comfort protected the Kurds from their Iraqi attackers and distributed food and medical supplies to them. A Kurdish-controlled zone for 4 to 5 million refugees was established in northern Iraq. Kurds hoped that the zone could eventually become the core of a self-governing Kurdistan.

Within the zone, approximately one million Kurds held an election in May 1992, to choose a 105-seat assembly. Thousands of armed guerrillas temporarily abandoned their positions opposite the Iraqi army in order to vote. Traditionally, tribal chiefs and Muslim sheikhs had held power among the Kurds, whose loyalties were further divided among eight political parties. The Kurdistan Democratic Party (KDP), the largest and oldest of the political groups, held strong appeal for the mountain Kurds, who were the backbone of the Kurdish military forces. Since its founding in Iran in 1945, the KDP had been under the control of the Barzani family. Massoud Barzani, the leader of the KDP in the 1990s, was distrustful of the West. He regarded Saddam Hussein as the real power with whom the Kurds must deal.

Among the other Kurdish political parties was the Patriotic Union of Kurdistan (PUK), led by Jalal Talabani and Ibrahim Ahmad. They were nationalists who sought to shape a political organization that could bypass tribal loyalties. There was also a Kurdish Communist Party and an Islamic Movement of Kurdistan. The latter group believed that Iraq should become an Islamic state.

After the election, Barzani and Talabani split control of the governing bodies that had been set up for Iraq's Kurds. Soon, however, a falling-out between the two men paralyzed decision making. By 1994, the Kurdish areas of northern Iraq had fractured into warring districts. Power was divided among numerous warlords, and, as had happened so often before, the Kurds were at one another's throats. Prospects for establishing a self-governing Kurdistan appeared dim.

Turkey, Iran, and Syria strongly oppose the creation of an independent Kurdistan. Since 1984, Turkey's armed forces have been fighting an insurgency by guerrillas belonging to the Kurdistan Workers Party (PKK). The PKK is a Marxist group that demands self-rule for Kurds inside Turkey. Turkey condemns its members as "terrorists." Human rights organizations have repeatedly criticized Turkey for its repressive measures against the PKK. In repeated forays beginning in 1992, Turkish troops crossed into northern Iraq to attack PKK bases. Coalition allies made protests but did not intervene.

Turkey has maintained good relations with the Iraqi Kurdish groups led by Barzani and Talabani. Both promised to help stop the PKK from using Iraq as a base for attacks on Turkey. In return, Turkey gave aid to the Iraqi groups and offered to mediate their disputes.

1. *Define or identify each of the following:*
   - a. *Operation Provide Comfort*
   - b. *PUK and PKK*
   - c. *Massoud Barzani*
   - d. *Islamic party of Kurdistan*
2. *Explain why you AGREE or DISAGREE with the following statement:*

   The United States and its allies should not be involved in the Kurdish effort to achieve autonomy (self-government).

Chapter 4 Review

A. *Write the letter of the correct response.*

1. *A goal of militant Islamic fundamentalists has been (a) peace with Israel (b) alliance with the United States (c) the overthrow of pro-Western Arab governments.*
2. *Efforts to make peace between Israel and its Arab neighbors have been hindered by (a) disagreements among Israelis (b) disagreements among Arabs (c) both of the above.*
3. *The Persian Gulf War was caused by (a) the Israeli conquest of*

the West Bank and Gaza areas (b) the Iraqi invasion of Kuwait (c) U.S. weapons sales to Saudi Arabia.

4. *A result of the Persian Gulf War was (a) greater Arab willingness to engage in U.S.-sponsored peace talks with Israel (b) the fall from power of Saddam Hussein (c) an independent Kurdish state.*
5. *A post-Gulf War problem was (a) Iranian aggression (b) an Israeli refusal to negotiate with its Arab neighbors (c) the slowness of democratization in Kuwait.*
6. *By 1990, Syria had become the dominant power in (a) Iraq (b) Kuwait (c) Lebanon.*
7. *Arab countries that have signed peace treaties with Israel are (a) Syria and Saudi Arabia (b) Egypt and Jordan (c) Lebanon and Iraq.*
8. *A country that spent billions of dollars to finance the coalition campaign in the Persian Gulf War was (a) Syria (b) Lebanon (c) Saudi Arabia.*
9. *A Marxist group fighting against Turkish government forces is the (a) PKK (b) PLO (c) Socialist Baath Party.*
10. *The largest ethnic group in the Middle East without a homeland are the (a) Sunni Muslims (b) Shiite Muslims (c) Kurds.*

B. *Reread "The Sword of Islam," on pages 69–73. Then write a paragraph to explain why most of the governments of the Middle East fear the militant Islamic fundamentalists.*

C. *Examine the maps of the Middle East in Chapter 4. Which of the following statements are true and which are false?*

1. *During the war in Afghanistan (1979–92), weapons for Afghan rebels could be slipped across the border from Pakistan.*
2. *In Egypt, the Nile River flows into the Mediterranean Sea.*
3. *The West Bank territory has borders with both Israel and Jordan.*
4. *Kuwait is governed from Baghdad.*
5. *Syria and Lebanon are separated by Israel.*
6. *Iraq can threaten the security of Saudi Arabia's border.*
7. *An independent Kurdish state might include land in northern Iraq.*
8. *The Golan Heights lie between Israel and Jordan.*
9. *Jordan occupies more territory than Israel.*

Chapter 5

Communism and Capitalism in Asia

In the 1990s, China remained Asia's largest Communist power, Hong Kong prepared for the end of British rule, and Japan experienced recession but retained its status as an economic superpower. Significant developments were seen in other parts of Asia as well. In India, overwhelming poverty, combined with violence between religious groups, continued to shake the stability of the country. North Korea, a nation near economic disaster, caused global alarm by its nuclear development policies. And in Southeast Asia, the Khmer Rouge, a group that brought terror and enslavement to Cambodia in the 1970s, waged a guerrilla war in an attempt to return to power.

The Modernization of China

In the 1990s, China began to emerge as an economic powerhouse. Throughout this large country, industrialization expanded at a rapid rate, moving from the coastal regions to the inland population centers along the Yangtze River and to the largely undeveloped areas beyond. At the national level, once powerful government ministries lost their monopolistic control of strategic industries and had to compete in the marketplace. Foreign investors received a warmer welcome than ever before. However, despite an unprecedented increase in prosperity, many factories and other enterprises remained under state control and were too inefficient to make money.

The leadership of the Communist Party continued the dictatorship established in 1949 by Mao Zedong. Throughout the

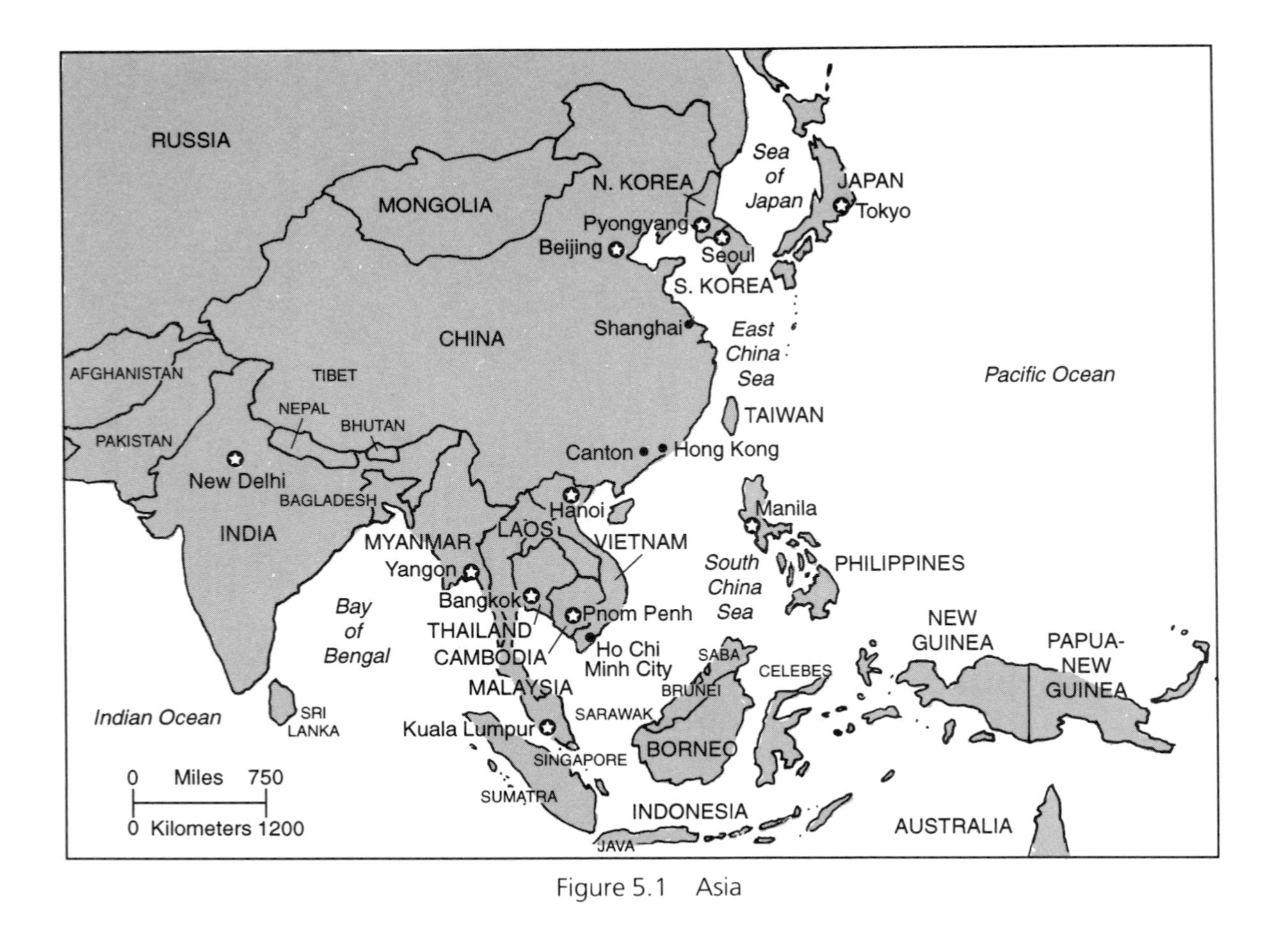

Figure 5.1 Asia

1950s and 1960s, the party combined political repression with rigid application of Mao's Marxist principles in government, industry, and society. The results were economic stagnation and severe human rights abuses.

Following Mao's death in 1976, a new, more practical Communist leadership began reforms in education, culture, and industry in an attempt to stimulate China's backward economy. Leaders also took steps to improve relations with non-Communist nations. Diplomatic relations with the United States, which had fought against China during the Korean War (1950–53), began in 1979. By the mid-1980s, economic reforms led to the abandonment of rigid central planning and the encouragement of private enterprise. As private ownership of businesses expanded, the country enjoyed more consumer goods and a rising standard of living. By 1994, China's gross national product of over $2.6 trillion was ten times what it had been in 1978. The country was regularly attaining economic growth rates of 10 percent or more each year.

Inefficient state-owned companies continued to be a problem, however. They employed nearly three-fourths of the urban labor force and accounted for half the nation's industrial production. Many state enterprises operated at a loss, pro-

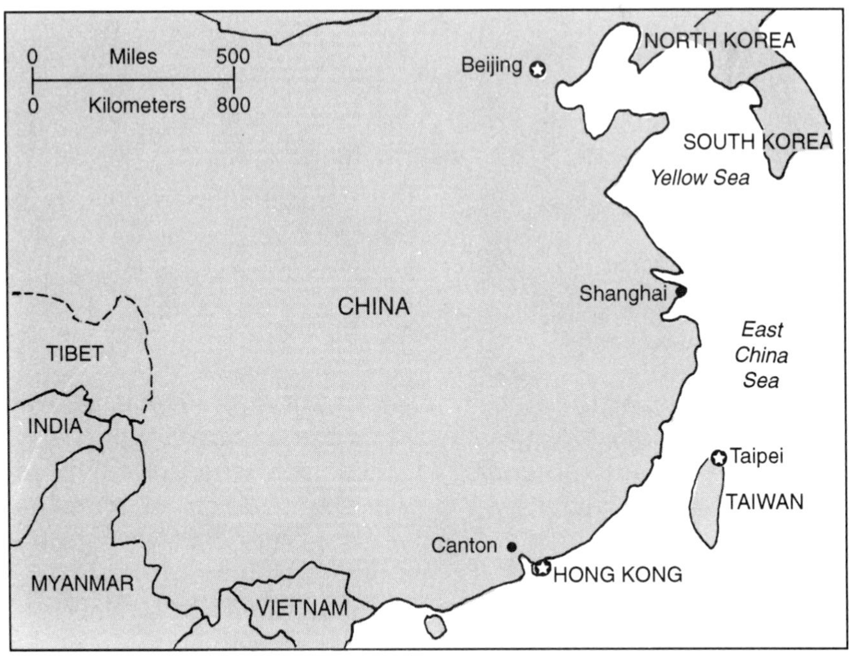

Figure 5.2 China

duced goods of inferior quality, and maintained more workers than they needed. They also ran schools, hospitals, and other public services. Only with the financial support of the state could these debt-ridden companies survive. Such subsidies cost the government about $6 billion a year.

Economic Reform. To make its state-owned businesses profitable, the government privatized many of them—sold them to private investors. The buyers invested new capital. Managers introduced modern production methods and dismissed many workers. At the same time, the government tried to improve the profitability of its remaining state-owned businesses by mergers, salary cuts, and layoffs. But privatization proved to be more effective.

- *Describe the economic changes that took place in China in the 1980s and 1990s.*

In order to modernize the economy, the Communist Party committed itself to a far-reaching restructuring. Although many senior party members saw privatization as the undoing of communism in China, the government permitted private investors to acquire state enterprises cheaply.

Many of the investors were foreigners, including overseas Chinese. Businesspeople from Hong Kong, Taiwan, and elsewhere improved China's economy by bringing to it new capital and advanced management skills. U.S. and other Western corporate giants also moved into China's huge market. They invested billions of dollars in the telecommunications, automobile, and electronics industries. Motorola and AT&T, for example, established research and development, manufacturing, and sales facilities in China. These investments boosted economic activity and contributed to a dramatic rise in Chinese exports.

Another departure from traditional Communist policies was the encouragement of private enterprise among ordinary Chinese. Throughout the country, individuals were urged to engage in business activity for profit. This sparked an economic and social revolution, which some observers compared to the reconstruction of Europe after World War II under the Marshall Plan. Economists predicted that China would be one of the world's top five economic powers by the beginning of the 21st century.

Hybrid

As a result of these changes, control of the economy shifted away from Beijing, the capital. Provinces and towns gained new importance. New "economic-development zones" sprang up, and construction boomed. Manufacturing activities moved increasingly into the provinces, where labor costs were low.

Despite the development of a market economy, however, the Communist Party remained firmly in power. China's new economic managers, more prosperous than ever before, retained membership in the Communist Party.

♦ *Describe the role of the Communist Party in the modernization of China.*

Political Freedom and Human Rights. In the areas of political freedom and human rights, the Chinese government clung to tradition. It remained an authoritarian regime with a huge propaganda machine and prison labor camps. Its repressive policies led to conflicts between China's leaders and many of its people.

A crisis occurred in May 1989. One million Chinese had gathered in Beijing to demand democratic reforms. Activists were demonstrating in 20 other cities as well. The Communist leaders imposed martial law and moved troops into Beijing. In Tiananmen Square, scene of the main demonstrations, hundreds were killed or injured. Authorities arrested large numbers of students and workers. Despite international outrage, Deng Xiaopeng, China's senior leader, allowed Communist Party conservatives to tighten control of cultural and media activities in order to discourage further demands for democracy. Deng's policies reflected his belief that the people would continue to accept Communist rule as long as their standard of living kept rising and the country's economic growth persisted.

Human rights concerns were one of several issues that clouded U.S.-Chinese relations in the 1990s. Presidents Bush and Clinton both pressed China to open up its political system. Other disputes centered on trade and military issues. China sold far more to the United States than it bought. Indeed, the U.S. trade deficit for China ran as high as $40 billion, second only to the deficit with Japan. U.S. leaders negotiated with China over ways to narrow the trade gap.

China's military policies also disturbed U.S. leaders. Determined to be the dominant military power in East Asia, China used some of its new wealth to build up its naval and air forces. U.S. strategists saw the Chinese buildup as a challenge to U.S. and Japanese interests in the region. The United States was one of many nations that protested Chinese underground nuclear tests in the mid-1990s.

Also drawing U.S. protests were China's population-control policies. With about 1.2 billion people, China has the largest population of any country in the world. The government has pursued a policy of only one child per couple, hoping to bring about a population decline in the 21st century. The United States denounced China's use of harsh methods to enforce birth control, including compulsory sterilization, forced abortions, and fines for unauthorized pregnancies.

Under a so-called responsibility system, local officials were held accountable for meeting family planning targets in their districts. As a result, the birthrate dropped to 18.2 infants per thousand people in the early 1990s, down from 21.1 in 1990 and 22.4 in 1988. (See Figure 5.3.) Government planners achieved goals they had not expected to reach until the year 2010. Some Chinese, especially in the countryside, where male babies are traditionally of great importance, opposed the birth control policy. Support was stronger in the cities, where the drop in fertility was credited with helping to boost the economy and with improving education and health standards.

	Year	Value
Birthrate (per 1000 people)	1988	22.4
	1994	18.2
Family Size	1988	15.5%
	1992	9.6%
Fertility Rate	1988	2.5
	1994	1.84

Figure 5.3 China's Population Growth Slows Down

1. *Describe the Chinese political crisis of May 1989.*
2. *What issues have dominated U.S.-Chinese relations in recent years?*
3. *PROVE or DISPROVE: China's program of population control has had the support of all Chinese.*

Hong Kong: A Colony in Transition

Located at the mouth of the Canton River in China, Hong Kong became a British crown colony after the Opium War of 1839–42, when Britain forced China to give up the island. In 1898, Britain and China negotiated a 99-year lease, running to June 30, 1997. Provisions for the island's return to Chinese control have been in the headlines in recent years. Hong Kong includes a main island, 235 smaller islands, and Kowloon Peninsula, which is part of China's mainland.

In the 20th century, Hong Kong became one of the great shipping, commercial, and manufacturing centers of Asia. Its port became vital to Asian trade. In addition to a major electronics industry, Hong Kong developed shipbuilding, iron and steel, and a highly competitive textile industry. Free trade, low taxes, a large labor force, and extensive communications made the colony prosperous. By the mid-1990s, Hong Kong had 6½ million inhabitants, including 20,000 British residents and approximately one million refugees from mainland China.

In 1984, Britain and China reached an agreement on what

would happen after 1997, when Britain's lease would expire and Hong Kong would revert to Chinese rule. The two nations agreed that Hong Kong's capitalist, free market economy and its local government would continue for 50 years.

As a British colony, Hong Kong was ruled by a legislative council, consisting of elected and appointed officials, and by a governor-general appointed by the British government. As the date for the turnover neared, Britain and China clashed over British efforts to introduce more democracy to Hong Kong. In 1994, Governor-General Christopher Patten pushed through a plan that allowed for the election in September 1995 of the colony's first fully elected legislature. China objected to the British changes, noting that it had already promised Hong Kong an elected legislature and a local chief executive. It said it would dissolve the bodies created by Governor Patten and hold new elections. Although many residents of Hong Kong expressed a desire for increased democracy, most also wished to avoid antagonizing China.

Hong Kong is valuable to China. It is a port through which the Communist giant can trade with Taiwan and other countries with which it has no formal diplomatic relations. China owns a number of hotels, department stores, and other business enterprises in Hong Kong. Half of the colony's food and water is imported from China.

Uncertainty over the future troubled Hong Kong residents and the Asian business community. The fate of democracy and capitalism in the colony could affect economic stability and investment confidence throughout East Asia.

1. *Explain why the future of Hong Kong is important to the Asian business community.*
2. *Complete the following sentence:*
   In 1994, Chinese leaders were angered by ____.
3. *Why do you think many businesspeople left Hong Kong in the 1990s?*

Japan: An Economic Superpower

Between 1931 and 1945, Japan used military force to conquer an empire in East and Southeast Asia. Japan's aggression, and its alliance with Nazi Germany and Fascist Italy, led to World War II. That conflict ended with the atomic bombing of two Japanese cities by the United States in August 1945.

At the war's end, most of Japan's cities and industries lay in ruins. Having defeated Japan, the United States acted quickly to democratize the country and to help it recover from the ravages of war. With help from American experts, the Japanese wrote a new constitution. It set Japan on a different course, away from the militarism and imperialism that had been such strong forces in its history. A democratic government, led by a prime minister, took office in 1947.

With American aid, Japanese industry grew rapidly. The automobile and electronics industries were especially successful. Japan found willing buyers all over the world for its cars and television sets. It became a leader in the development and manufacture of computer chips and other high-tech products. In addition, Japanese investors became influential in the economies of the United States and other countries.

One reason for Japan's success was its high rate of savings. The savings contributed to heavy investment in new plants and capital equipment—at a rate far exceeding that of the United States. Another factor was Japan's dynamic pursuit of

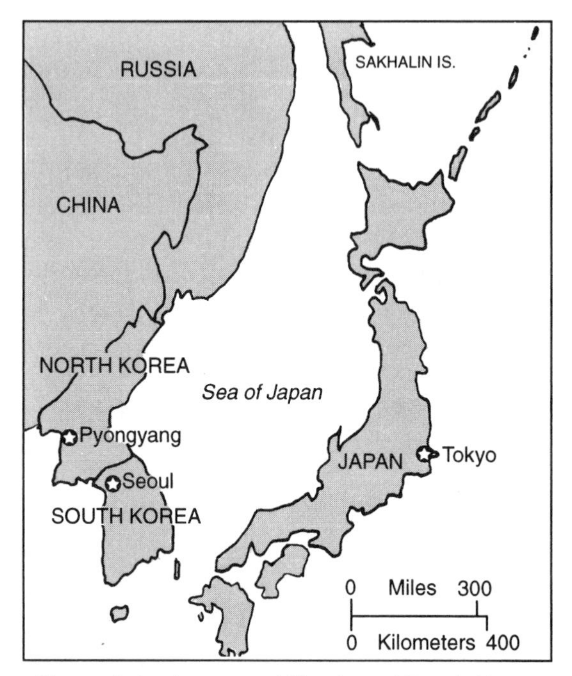

Figure 5.4 Japan and North and South Korea

investment opportunities, especially in Asia. In China, Korea, Taiwan, Hong Kong, Vietnam, Thailand, Malaysia, Singapore, and Indonesia, Japanese firms invested and sold far more than did U.S. and European companies.

Japan's economic success drew on a disciplined and educated workforce and on a traditional unity of purpose among industry, labor, and government. In Japan's unique form of capitalism, government and industry cooperated in laying plans for the future and seeing that they were carried out.

By the 1980s, Japan had become an economic superpower. It ranked second only to the United States in total output, a position it still holds today.

However, Japan's economy became stuck in a deep downturn from 1990 onward. Land prices dropped to half their former levels. So did stock prices on the Tokyo stock exchange. Prospects for recovery seemed no brighter in the mid-1990s than at the start of the decade.

The stumbling economy sent shock waves through Japan's political system. Public exposure of corruption in government circles, especially among leaders of the long-dominant Liberal Democratic Party (LDP), touched off a series of political scandals that contributed to the disarray. In 1993, the LDP lost its majority in the lower house of parliament. For the first time in 38 years, it was not in control of the government.

A reformer named Morohiro Hosokawa became prime minister, but his government lasted only a short time. The LDP still held the largest block of seats in parliament, and it threw its support behind the leader of Japan's small Socialist Party. In June 1994, the lower house chose the Socialist leader, Tomiichi Murayama, to be prime minister. However, Murayama's power was sharply restricted by his dependence on LDP votes for staying in office. LDP leaders assumed many key government positions, and in 1996 LDP leader Ryutaro Hashimoto became prime minister.

♦ *List the problems that brought a new government to power in Japan in 1993.*

For all its recent problems, Japan remains an economic superpower—and one that is not always loved by its competitors. Japan has frequently run up large trade surpluses with the United States and Europe. Japan's surplus with the United

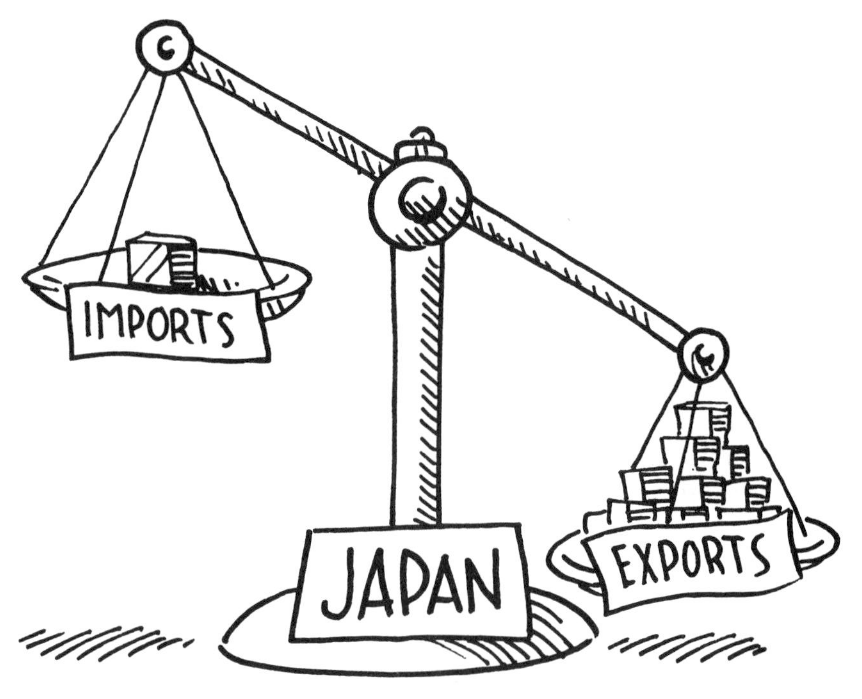

Trade Imbalance

States exceeded $65 billion a year in the mid-1990s. That meant that Japan received $65 billion more for the goods it sold to the United States than Americans received for the goods they sold to Japan. Many of Japan's trading partners argued that Japan's policies were unfair. They said Japanese business practices froze out competition from non-Japanese business firms that tried to break into the Japanese market.

Ever since the presidency of Ronald Reagan in the 1980s, U.S. leaders have been pushing the Japanese to make changes. Under Presidents Bush and Clinton, the dialogue grew sharper. American efforts to reduce the Japanese surplus by economic and diplomatic means were sometimes called a *trade war.*

The United States tried many different approaches. In the 1980s, it persuaded Japan to set quotas, or limits, on the number of cars it sold to the United States. Japanese manufacturers got around the limits by building factories in the United States. In the 1990s, U.S. leaders threatened to set high tariffs on certain Japanese products unless Japan opens up its internal markets to U.S. companies. Under pressure, Japan made certain concessions. U.S. leaders said Japan needed to do more.

From 1993 to 1995, President Clinton tried to force an increase in the value of the Japanese yen. That meant a corresponding decrease in the value of the U.S. dollar. The goal was to make it harder for Japan to sell to the United States by making its products more expensive for U.S. consumers. The tactic did manage to make the yen more costly. A dollar bought about 100 yen in 1993, but by early 1995 it was buying only about 80 yen. (The dollar was also buying less German and French and British currency.) However, the changes in currency rates did little to curb Japanese sales to the United States. In mid-1995, the United States quit intervening in the currency markets, and soon the dollar again bought about 100 yen.

♦ *Explain why Japan's trade surplus with the United States caused tension between the two nations.*

After World War II, Japanese foreign policy was conducted beneath a U.S. nuclear "umbrella." Japan granted the United States valuable military bases. It paid most of the cost of stationing U.S. troops in Japan. Today, despite its recent trade disputes with the Americans, Japan supports a post-cold war U.S. military presence in East Asia. Japan leads this region economically but has not attempted to dominate it politically.

Japan has no large military forces of its own. After World War II, the United States encouraged Japan to write into its constitution a ban on having an army. The purpose was to avoid a revival of Japanese militarism. In the 1950s, Japan created its own Self-Defense Forces but barred them from going overseas. Today some Japanese favor changing the constitution to allow Japan to take a stronger military role in world affairs. However, most Japanese oppose any change that might risk a revival of militarism.

Japan's policies have kept it from taking an active part in international military missions. Japan had a keen interest in the Persian Gulf War of 1991 because it depends heavily on oil from the Persian Gulf. However, Japanese soldiers did not join the U.S.-led coalition fighting against Iraq. Instead, Japan contributed money to pay for the war. Later, the Japanese Self-Defense Forces did take part in a United Nations military mission to Cambodia. But the Japanese troops were limited to noncombat tasks.

In recent years, Japan has been the world's largest foreign aid donor. It has also been the second largest contributor to the United Nations budget, after the United States.

♦ *Which of the following are correct statements? Revise the incorrect statements.*

a. After World War II, Japan and the United States cooperated closely on military matters.
b. Disputes over Japan's trade surplus in the 1990s led to Japan's asking the United States to remove its troops from Japan.
c. Japan's constitution has prevented Japan from maintaining any military forces at all.
d. Japan contributed money but not soldiers for the Persian Gulf War.
e. Japan spends more on foreign aid than does the United States.

North and South Korea

Korea was part of the Japanese empire until the end of World War II in 1945. Following occupation by Soviet and American forces, the former colony was divided into two separate countries.

In June 1950, Communist North Korea invaded noncommunist South Korea. During the ensuing Korean War (1950–53), United Nations military forces, led by the United States, halted North Korea by forcing its troops to withdraw behind the 38th parallel, the border between the two nations.

North Korea became one of the most rigidly run Communist states in the world. Despite aid from China, the economic development of the Democratic People's Republic of Korea was limited. The country became largely self-sufficient in food production. Some 36 percent of the labor force is engaged in agriculture, and rice is the major crop. Because North Korea remains committed to continuing the Communist struggle against Western capitalism, its economic resources have been largely directed toward military production. In the 1990s, a severe fuel shortage reduced industrial and agricultural output, hampered fishing, and caused a serious shortfall of food.

For North Korea's first 46 years, supreme power was in the hands of Communist party leader Kim Il Sung. Kim died in July

1994, at the age of 82. His son, Kim Jong Il, who had been commander of North Korea's military forces, took his place. Thus, North Korea became the world's first Communist dynasty.

South Korea was not a model of democracy either. It became a police state under the control of a military junta led by General Park Chung Hee in 1961. Park was assassinated in 1979. He was eventually replaced by General Chun Doo Hwan, who continued to rule by imposing martial law. In 1987, weeks of protest by middle-class workers, businesspeople, and students against authoritarian rule resulted in the election of President Roh Tae Woo by direct popular vote.

Since 1990, South Korea has evolved toward a relatively stable state in which two large parties compete for votes. Kim Young Sam, elected president in 1993, was the first civilian president in three decades. During Kim's term of office, former presidents Chun and Roh went to jail. They faced criminal charges for their roles in the 1979 military coup. Roh was also accused of accepting millions of dollars in bribes.

In contrast to North Korea, the Republic of Korea experienced extensive economic growth, with textiles and automobiles becoming major industries. Some 79 percent of the labor force is engaged in manufacturing and service industries. Since World War II, the economy has been controlled by *chaebol,* large family-run business organizations with great political influence. South Korean companies like Samsung and Hyundai have won a growing share of world markets.

In 1972, South and North Korea agreed on a common goal of reunifying their two nations by peaceful means. They made little progress toward that goal until 1985, when they reached an agreement to discuss economic issues. The two countries opened trade relations, and South Koreans began investing in North Korea. In June 1994, the two Koreas set a date in the following month for the first summit meeting between their two leaders. However, North Korean dictator Kim Il Sung died a week and a half later and the meeting was put off indefinitely.

During the 1990s, North Korea's nuclear program alarmed both Western and Asian governments. A crisis erupted in 1993, when North Korea rejected international demands for inspection of its nuclear power facilities and announced its intention to withdraw from the 1968 Nuclear Nonproliferation Treaty. That agreement has been the mainstay of efforts to prevent the spread of nuclear weapons. North Korea was the first nation to threaten to withdraw from the treaty.

After U.S. warnings of dire actions if North Korea went ahead with its plans, North Korea and the United States reached an agreement in October 1994. North Korea promised to freeze its nuclear weapons development program and then shut it down. In return, the United States promised to arrange more than $4 billion in energy assistance for North Korea, mainly from Japan and South Korea. Included in the assistance would be two nuclear reactors for producing electricity. They would be so-called light-water reactors, whose by-products would be hard to use in a nuclear weapons program. Before, North Korea had been building a type of nuclear reactor whose by-products would be relatively easy to use in weapons.

Negotiations on how to carry out the nuclear agreement began late in 1994, but quickly ran into snags. Moreover, new disputes erupted between North and South Korea. The Korean peninsula remained a hot spot in the mid-1990s.

1. *Contrast North and South Korea politically and economically.*
2. *Explain why North Korea caused concern for Western and Asian governments in 1993.*
3. *Identify:*
   a. *Kim Young Sam*
   b. *Kim Il Sung*
   c. *Kim Jong Il*

Terror in Southeast Asia

Cambodia. As a result of the Vietnam War (1959–75), Communist governments were established in the Southeast Asian nations of Vietnam, Laos, and Cambodia. The most radical of those governments was the Khmer Rouge regime in Cambodia, led by Pol Pot. Military conflicts and economic problems have continued to trouble the region.

The Khmer Rouge killed or enslaved more than a million Cambodians suspected of opposition to communism. It aroused fierce opposition both within Cambodia and in other countries of the region.

In 1977, fighting broke out between Vietnam and Cambodia, two nations that had been antagonistic toward each other for

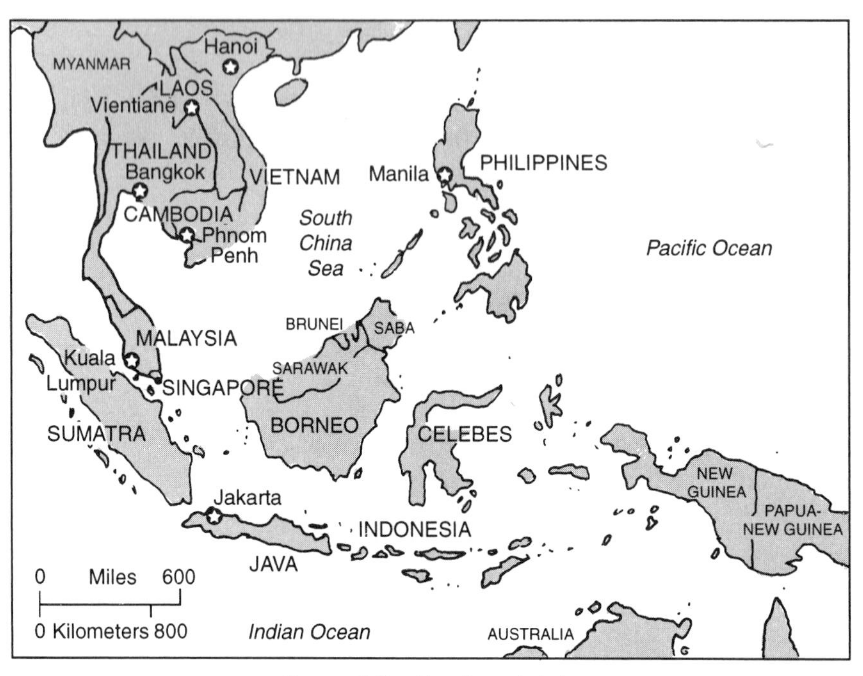

Figure 5.5 Southeast Asia

centuries. Each side charged the other with aggression, border violations, and atrocities against civilians. Two years later, Vietnamese forces invaded Cambodia. They ousted the brutal Khmer Rouge government and replaced it with a Vietnamese-supported regime of moderate Communists.

Cambodia plunged into a state of civil war. On one side was the new Cambodian government, backed by Vietnamese troops. On the other side were the remnants of the Khmer Rouge, supported by China, and two noncommunist groups. One of those was headed by Prince Norodom Sihanouk, who had been Cambodia's head of state from 1960 to 1970. The United States helped to arm the noncommunist groups.

In 1989, Vietnam began to withdraw its forces from Cambodia. The Vietnamese government acted in the hope of being rewarded with badly needed Western economic aid. In 1991, the four rival Cambodian factions declared a cease-fire. They signed a peace agreement drawn up by the United Nations. This accord created a transitional coalition government to serve until a new government was democratically chosen in elections to be supervised by the United Nations in 1993. A *United Nations Transitional Authority in Cambodia* (UNTAC) was appointed to police the cease-fire, control several government ministries, and disarm the forces of the rival factions.

The Khmer Rouge refused to place its troops under U.N. supervision. Instead, the Communists began a campaign to regain power by appealing to Cambodians' hatred of the Vietnamese, their traditional enemies. In 1992 and 1993, the Khmer Rouge carried out brutal massacres of Vietnamese civilians, many of whom had settled in Cambodia after 1979. They also attempted to discredit UNTAC and to persuade Cambodians that the 1993 elections were a plot to legitimize Vietnamese control.

Nevertheless, elections sponsored by the U.N. were held successfully in May 1993. Although the Khmer Rouge officially boycotted the elections, the disruption and violence feared by many did not occur. In Phnom Penh, Cambodia's capital, the National Assembly adopted a new constitution in September 1993. It made Cambodia a constitutional monarchy. Prince Sihanouk became King Sihanouk. His son, Prince Ranariddh, leader of one of the two major political parties, became prime minister. Hun Sen, leader of the other party, became deputy prime minister.

These leaders offered to share power in the new government with the Khmer Rouge, led by Pol Pot. However, this was opposed by the U.N. and the United States. The Khmer Rouge continued to oppose the new government from armed camps along Cambodia's border with Thailand.

The Cambodian government had frequently accused the Thai military of supporting the Khmer Rouge. Thai military commanders saw the Khmer Rouge as a useful buffer against its traditional enemy, Vietnam.

Into the Light

The rigid control of the economy and the massive collective farming that had been imposed by the Khmer Rouge during the 1970s have been abandoned. Since 1990, 70 percent of Cambodia's economic resources have been controlled by private businesspeople.

Literacy and education have suffered serious setbacks in Cambodia. In 1975, the Khmer Rouge closed down all schools and killed most of the teachers. A severe shortage of teachers and textbooks continued in the 1990s. Only about 48 percent of the population is literate. Although the government has promised to make education a high priority, the solution to this and other national problems depends on Cambodia's political future.

1. *Describe the effect of the Vietnam War on Cambodia.*
2. *Explain the role of the United Nations in Cambodia.*

Vietnam. In August 1995, U.S. Secretary of State Warren Christopher flew to Vietnam's capital, Hanoi, to sign a piece of paper. Twenty years after the Communists won the Vietnam War, the United States and Vietnam were opening formal diplomatic relations. The bitterness of war was being consigned to the past. A few blocks away from the signing ceremony, dust flew as workers tore down the notorious prison known as the "Hanoi Hilton." There, U.S. airmen and other captives were imprisoned and tortured during the war. In its place was to rise a multistory office and shopping complex.

Since the war ended in 1975, Vietnam's chief concern has been its economic well-being. Agriculture predominates. In 1989, Vietnam became the world's third largest exporter of rice. In addition, offshore oil and mineral deposits are significant. However, many of its natural resources remain undeveloped.

Vietnam experienced continuous warfare from 1940 to 1975. The Vietnamese fought the Japanese during World War II, French colonialists during the 1950s, and the Americans who intervened in their civil war in the 1960s and 1970s. As a result, economic development was limited, and Vietnam remained one of the world's poorest countries in the 1990s. Poverty was accompanied by a high birthrate. Government efforts to impose a limit of two children per family were ineffective, despite cuts in food rations for those who did not cooperate.

In 1987, Vietnam's leaders departed from traditional Communist economic control and began to permit privately owned, profit-making enterprises. Under a program called *doi moi*, or renovation, farmers were allowed to lease land on long-term contracts that could be passed on to their children. Family-owned farms replaced some of the nation's farm collectives. Increased agricultural production and higher incomes resulted.

Doi moi made more progress in the southern portion of the country than in the north, which had been under Communist control for a longer time. A new prosperity arose in Ho Chi Minh City (formerly Saigon), the largest city of the south. In its elegant restaurants, American and other Western businesspeople began to appear in increasing numbers. In the north, by 1990, free market activity led to the emergence of a variety of new businesses in Hanoi.

The end of the cold war deprived Vietnam of the aid it had been receiving from the Soviet Union. The Vietnamese tried to make up for the loss by attracting Western investors. In 1992, the United States offered humanitarian aid in exchange for cooperation with efforts to locate M.I.A.'s, American servicemen missing in action during the Vietnam War and unaccounted for since. Agreements also were reached for the repatriation of "Amerasians," the children fathered by U.S. servicemen.

A new constitution adopted in 1992 introduced several political reforms. First, it provided for a president to be chosen by and from the membership of the National Assembly, the lawmaking body. Assembly members are elected for five-year terms by popular vote. Second, it provided for a prime minister to head the government, assisted by a cabinet. Although no opposition parties were permitted, the constitution limited Communist Party involvement in government operations.

Improvements in Vietnam's relations with the United States were paralleled by better relations with China. In 1979, Vietnam and China had fought a short, bitter border war. Tensions remained high until Vietnam began to remove its troops from Cambodia. In 1991, Vietnam and China agreed to normalize their relations.

By also normalizing its relations with the United States, Vietnam hopes to obtain access to Western markets and to expand Western investment in Vietnam. It has also courted the business of other capitalist nations. Billboards in Hanoi advertise the products of companies from Japan to Great Britain. At the Hanoi airport just before Christopher's visit, pictures of giant Coca-Cola bottles greeted visitors, and the Vietnamese sign declared: "Coke welcomes you to Hanoi."

1. *Contrast present-day Cambodia and Vietnam, politically and economically.*
2. *Complete the following sentences:*
   a. *The mission of UNTAC in the 1990s in Cambodia was ____.*
   b. *After the end of the cold war, Vietnam attempted to ____.*
3. *Identify:*
   a. *Khmer Rouge*
   b. *UNTAC*
   c. *Norodom Sihanouk*
   d. *Phnom Penh*
   e. doi moi

Religious Strife in India

Religious conflict has raged in India for centuries. When Britain prepared to grant independence to India in 1947, thousands died in violence between Hindus and Muslims. Muslim

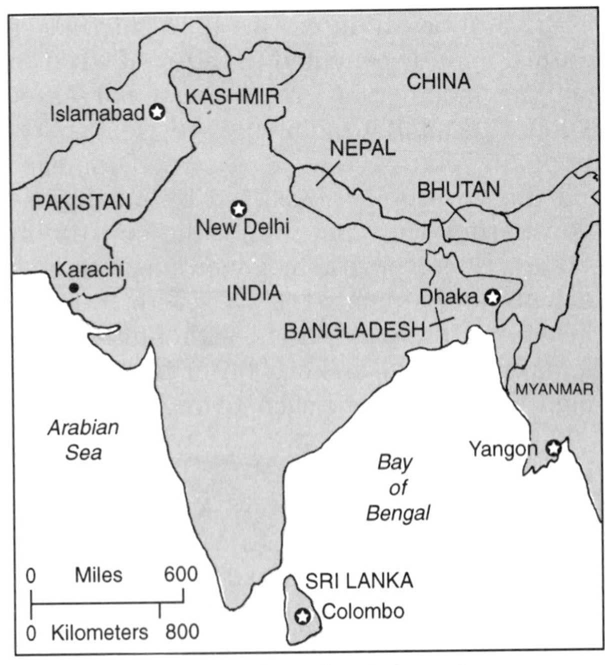

Figure 5.6 The Indian Subcontinent

leaders refused to cooperate in the establishment of an Indian nation led by a Hindu-controlled government. As a result, Pakistan was created out of portions of India inhabited by a Muslim majority.

The division of British India into Hindu- and Muslim-governed nations did not end religious conflict in the region. From 1971 to 1973, India and Pakistan were at war. During the 1980s, violence broke out between Hindus and Sikhs in Punjab state, in western India. The Sikhs form a distinct religious community, with beliefs that combine Hindu and Islamic elements. The Indian government sent troops into Punjab to put down a wave of terrorism by Sikh secessionists. The troops seemed to have crushed the Sikh secession movement in 1992, but militant Sikh groups reorganized. In 1995 they assassinated the top elected official in Punjab.

Other assassinations targeted officials at the national level. In 1984, two Sikh bodyguards killed Indian Prime Minister Indira Gandhi. In 1991, other assassins killed her son, Rajiv. Rajiv Gandhi had served as prime minister after his mother's death and was campaigning to win back the post. His killers do not seem to have had religious motives.

Another religious crisis exploded in Kashmir in 1989, when separatist Muslims began a guerrilla war against Indian domination. Kashmir, on India's northwest frontier, is inhabited by Hindus and Muslims. Since 1949, two thirds of the area has been controlled by India and the remainder by Pakistan. India poured troops into Kashmir until it resembled a battle camp. Yet the troops made little headway in controlling the rebellion. The conflict further strained relations between India and Pakistan.

Yet another religious crisis began in December 1992. Hindu extremists in the northern holy city of Ayodhya destroyed an ancient mosque, sacred to Muslims. The Hindus believe the site on which the mosque was built was the birthplace of Lord Ram, a Hindu god. In March 1993, unknown terrorists bombed the Bombay stock exchange. These acts of destruction touched off new waves of religious hatred, which spread rapidly throughout India. Riots in Bombay, Delhi, and other cities brought death to more than 1,200 people. The violence also spread to Pakistan and Bangladesh. India's media and politicians blamed Pakistan for the Bombay bombing. They also suggested other possible suspects, ranging from Kashmiri militants to Arab and Iranian extremists.

The religious strife that periodically sweeps India has intensified the nation's problems. A country of 850 million people, in which poverty is widespread, India faced many problems in the 1990s because of rapid population growth. Millions of India's people are not part of the cash economy. They grow their own food, bartering surplus produce for clothing and other necessities. About 70 percent of India's population is engaged in agriculture. More and more of India's farmers have been adopting modern equipment and methods. India's food output has risen sharply since the 1970s, lessening the country's need for outside aid.

India needs both foreign investment and popular support for economic reforms. The religious conflicts, and the accompanying breakdown in public safety, have damaged India's standing in the international community and reduced its ability to attract foreign investors. Those and other factors resulted in periodic demands for the resignation of Prime Minister Narasimha Rao, whose government took office in 1991.

Rao was a member of the Congress Party, which led India to independence from Britain in 1947 and has ruled most of the time since. Lately, evidence of corruption and incompetence within the party has caused many Indians to reject it. A major rival, the Bharatiya Janata Party (BJP), rose rapidly in the 1990s on a platform of Hindu nationalism. Many believed it could end the dominance of the Congress Party. The BJP's popularity was fueled by Hindu rage against India's Muslim minority.

The government of Prime Minister Rao turned its back on many Congress Party traditions, including a commitment to socialism. Under Rao, India reduced the government's role in the economy and invited more foreign investment. As India's economy opened to the world, new industries developed. India began to make its mark in the production of computer software and other high-tech endeavors.

1. *PROVE or DISPROVE: Religious violence is India's only major problem.*

2. *Which are the correct statements? Revise the incorrect statements.*

   a. *India and Pakistan are both Hindu nations.*
   b. *The Sikhs are Indians, but they constitute a separate religious community.*
   c. *Ayodhya was the scene of religious violence in late 1992.*

d. India's government has succeeded in controlling population growth.
e. Kashmir gained independence in 1989.

Chapter 5 Review

A. *Select the letter of the correct response.*

1. *In the 1990s, China's economic policies stressed (a) rigid state control (b) development of privatization and a market economy (c) rejection of foreign investors.*
2. *Since 1991, China's program of population control has (a) reduced the birthrate (b) won international approval (c) failed to be effective.*
3. *Democratic reforms caused conflict, in 1994, between China and (a) Cambodia (b) Korea (c) Hong Kong.*
4. *From 1993 to 1995, the United States followed a policy designed to (a) increase the value of the Japanese yen (b) increase the value of the dollar (c) remove U.S. bases from Japan.*
5. *During the post-World War II years, Japanese firms eagerly pursued investment opportunities in (a) Latin America (b) Eastern Europe (c) Asia.*
6. *In 1972, North and South Korea agreed on a process of (a) arranging joint military maneuvers (b) reunifying their two nations (c) merging university systems.*
7. *In 1993, North Korea caused international alarm by announcing its intention to (a) withdraw from the Nuclear Nonproliferation Treaty of 1968 (b) send its troops across the 38th parallel (c) break diplomatic relations with China.*
8. *Violence erupted in Cambodia in 1992 and 1993 because of (a) Vietnamese military activity (b) food riots in Phnom Penh (c) Khmer Rouge attacks on Vietnamese civilians.*
9. *The term* doi moi *refers to (a) the Vietnamese program of economic reform (b) the majority political party in Hanoi (c) overseas Vietnamese anticommunists.*
10. *India has long been troubled by religious strife between (a) Hindus and Jews (b) Hindus and Christians (c) Hindus and Muslims.*

B. *Reread "The Modernization of China" on pages 91–97 and examine the graph on page 97. Then answer these questions:*

1. *What happened to the birthrate in China between 1988 and 1992?*
2. *How did family size change between 1988 and 1992?*
3. *Why have changes in the fertility rate pleased China's family planners?*

C. *Which of the following statements are* true *and which are* false*? Revise the incorrect statements. (Examine maps in this chapter.)*

1. *Nepal and Mongolia are both part of the People's Republic of China.*
2. *Yangon, Colombo, and New Delhi are cities in India.*
3. *Japan is a group of islands.*
4. *Pyongyang is the capital of South Korea.*
5. *Hong Kong and Vietnam both have access to the South China Sea.*

D. *Write a composition on "Asia in the 1990s." Include statements about each of the following:*

1. *the growth of democracy and free market economies.*
2. *political and economic relations with the West.*

Chapter 6

Drugs and Politics in Latin America

Poverty, inequality, and political repression made revolutions common in Latin America in the 19th and 20th centuries. During the cold war, fear of communism prompted the United States to support a number of right-wing, anti-communist dictatorships. At the same time, U.S. leaders spoke out in favor of democracy and respect for human rights, as they continue to do. Meanwhile, the United States has been assisting Latin American governments in their struggle against the growing power of drug *traficantes* (dealers).

Preventing the shipment of narcotics from Latin American laboratories and processing plants to criminal distributors in North America has been a major goal of the United States in recent years. U.S. military and law enforcement personnel have worked closely with their Latin American counterparts in the war against the *traficantes*.

In the 20th century, the United States has played a strong role in Latin American affairs, often exercising police power. Many Latin American governments have cooperated with their powerful northern neighbor. But resentment of Yankee interference is strong in the 1990s.

Throughout Latin America, the military has continued to wield immense political power. Venezuela experienced two military coup attempts in 1992. Rumors of coups swept other nations from time to time. The civilian government of Chile, elected in 1989, was unable to remove General Augusto Pinochet, the former dictator, from his post as commander-in-chief of the army. In Uruguay, Bolivia, and Paraguay, high-ranking military officers have repeatedly warned civilian

Figure 6.1 Latin America and the Caribbean

governments not to investigate past human rights abuses. In all cases, the growth of democracy has depended upon a balance between the determination of the people for more political power and the determination of military leaders to retain their special status.

- *State the goals of the United States in Latin America.*

Peru and the Shining Path

The troubled history of Peru has included military dictatorship from 1968 to 1980, food shortages and labor strikes in the 1970s and 1980s, and a cholera epidemic that began in 1991.

Since 1980, Peru has suffered from a brutal guerrilla war against the elected government. A Maoist organization named the Shining Path, led by Abimael Guzman, fought its way from the rural highlands to the streets of Lima, the capital. Specializing in political assassinations, kidnappings, and car bombings, the guerrillas killed tens of thousands of Peruvians.

At their strongest, the guerrillas numbered about 8,000. They financed themselves by charging "landing fees" to drug traffickers who flew coca leaves (the source of cocaine) out of Peru. They also received money from overseas groups. The rebellion arose out of years of resentment caused by political corruption, unemployment, and racial discrimination. Another issue was inflation, which climbed as high as one million percent in the 1980s. The combined effect of a high rate of population growth and limited arable land also contributed to discontent.

Alberto Fujimori, an agricultural engineer of Japanese descent, was elected president in 1990 with broad support from the lower and middle classes. Once in office, Fujimori turned to the military for support of his efforts to improve the economy and combat terrorism. Tension developed between him and the Congress, which the president criticized for not doing enough to resolve Peru's political and economic problems.

In April 1992, Fujimori dissolved Congress and the courts, claiming that they were obstructing the fight against terrorism. Fujimori assumed dictatorial powers. For nine months he ruled by decree. The president gave police and military

Figure 6.2 South America: North and West

agencies sweeping powers to arrest and interrogate suspected terrorists, without regard to their constitutional rights. Criticizing his actions, the United States reduced its economic aid to Peru.

As more arrests were made, terrorist violence subsided and economic growth improved. To many Peruvians, Fujimori became a hero. His popularity soared with the capture of Abimael Guzman, the guerrilla leader, in September 1992. In a 1993 poll, 64 percent of Peruvians approved Fujimori's policies.

Guzman's capture dealt a devastating blow to the Shining Path, although battles between the army and the guerrillas continued. In April 1993, the president claimed that 95 percent of the Shining Path's leadership was in prison. He said Peru's increased stability would attract foreign investments and help Peru to become a strong industrial nation.

With the inauguration of a new Peruvian Congress in 1993, Fujimori gave up his dictatorial powers. The United States restored its economic aid. Peru repaid debts to the World Bank and to the International Monetary Fund. It reentered the international financial community for the first time since 1986.

Human rights groups, however, continued to protest Fujimori's antiterrorism policy. They accused him of allowing the police and military to imprison, torture, and kill hundreds of innocent people.

To further stimulate the economy, the Peruvian government developed a plan to sell state-owned electric and telephone companies. The funds raised were used to help balance the national budget, reduce inflation, and support social welfare programs. The president, for example, began a program of opening one new school each week.

Peru's economy grew briskly in the years that followed. In 1994, the gross domestic product (GDP) soared by 12.7 percent, giving Peru the fastest-growing economy in the world. Peruvian voters, duly impressed, gave Fujimori a landslide victory in the April 1995 presidential election. The president won 65 percent of the vote, and his independent political party won a majority of the seats in Congress.

Many Peruvians hoped that Fujimori would make headway against the country's immense social problems. Despite the booming economy, half of Peru's people lived in poverty and only one worker in seven held a full-time job.

During his second term, Fujimori tried to keep the military happy. In June 1995, Congress passed and Fujimori signed a broad amnesty for the military. It meant that soldiers who had tortured or killed in the war against the Shining Path could never be brought to trial. The United States registered a strong protest, as did human rights groups.

1. *Explain how President Alberto Fujimori became a hero to many Peruvians.*
2. *State two developments in Peru in the 1990s that could not happen in the United States.*
3. *Explain why you AGREE or DISAGREE: By the summer of 1995, President Alberto Fujimori had become a prisoner of the Peruvian military.*

The Misery and Hopes of Haiti

In the 1990s, the Caribbean island nation of Haiti began to break free from years of oppression. Haiti had a long, proud history. When a slave rebellion brought it to independence in

1804, it was hailed as the world's first black republic. Later it fell under military rule and dictatorship. But a path to greater freedom opened in 1986, when unrest provoked by crop failure and famine put an end to 28 years of dictatorship. The dictators were François Duvalier, who died in 1971, and his son, Jean-Claude Duvalier, who fled to Europe in 1986. Four years of military rule followed. In 1990, a left-wing Catholic priest named Jean-Bertrand Aristide became the first democratically elected president to lead Haiti since 1950.

Aristide ruled only briefly. His proposed democratic reforms alarmed both the military and Haiti's small educated elite, who saw them as a threat to their power and wealth. In September 1991, the military arrested Aristide and expelled him from Haiti. General Raoul Cédras assumed power at the head of a military junta.

Although some U.S. officials distrusted Aristide for his leftist ideas, the United States and the Organization of American States demanded that he be restored to power as Haiti's rightful ruler. They placed an economic embargo on Haiti in October 1991. The embargo caused serious damage to Haiti's economy, the poorest in the Americas. The damage worsened after the United Nations put an embargo on oil and arms sales to Haiti in June 1993.

Even before the embargoes, the majority of Haitians had lived in poverty. They crowded into urban slums or scratched out meager livings on small farms. An upper class of less than

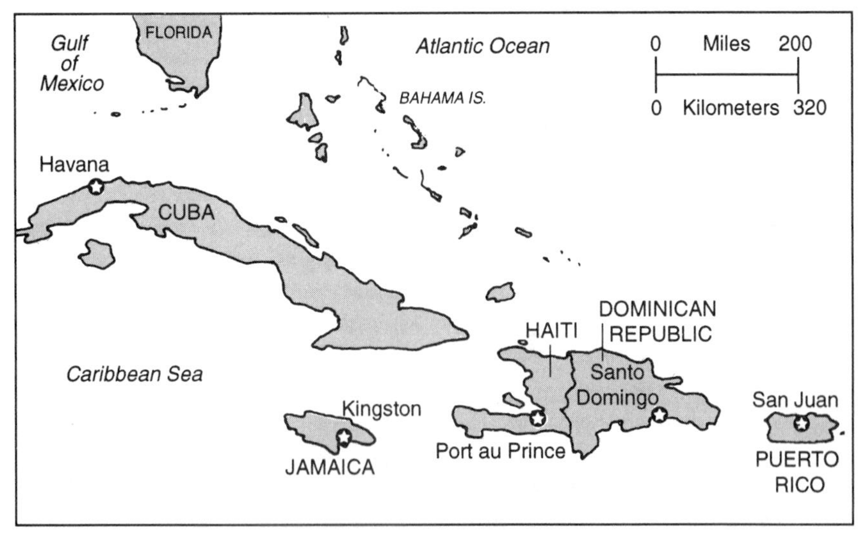

Figure 6.3 The Caribbean

5 percent of the population controlled Haiti's limited wealth. The embargoes made life even harder for most Haitians. Unemployment and starvation spread. Despite the suffering brought by the embargo, many Haitians supported it, in the hope that it would bring back Aristide.

Fearing rebellion, the army terrorized the slums and countryside. Thousands of Haitians attempted to flee to the United States by boat. However, Presidents Bush and Clinton refused to admit most of the boat people, saying the Haitians were motivated by hope for economic gain rather than fear of political persecution. The Coast Guard returned many boatloads to Haiti. It took others to "safe havens" in Latin America. Some critics claimed the U.S. policy was racially biased.

The United Nations tried to work out an agreement between Cédras and Aristide for a peaceful return of the president to power. A tentative agreement in 1993 did not hold up. In May 1994, U.N. sanctions were tightened.

The United States positioned Marines near Haiti and announced they were practicing for an invasion. That news inspired mixed reactions among Haitians. Even Aristide supporters were leery of U.S. military action, recalling that U.S. soldiers had occupied Haiti from 1915 to 1934. To some Haitians, U.S. intervention smacked of old-fashioned imperialism. Others saw it as the only way to restore Aristide to power.

In July 1994, the U.N. Security Council authorized the use of force against Haiti. On the eve of an announced U.S. invasion, a team of U.S. negotiators persuaded General Cédras to let U.S. troops land peacefully and to step down within 30 days. This time the agreement held up. Some 20,000 U.S. soldiers entered Haiti, without military opposition.

On October 15, 1994, President Aristide returned to Haiti on a U.S. government plane. Cheering crowds greeted him. The president urged his supporters not to seek revenge against Haitian soldiers for their past acts. "No to violence, no to vengeance, yes to reconciliation," Aristide declared.

Haiti began the long, slow process of rebuilding its economy and strengthening its democratic institutions. U.N. peacekeeping troops arrived, replacing most of the U.S. soldiers. At parliamentary elections in June 1995, a coalition of Aristide supporters won two thirds of the seats. Voters went to the polls again six months later to elect René Préval as the president's successor. Préval was a close associate of Aristide and had his endorsement in the race. The road ahead would be long and hard. But the prospects for democracy in Haiti seemed brighter than they had been in a long time.

1. *Explain why a citizen of Haiti might have mixed feelings about the arrival of U.S. soldiers.*
2. *Complete the following sentence:*
   After his return, President Aristide faced the following problems: ______.
3. *Identify each of the following:*
   a. *Jean-Bertrand Aristide*
   b. *Raoul Cédras*
   c. *François Duvalier*
   d. *René Préval*

Colombia and the Drug War

Colombia is one of the world's largest suppliers of illegal narcotics. It leads the world in the production of cocaine. It is the home of the Medellín and Cali drug cartels (named for the cities in which they have headquarters). Colombian drug lords control private armies, airplanes, ships, laboratories, and processing plants.

Although a democracy, Colombia has had large-scale economic and social problems, worsened by a high birthrate. For years, impoverished peasant guerrillas have waged war against the national government. Their objective has been to break the power of wealthy landowners.

The 1990 election of President César Gaviria marked a turning point in the guerrilla war. Gaviria's policies of land redistribution and other social reforms brought the voluntary demobilization of some of the guerrilla forces. Those groups became political parties and sought power in rural areas through democratic elections. Other rebel groups, however, continued their war against the government. In 1994, Colombians elected a new president, Ernesto Samper Pizano, who promised to increase social spending under a policy that he called "social capitalism." He continued peace talks with the remaining guerrillas.

A related war has also been fought by government forces against the drug lords. Campaigns of violence by the drug cartels against government and civilian targets are known as *narcoterrorism.* Hundreds of political and military officials have been murdered. Such killings reached a peak in 1989 and 1990, when three presidential candidates were assassinated.

Elected in 1990 as a strong opponent of the drug cartels, President Gaviria tried to reduce Colombia's violence by offering lenient treatment to narcoterrorists who surrendered. By 1991, the number of political murders was on the decline. President Gaviria's policies helped lead to the surrender of Pablo Escobar, the billionaire leader of the Medellín cartel.

Gaviria's policies won the approval of most Colombians. However, Escobar's escape from a custom-designed luxury prison in 1992 drew sharp criticism from the police and the military. They contended that the decision to provide special treatment for Escobar had weakened the war on the drug lords.

Subsequently, Escobar became Colombia's most wanted fugitive. Following his escape, more than one hundred Medellín policemen were killed on his orders. By March 1993, however, police and military units had eliminated much of the drug lord's organization, and Escobar offered to surrender again if the government would allow his family to seek safety in the United States. That was refused. In December 1993, the Colombian security forces found and killed Escobar. His death, however, did little to diminish the trade in cocaine.

1. *Define the term* narco-terrorism.
2. *Identify:*
    a. *César Gaviria*
    b. *Pablo Escobar*
    c. *Ernesto Samper*

The growing importance of oil to the Colombian economy changed the nature of the government's war against narcoterrorists and guerrillas. In 1991, oil replaced coffee as Colombia's largest export product. A newly discovered underground sea of crude oil in the foothills of the Andes Mountains attracted large foreign investments. Economists predicted that Colombia would become South America's second largest exporter of oil, after Venezuela.

The oil pipelines became targets of antigovernment guerrilla attacks. The government retaliated aggressively with a new set of strategies. Among them: (1) offering bounties for the capture of guerrilla leaders, (2) freezing the assets of the families of kidnapped people to forestall ransom payments, (3) imposing

Buying Influence

penalties on banks found guilty of handling guerrilla accounts, and (4) canceling state oil and mining contracts with foreign companies caught paying protection money to guerrillas. The government also began auditing state and city financial records to stop governors and mayors from paying protection money to narcoterrorists and other criminal organizations.

Although he was popular early in his administration, during his second year in office President Samper faced a serious crisis of confidence. Had drug dealers bought off the president? That's what critics claimed. They said Samper received nearly $6 million in campaign contributions from *traficantes* during the 1994 campaign. In exchange, the critics alleged, Samper promised lenient treatment to drug dealers in the courts. Police raids against drug leaders turned up documents that seemed to show $25 million in payments to 2,000 politicians, journalists, soldiers, police officers, soccer players, and entertainers.

Despite repeated denials by Samper, who pointed out that his administration had jailed six of the top seven leaders of the Cali cartel, the dispute over the alleged payoffs dragged his administration through the mud. Investigators brought criminal charges against several top officials, some of whom backed up the accusations against the president. Some observers compared Samper's position to that of U.S. President Nixon during the Watergate scandal of the 1970s. Many Colombians said the president should resign. Refusing to do so, Samper declared a state of emergency in August 1995, and announced a stepped-up war against the drug dealers and the guerrilla armies.

Despite this, U.S. President Clinton cut off most economic aid to Colombia in March 1996. He cited the country for failing to cooperate in the fight against illegal drugs.

♦ *Find out what is wrong with each of the following statements. Then rewrite each as a correct statement.*

a. *Drug trafficking has played only a minor role in the history of Colombia.*
b. *Antigovernment guerrillas saw the rise in Colombian oil production as a way for the government to finance new social measures.*
c. *President Ernesto Samper's war on drug dealers brought him rising popularity.*

The United States and the Drug War

Mexico. Several Latin American countries have been centers of narcotics production and distribution. That fact has complicated, and often strained, relations between Latin America and

Figure 6.4 Central America

the United States. In 1993, for example, Mexico drew closer to its northern neighbor by entering into the *North American Free Trade Agreement* (NAFTA). But tension continued between officials of the U.S. Drug Enforcement Agency (DEA) and Mexican security forces. The operations of *traficantes* in Mexico City and in other Mexican centers, where the drug lords lived in open luxury, were a source of frustration to the U.S. officials who tried to intercept the drugs being smuggled across the border.

Carlos Salinas de Gortari, Mexico's president from 1988 to 1994, cooperated with U.S. officials in their war on drugs. Salinas declared that drug trafficking should be regarded as a threat to national security. He created military and police organizations to carry out antinarcotics operations.

Under Salinas, Mexican agents worked closely with U.S. officials. Mexican agents destroyed crops of marijuana and opium poppies. They intercepted drugs being smuggled from South America through Mexico to the United States. However, drug lords sometimes were able to bribe Mexico's antidrug officials. U.S. agents suggested that corruption reached into high levels of the Mexican government.

Some Mexicans objected to the U.S. involvement in their country's internal affairs. Others worried about the rising power of the military as a result of the antidrug campaign. Was local civilian authority being undercut? Some questioned the wisdom of giving more weapons, equipment, and training to the Mexican military, which had a poor record on human rights.

Ernesto Zedillo, who succeeded Salinas in 1994, continued the policy of close cooperation with the United States. In truth, he had little choice. Mexico's economy took a sharp nosedive soon after President Zedillo took office, and President Clinton insisted on a promise of closer cooperation in the drug war before agreeing to a multibillion-dollar rescue of Mexico's economy. Zedillo also had to deal with a challenge from leftist rebels who launched a guerrilla war in the southern state of Chiapas in 1994. The rebels, who called themselves *Zapatistas* (after the early 20th-century Mexican revolutionary Emiliano Zapata), suspended military operations to enter into peace talks with the government. But the two sides seemed to be far apart.

♦ *Describe Mexico's efforts to reduce drug trafficking.*

Peru. U.S. officials criticized the administration of Peruvian President Alberto Fujimori for ineffective use of antidrug funds provided by Washington. Peru, like Bolivia and Colombia, has been a center of coca leaf production. To encourage peasant farmers to switch from coca leaf to the cultivation of such legal crops as rice and corn, Fujimori has requested additional U.S. aid.

Bolivia. Such alternative development has been pursued, with limited success, in Bolivia. The peasants of that Andean nation live in grinding poverty. They have the shortest life span in the Americas. Less than half the population of Bolivia has access to safe drinking water. The sale of coca leaves to drug traffickers has kept alive whole communities of farmers.

The United Nations Drug Control Program (UNDCP) has supported alternative development in portions of Bolivia by providing coca growers with the tools and training needed to change over from coca to tea, bananas, and livestock. UNDCP has also funded the building of roads to take the goods to market. Hospitals and basic medical services have also been provided as part of an effort to reduce poverty.

Coca growing has been reduced in many parts of Bolivia. Much of the decline, however, is due to a U.S.-trained antidrug

Alternative Development

police force. It has made the farmers fear the police more than the *traficantes*. U.S. officials working in Bolivia say the war against drugs in the Andes can be won if alternative development is combined with tough policing and eradication of drug-processing factories and support facilities.

U.S. policy in recent years has been aimed at reducing the flow of illegal drugs into North American cities. To accomplish this, the Drug Enforcement Agency (DEA) and other U.S. agencies have sent officers to Latin American countries to work with the local security services. The U.S. officers have coordinated raids on coca farms, factories, and illegal airstrips and participated in the arrest of *traficantes*. Such joint efforts have won some support but have also aroused resentment.

Many Latin Americans blame the United States for causing Latin America's drug problems, and denounce the United States for meddling in local affairs. Critics say the North Americans should focus on reducing the demand for cocaine in their own country. Then they would not have to attack the sources of supply in Latin America.

Political leaders in Peru, Bolivia, and elsewhere point to the economic and political sides of the drug problem. The farmers who grow coca, and others who are involved in the drug trade, are often taxpayers and voters. Many of those employed by the *traficantes* have no other source of income. Given those realities, and the urgent need to use military resources to combat politically motivated terrorism, some Latin American leaders have preferred to negotiate with the drug lords rather than continue destructive wars against them.

Therefore, despite American pressure and offers of economic assistance, many Latin American governments are reluctant to cooperate with the United States in the drug war. Resentment of the U.S. military presence and suspicion of U.S. motives strengthened in the 1990s. Also, critics of the U.S. war on drugs pointed out that a decade of interdiction and enforcement programs had failed to stop the flow of narcotics from the Southern Hemisphere to the drug-consuming populations of North America.

1. *Define "alternative development" and explain how it was implemented in Bolivia in the 1990s.*
2. *AGREE or DISAGREE: The drug policy of the United States should be focused on reducing the demand for narcotics in North America rather than on eliminating the sources of supply in Latin America.*

Turmoil in Venezuela

When Rafael Caldera Rodríguez took office as Venezuela's democratically elected president in February 1994, he already knew he faced an immense challenge. Since the mid-1980s, slumping world oil prices had plunged Venezuela into an economic tailspin. But worse was yet to come. Within days, a banking crisis struck. Eighteen banks failed. Venezuela's economy spiraled even lower, as unemployment spread and inflation worsened. Before the year was out, prices had risen by 70 percent. What was the background to Venezuela's crisis? Was there anything Caldera could do to end it?

A civilian-run democracy since 1958, Venezuela has the largest oil reserves outside the Persian Gulf. When oil prices soared in the 1970s, Venezuela prospered. The government found itself awash with money, which it used to finance generous social welfare programs.

As president from 1974 to 1979, Carlos Andrés Pérez used oil revenues to launch ambitious construction projects and to provide jobs and social services for most of the population. Pérez also carried out a generous foreign policy, offering economic aid to Venezuela's needy neighbors.

Figure 6.5 South America: North and East

After ten years out of office, Pérez won reelection in December 1988, at the head of his Democratic Action Party. But times had changed. The easy money was long gone, oil revenues were pinched, and Venezuela was deeply in debt. To address those problems, Pérez began a free market austerity program that angered many Venezuelans. It included the lifting of price controls on consumer goods and public services, the gradual elimination of import duties (which protected Venezuelan products from foreign competition), a freeze on public service jobs, and increased gasoline prices and urban transport fares.

Angry Venezuelans rioted in Caracas, the capital. Pérez dismissed the protests as the actions of criminals. Neither of the major political parties responded to the discontent. Instead, the army moved in, using muscles and guns to restore order. As a result, many middle-class Venezuelans began to regard the armed forces, rather than the political leaders, as the guarantors of order and stability.

Continuing with his free market reform program, Pérez tried to reduce the nation's debt and attract new capital. Although petroleum sales remained a major source of revenue, Pérez increased income from other exports, including agricultural products. Starting in August 1990, the crisis in the Persian Gulf raised oil prices and increased Venezuelan revenues. By 1992, the Venezuelan economy had improved.

Nonetheless, Pérez grew increasingly unpopular, and Venezuelans turned away from the two main political parties, the Democratic Action Party and the Social Christian Party. Many hated the major parties' total control of the electoral system. In all elections, lists of candidates were prepared by the party bosses. Voters cast their ballots for the party, not the individual candidate. Those elected, therefore, were more responsible to the political leaders than to the voters. People also resented the widespread practice of political patronage (the distribution of political offices to party loyalists and friends). And people were shocked by the scandalous behavior of public officials. Critics accused close associates of the president of corrupt financial dealings.

Furthermore, many civilians and military leaders objected to Pérez' attempts to negotiate a dispute over the Venezuela-Colombia boundary in the oil-rich Gulf of Venezuela. Critics insisted that the entire body of water must be Venezuela's.

Much of the public welcomed two attempts by members of the armed forces to overthrow Pérez in 1992. Although the coup attempts failed, with heavy loss of life, Pérez responded with efforts to satisfy some civilian and military complaints. Military salaries and social security benefits went up. Steps were taken to keep the prices of foods and medicines from rising. Planned increases in gasoline prices were canceled.

But Pérez' time was running out. In May 1993, the Venezuelan Senate stripped him of his presidential powers. Pérez was ordered to stand trial on charges of embezzling $17 million in government funds. In Caracas, crowds cheered the president's downfall.

1. *Explain the importance of oil to the Venezuelan economy.*
2. *State three reasons why Venezuelans were dissatisfied with President Carlos Andrés Pérez.*

After a period when an interim president headed the country, the voters elected Rafael Caldera Rodríguez as president. The grandfatherly Caldera was a familiar figure, having served as president in 1969–74. In those days, he headed the important Social Christian Party. But by 1994 voters were fed up with the old party system. Caldera cut his party ties and ran as an independent, in alliance with several small parties of the left and right. Caldera had a populist style that appealed to many Venezuelans, and he won in a field of 18 candidates. But he received less than 30 percent of the vote and controlled only one of the five groups in Congress.

Before the election, Venezuela had adopted a new voting system aimed at weakening the party bosses' control. For the first time, half the members in the lower house were elected not on party lists but as individuals.

Although Caldera had criticized the free market reforms introduced by Pérez, his response to the economic crisis of 1994 followed standard free market doctrine. First, he cut the budget. Then, he announced plans to privatize several state-owned businesses—an airline, hotels, power plants, a steel and aluminum company. When the economic downturn continued, Caldera introduced price and exchange controls.

Responding to public concerns about crime and corruption, Caldera resorted to authoritarian measures. In June 1994, he suspended constitutional rights. The suspension allowed police to make illegal searches and arrest and hold suspects without warrants. They could block the right to travel freely. Although Congress voted weeks later to restore constitutional rights,

Caldera immediately suspended them again—and Congress let the suspension stand.

By 1995, the bloom was off the Caldera presidency. Public opinion polls showed a sharp drop in the president's ratings. Many Venezuelans looked for a savior, and their favorite seemed to be a former military officer who had led one of the 1992 coup attempts. The officer, Hugo Chávez Frías, was released from prison in 1994 on the orders of President Caldera, who hoped to keep the military from revolting again. Chávez had strong backing within the military and among a public that was disgusted with political corruption and economic hard times. Openly expressing political ambitions, he assembled a body of leftist followers eager to help him win power.

1. *PROVE or DISPROVE: Venezuela prospered during the presidency of Rafael Caldera.*
2. *Which statements are correct?*
   a. *Venezuela is an oil-rich nation.*
   b. *The military coup attempts of 1992 were successful.*
   c. *Venezuela and Colombia have had a dispute over boundary lines.*
   d. *President Pérez was forced out of office because of charges of corruption.*
   e. *President Caldera was more successful than President Pérez in rescuing Venezuela's economy.*

A Democratic Brazil Chooses Free Market Reforms

After centuries of being dominated by the government, Brazil's economy is breaking loose. Fernando Henrique Cardoso, a candidate who preached the free market gospel, won election as president in October 1994. Cardoso quickly put his ideas into practice. During 1995, Brazil's Congress gave preliminary approval to five free market amendments to the constitution. The amendments called for an end to government monopolies in the oil, natural gas, shipping, mining, and telecommunications industries. In addition, the measures would open Brazil's economy to investment by foreigners. Back in the 1950s, Brazilian army general Leónidas Cardoso had rallied public support for government controls with the slogan, "The Oil Is Ours." Now his son, as president, was ready to let foreigners and private companies have a crack at Brazil's oil and other resources.

The trend to a more free market economy was one of two key facts about Brazil in the 1990s. The other was its newfound commitment to democracy.

Like other Latin American nations, Brazil had a tradition of relying upon the military to provide "strong government." Between 1964 and 1985, military leaders governed Brazil by issuing decrees and by appointing promilitary politicians to key posts. The military rulers concerned themselves chiefly with state-guided economic development. Civilian society was organized to provide support for government economic projects.

A country with a wide gulf between the very rich and the very poor, Brazil discovered that economic progress could not come about without democratic reforms. Such progress was needed to gain the support of foreign governments and investors. During the 1980s, the armed forces began a program of *abertura*, or "political opening." The government offered amnesty to its critics and opponents, granted increased freedom of the press, and encouraged popular elections of regional and local officials. The military regime ended in 1985, with an electoral college choosing a civilian president. Brazil adopted a new constitution, and in 1989 voters elected a new president. Fernando Collor de Mello became Brazil's first directly elected president in 29 years.

- *PROVE or DISPROVE: The military has had a leading role in Brazilian politics.*

Millions of Brazilians regarded Collor as their best hope for change. In his presidential campaign, Collor presented himself as a candidate who would fight against corruption and privilege. However, Brazil's Congress soon began to investigate charges that Collor had accepted bribes. Angry crowds took to the streets to demand the president's removal from office. To avoid an impeachment trial, Collor resigned in December 1992. The Senate impeached Collor anyway, and stripped him of his right to hold political office until 2001. Although the Supreme Court eventually found Collor not guilty of corruption, it let stand the removal of his right to hold office.

The peaceful removal of a disgraced president was regarded as proof of the strength of Brazilian democracy. For once, the military was not considered the solution to a political crisis. Also, when the charges against Collor appeared in newspapers and magazines, the government took no action to curb freedom of the press. Finally, the political parties acted responsibly and without disruption to public order.

However, public resentment against Collor left Brazilians with distrust of the democratic process. They were also upset about galloping inflation and rising unemployment. President Itamar Franco, who succeeded Collor, called on Fernando Henrique Cardoso to shape an economic recovery program. Cardoso was a sociologist by training. As minister of finance, he revamped the nation's finances, replacing the old currency (the *cruzeiro*) with a new currency (the *real*) and linking the currency loosely to the U.S. dollar. Within a brief time, inflation had been curbed and Brazilians had gained new hope.

Cardoso's reputation as the "inflation killer" propelled him into the presidency. Against an opponent who carried the socialist banner, Cardoso offered a mixture of free market reforms and social welfare programs. "We are an unjust country," Cardoso declared. "The great Achilles heel [weak spot] of Brazil is injustice." He proposed spending billions of dollars on better schools, health care, roads, and other projects.

President Cardoso's free market reforms aroused strong reactions from Brazil's people. Many people saw them as a means to modernize the country's old-fashioned economy. But union members and others on the left voiced vigorous opposition. Critics said that the government was undermining Brazil's sovereignty—it was more interested in luring foreign investors than in helping average Brazilians.

Brazil's economic, social, and political future will affect far more than Brazilians. As the tenth largest economy in the world, Brazil is an emerging industrial power. Yet about 40 percent of its 159 million people live in deep poverty, and more than half lack adequate means of disposing of sewage.

1. *Explain why the removal from office of President Fernando Collor de Mello in 1992 was considered a triumph for Brazilian democracy.*
2. *Complete the following sentence:*
   President Fernando Henrique Cardoso sought to bring change to Brazil's economy by ____.
3. *List two problems that President Cardoso faced.*

Central America, Cuba, and the United States

During the cold war, fear of the spread of communism made Central America and Cuba areas of ongoing involvement for the United States. U.S. involvement continued in the post-cold war period of the 1990s, with frequent expressions of concern about democracy and human rights.

Nicaragua. In 1979, the Sandinista National Liberation Front overthrew the U.S.-supported military dictatorship that had ruled Nicaragua for 50 years. The United States and some Latin American countries opposed the Sandinistas because they were Marxists. The Sandinistas received aid from Cuba and sent weapons to revolutionary groups in neighboring countries. In the 1980s, the United States aided anti-Sandinista insurgents, known as the Contras. Using weapons provided by the United States, the Contras fought to overthrow the Nicaraguan government. In 1989, President George Bush and the U.S. Congress agreed to limit Contra aid to medical supplies, food, and clothing. Sandinista rule ended peacefully in 1990 with the election of Violeta Barrios de Chamorro, an opponent of the Sandinistas, as president of Nicaragua.

However, Nicaragua remained a sharply divided society. Continuing poverty and unemployment caused strikes and political kidnappings. In an attempt to strengthen the nation's fragile democracy, President Chamorro and the often hostile National Assembly agreed on constitutional changes in 1995. The changes strengthened the legislature at the expense of the presidency and barred Chamorro from running for reelection.

El Salvador. Another area of concern for the United States was El Salvador. In 1979, that tiny nation was ruled by a junta of military officers and civilians, representing the wealthy landowners and coffee plantation owners. A well-organized Communist guerrilla movement arose to challenge the government.

During a 12-year civil war that lasted through the 1980s, political assassinations and social and economic disruption brought El Salvador to the brink of ruin. The United States backed the government of El Salvador with military equipment and economic aid. The guerrilla forces received weapons and military supplies from the Soviet Union, Cuba, and the Sandinista government in Nicaragua. An estimated 70,000 people, mostly civilians, died before the war ended in a United Nations-mediated settlement.

The transition to peaceful democracy brought many new challenges. Democratic elections in 1994 produced a victory for the right wing's presidential candidate, Armando Calderón Sol. But a coalition of former leftist rebel groups became the second most powerful bloc in the national legislature.

♦ *List the major problems faced by Nicaragua and El Salvador in the 1990s.*

Panama. In 1990, U.S. forces invaded Panama in order to arrest that country's dictator, General Manuel Noriega. He had been aiding drug dealers who were moving drugs from South America to the United States. The U.S. forces helped to install a new, more democratic government in Panama. Tried in a U.S. court, Noriega was convicted of racketeering and drug trafficking.

Guatemala. Another Central American country with deep U.S. involvement is Guatemala. In the 1950s, Guatemala had an elected president. When he nationalized the property of powerful U.S. companies and bought arms from a Communist country, U.S. agencies secretly backed an invasion. The invading force quickly overthrew the government.

From 1954 to 1986, a succession of Guatemalan military officers held power, with the support of the United States. Power often changed hands in military coups. Leftists organized a guerrilla army in the mountains and hills of rural Guatemala, demanding social reforms to aid the desperately poor peasants. The army responded with brutal repression. Many rural people fled across the Mexican border and spent years in refugee camps.

Democratic government returned in 1986 under a new constitution. But the war in the countryside went on, and civilian presidents had little control over the military. In 1993, an elected president tried to suspend constitutional rights. The military forced him to step down. A weak caretaker president, Ramiro de León Carpio, took over. Peace talks with the guerrilla leaders produced preliminary agreements and, in 1995, a temporary cease-fire.

Meanwhile, U.S.-Guatemalan relations suffered a shock during 1995 with new revelations about secret deeds. A U.S.

member of Congress revealed that the Central Intelligence Agency had made payoffs to Guatemalan military officials. One of those officials was alleged to have been involved in the slayings of an American and of a guerrilla leader who was married to an American lawyer.

Cuba. Another vivid example of U.S. involvement in the affairs of a Latin American nation is provided by Cuba. During the first half of the 20th century, Americans owned many businesses in Cuba, including most of the crucial sugar industry. In 1959, a rebel army led by Fidel Castro overthrew the Cuban government. Castro took control of U.S.-owned businesses. When the United States responded by putting an embargo on trade with Cuba, Castro proclaimed himself a Marxist and sought economic help from the Soviet Union.

In 1961, the United States trained an army of anticommunist Cubans and organized an invasion aimed at overthrowing the Castro dictatorship. The Bay of Pigs invasion failed because the Cuban people did not support the American-trained force.

The next year, the United States and the Soviet Union nearly went to war over Cuba. Soviet Premier Nikita Khrushchev had placed nuclear missiles in Cuba. President John F. Kennedy demanded their removal and ordered a naval blockade of Cuba. Finally, the Soviets gave in to Kennedy's demand.

Soviet economic aid to Cuba continued until the dissolution of the Soviet Union in 1991. When aid was cut off, the Cuban economy went into a sharp decline. Cuba's problems were made worse by a drop in trade with Eastern Europe. Serious shortages of fuel developed, limiting both industrial and agricultural production.

In 1993 and 1994, President Castro and the Communist Party leadership introduced limited free market reforms modeled after those in China. People were allowed to form small private businesses, legally possess foreign currency, and establish their own agricultural cooperatives. However, the reforms caused little immediate improvement in Cuba's economy.

In August 1994, some 35,000 Cubans crowded into flimsy boats and headed for the United States. The Cuban government did nothing to stop them. After secret talks with Cuban representatives, President Bill Clinton announced in May 1995 that he was ending a 35-year-old policy of granting Cuban refugees free entry to the United States. And the United States toughened its longstanding embargo on Cuban trade in early

Boat People

1996 after two aircraft owned by U.S. citizens were downed by the Cuban air force.

With the aging Castro facing political challenges from inside and outside Cuba, the political and economic future of this Latin American nation was very much in doubt.

1. *Explain how the involvement of the United States in Central America and Cuba has changed in the post-cold war period.*
2. *Identify each of the following:*
   a. *Sandinistas*
   b. *Contras*
   c. *Manuel Noriega*
   d. *Violeta Barrios de Chamorro*
   e. *Fidel Castro*

Chapter 6 Review

A. *Write the letter of the correct response.*

1. *The country terrorized by the Shining Path guerrillas since 1980 is (a) Bolivia (b) Colombia (c) Peru.*
2. *In 1994, President Jean Bertrand Aristide was restored to power in (a) Haiti (b) Panama (c) the Dominican Republic.*

3. *The country that has been the world's largest supplier of illegal narcotics and the home of the Medellín drug cartel is* (a) *Peru* (b) *Bolivia* (c) *Colombia.*
4. *Two other countries that have also been centers of narcotics production and distribution are* (a) *Peru and Bolivia* (b) *Cuba and El Salvador* (c) *Nicaragua and Haiti.*
5. *The country that has been trying to get Latin American farmers to stop growing coca leaves is* (a) *France* (b) *the United States* (c) *Britain.*
6. *During the 1980s, Sandinistas and Contras fought for power in* (a) *Nicaragua* (b) *El Salvador* (c) *Panama.*
7. *In 1991, a 12-year civil war was ended in* (a) *Nicaragua* (b) *El Salvador* (c) *Panama.*
8. *In 1995, President Clinton changed U.S. policy that affected refugees from* (a) *Mexico* (b) *El Salvador* (c) *Cuba.*
9. *The country invaded by U.S. forces, in 1990, to arrest its dictator was* (a) *Panama* (b) *Haiti* (c) *Cuba.*
10. *In the 1990s, the termination of Soviet aid caused a decline in the economy of* (a) *Panama* (b) *Haiti* (c) *Cuba.*

B. *Write two or three sentences to further explain each of the following statements. Give specific examples from the chapter to support your information.*

1. *In the 1990s, the United States was concerned about drug trafficking in Latin America.*
2. *Terrorism has been a major problem in Latin America.*
3. *In both Brazil and Guatemala, the military has played a significant role in politics.*

C. *Examine the maps of Latin America in Chapter 6 and indicate which of the following statements are* true *and which are* false.

1. *Caracas, Bogota, and Lima are South American capitals.*
2. *Bolivia is a landlocked nation.*
3. *Cuba and Haiti share the same island.*
4. *San José is the capital of Mexico.*
5. *Nicaragua borders Costa Rica and Honduras.*

D. *Select two Latin American leaders. Describe their problems and policies.*

Unit I Review

A. *Examine the maps and the list of events below. For each description, write the letter of the region in which the event occurred.*

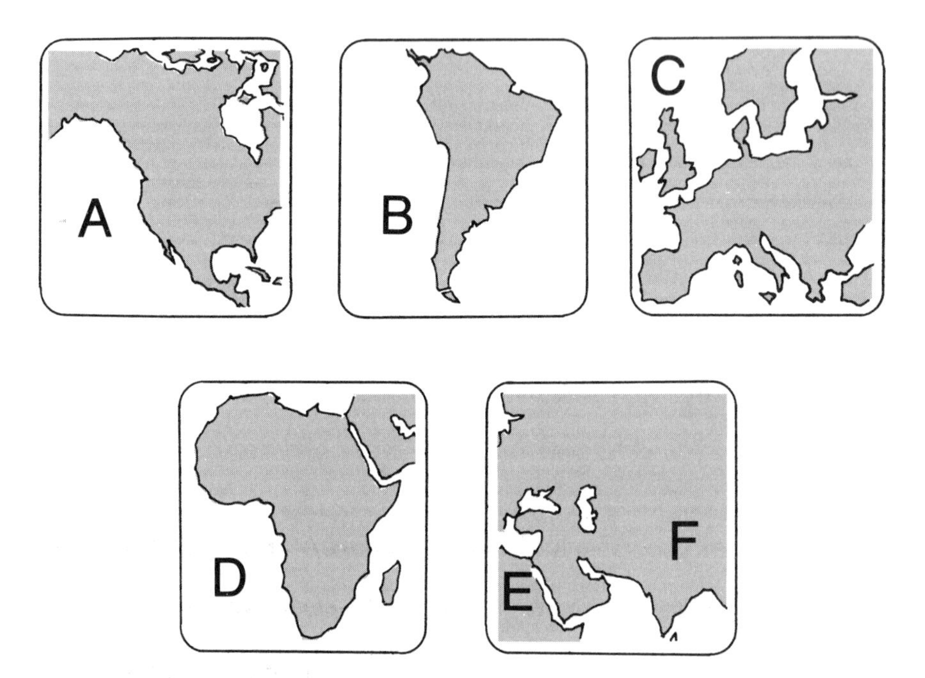

1. *Following the abandonment of communism by its satellite nations, the Soviet Union collapsed. These events ended the cold war.*
2. *Islamic fundamentalism threatened the stability of governments in this oil-rich region.*
3. *A major breakthrough was made in ending white minority rule and terrorism. However, tribal and clan rivalries, combined with drought and famine, brought misery to thousands in this region.*
4. *While Japan led the region in economic development and China pursued increased private enterprise, India struggled with religious rivalries and Cambodia held elections to determine its political future.*
5. *The United States attempted to end its trade war with Japan, while bringing food to starving Somalis and seeking ways to end the bloodshed in Bosnia-Herzegovina.*
6. *Increased democracy under civilian governments was pursued in a region in which military leaders have traditionally played a strong role in political affairs.*

B. *Use information from Unit I to complete the chart below.*

National Leader	*Nation*	*Major Problem*
Boris Yeltsin		
Nelson Mandela		
Jerry Rawlings		
Hosni Mubarak		
Shimon Peres		
Saddam Hussein		
Deng Xiaopeng		
Ryutaro Hashimoto		
Kim Jong Il		
Alberto Fujimori		
René Préval		

C. *Use information from Unit I to explain the significance of each of the following newspaper headlines.*

BERLIN SUSPECTS NEO-NAZI ARSON AS FIVE TURKS DIE

FIGHTING IN SUDAN HALTS FOOD RELIEF

PLO CRACKS DOWN ON HAMAS TERRORISTS IN GAZA

HOPE AND VIOLENCE BOTH PROMINENT AS CAMBODIA STARTS SIX DAYS OF VOTING

ARISTIDE IN TRIUMPHAL RETURN; URGES RECONCILIATION, NOT VENGEANCE

D. *Review Chapter 2, "The Rise of the New Europe," beginning on page 14. Then select TWO of the statements below. For each, write a paragraph to explain why you agree or disagree with it.*

1. *The Russians were better off economically under communism than they have been under the free market system of the post-cold war period.*
2. *Under communism, consumer goods were available to Russians in greater quantity.*
3. *While the movement toward a free market economy has given some Russians the opportunity to earn more, inflation*

has placed consumer goods beyond the reach of many Russians.

4. *The movement toward a free market economy in Russia has stimulated the production of food and other consumer goods. However, consumer purchasing power has not kept pace with production.*
5. *Under communism, most Russians had a higher income.*

UNIT II

THE SEARCH FOR INTERNATIONAL SECURITY

Among the global struggles of the late 20th century have been attempts (1) to reduce the threat of atomic disaster by seeking to limit the number of nations possessing nuclear weapons; (2) to prevent human rights abuses by governments, and to bring perpetrators of this type of criminal action to justice; and (3) to curb international terrorism.

In the 1990s, world leaders and a variety of organizations have labored to attain these objectives. Their fulfillment would strengthen international security, and permit nations and their citizens to pursue political, economic, and social goals without fear of repressive governments, brutal terrorists, or destructive leaders armed with nuclear weapons.

Chapter 7

Nuclear Proliferation

The nuclear age began in August 1945, when the United States ended World War II by dropping atomic bombs on the Japanese cities of Hiroshima and Nagasaki. Horrified by the enormous death and destruction in these cities, the Japanese government surrendered. Since 1945, the United States has sought to limit the spread of nuclear weapons.

Cold War Strategies

Missiles. Strategic nuclear weapons deliver warheads to their targets in a variety of ways. Intercontinental ballistic missiles (ICBM's) carry a warhead into space and release it on a trajectory toward its target. Submarine-launched ballistic missiles (SLBM's) work in the same way, but are fired from submarines. Bombers transport a warhead to its target by air. Cruise missiles also travel to their targets by air, flying a preprogrammed route close to the ground. Atomic explosives have also been adapted to other weapons systems, including artillery shells, land mines, short-range missiles, and depth charges.

Throughout the late 1940s and the 1950s, the United States had overwhelming nuclear superiority. By 1960, however, the Soviet Union had built a nuclear stockpile large enough to ensure that any attack upon it would be met with full retaliation. By the late 1960s, the Soviet nuclear arsenal was roughly equal to that of the United States. Out of this balance of power arose the belief in *mutual assured destruction* (MAD). Its proponents reasoned that neither the U.S. nor the U.S.S.R. would resort to the use of nuclear weapons if each had the ability to destroy the other. Nuclear weapons, therefore, were developed and maintained to enable each nation to deter an attack by the other. MAD provided both the United States and the Soviet Union an incentive to maintain the nuclear balance. It was recognized that the development of an imbalance would jeopardize international security.

This interdependence led the United States and the Soviet Union to seek ways to assure stability. From 1963 until the Soviet Union collapsed in 1991, they negotiated arms control agreements to maintain a balance of nuclear weapons and to curb weapons systems that might upset the balance of power. Limitations on antiballistic missile systems, for example, were established in 1972 and 1974.

- *Explain how a "nuclear interdependence" developed between the United States and the Soviet Union.*

Nuclear Arms Control. Beyond treaty arrangements, a strong international opposition to the use of nuclear weapons developed. A nuclear freeze movement arose in the United States. Local and national campaigns against nuclear weapons research, production, and testing reached a peak between 1982 and 1984. Eighty-one percent of U.S. citizens polled in April 1982 voted in favor of a freeze. The movement in the United States reached out to peace movements in Western Europe, Eastern Europe, and the Soviet Union. But it declined after the 1984 reelection of President Ronald Reagan.

Nuclear weapons have not been used in warfare since 1945. The Soviet Union did not use them in Afghanistan. The United States did not use them in Vietnam or Iraq. However, the possibility that nations with nuclear arsenals would use them against nations lacking such weapons caused general concern.

In 1957, the *International Atomic Energy Agency* (IAEA) was founded. It is an independent United Nations agency whose 122 member countries work to encourage peaceful uses of atomic energy. The agency attempts to discourage the building of nuclear weapons and to prevent the conversion of nuclear plants from civilian to military use.

The *Nuclear Nonproliferation Treaty* (NNT) of 1968 is an agreement among more than 175 nations to halt the proliferation (spread) of nuclear weapons to other countries and to support an international authority for the development of peaceful nuclear technologies. The signers of the treaty pledged to allow inspections of their nuclear facilities. Those inspections are conducted by the IAEA.

In addition, the *London Suppliers Agreement* of 1976 is designed to prevent the export of any nuclear materials or technology with military potential to nations that do not possess nuclear weapons. Also, EURATOM, the Western European nuclear authority, has an independent legal responsibility for insuring that nuclear material in its nonweapons state is not diverted to nuclear weapons or nuclear explosives. The EURATOM Commission can directly penalize any person or organization that violates its rules and bring an offending nation before the European Court of Justice. Despite these agreements and safeguards, nuclear proliferation has not been stopped.

1. *What are the goals of the International Atomic Energy Agency?*
2. *Define nuclear proliferation.*
3. *List the measures taken to prevent nuclear proliferation.*

The Spread of Nuclear Arsenals

Following the dissolution of the Soviet Union and the end of the cold war, the nations that admitted possessing nuclear weapons were the United States, Russia, China, France, and Britain. Parts of the Soviet nuclear stockpile remained in Ukraine and in Kazakhstan.

Several other nations are also believed to have nuclear arms. India exploded a "peaceful nuclear device" in 1974. It may have a small nuclear arsenal for possible use against Pakistan, with which India has frequently quarreled. Pakistan has pursued the development of its own nuclear weapons. Israel reportedly has built several hundred nuclear weapons for use as a last resort against its Arab enemies. South Africa's white-minority government built atomic weapons in the 1980s. However, it gave them up voluntarily while negotiating an end to apartheid in 1991. Libya, North Korea, Iraq, Iran, and Argentina are among other nations believed to have started programs to develop nuclear weapons.

- *List the nations with known or suspected nuclear arsenals in the 1990s.*

Cause for Worry

Iraq: Foiled by U.N. Inspectors

On a television screen at a United Nations office in Baghdad, a flickering image showed a room in a factory somewhere in Iraq. The screen was part of a highly complicated system by which U.N. observers monitored Iraq in the period following the Persian Gulf War of 1991. The U.N. wanted to make sure Iraq was destroying all vestiges of its programs to build nuclear, biological, and chemical weapons, as Security Council resolutions required it to do.

Iraq's case was unusual. A U.N.-sponsored military force had defeated Iraq in war. The Iraqi government could hardly say no when the Security Council sent in a group of observers called the United Nations Special Commission. The commission was created with the sole purpose of checking up on Iraq. As a result, the world now knows more about Iraq's former nuclear efforts than it does about the efforts of any other potential nuclear weapons holder.

The U.N. commission made a number of startling discoveries. For example, at the industrial center of Zaafarania, Iraq was preparing to use advanced computer-controlled machinery to build nuclear weapons. The precision equipment at Zaafarania was manufactured by a British firm with offices in London and Ohio. The firm had provided military technology to Iraq. Sophisticated machinery made by German companies was also found in Zaafarania.

The Zaafarania incident points up how hard it is to prevent nuclear proliferation. Iraq is a signer of the Nuclear Nonproliferation Treaty. So are Britain, the United States, and Germany. Nevertheless, Iraq seemed to have no qualms about starting a nuclear weapons program, and little trouble buying the highly specialized equipment it needed. Iraqi officials later stated that Iraq was within four months of producing its first atomic bomb when the U.S.-led coalition began the Persian Gulf War in January 1991.

Inspectors of the International Atomic Energy Agency were supposed to have been making regular inspections to spot any suspicious nuclear activities in Iraq. Why didn't the IAEA know what Iraq was doing? Opponents of nuclear proliferation question the agency's ability to stop a determined country from building weapons in violation of the treaty. Defenders of the IAEA argue that proliferation can only be stopped if the industrialized nations take stronger steps to prevent exports of bomb-making materials and technology.

Supplying the Parts

In fact, the IAEA has a limited role. Its task is to inspect nuclear facilities that a host country declares it has, and to make a careful accounting of nuclear materials. The agency also has the authority to inspect undeclared facilities. Before the 1991 war, neither the atomic energy agency nor any government had information about the Iraqi attempt at nuclear weapons development.

After the war, U.N. and IAEA inspectors found and destroyed Iraq's nuclear weapons production facilities. But how could they be certain they had done a thorough job? And what was to keep Iraqi technicians who had developed the program from starting over?

♦ *Complete the following sentences:*

1. *The United Nations Special Commission tried to make sure Iraq could no longer build ____.*
2. *At Zaafarania, U.N. inspectors found ____.*
3. *A weakness in the regulation of nuclear proliferation, revealed by the disarming of Iraq, was ____.*

Ukraine: No More Missiles

When the Soviet Union broke apart at the end of 1991, 1,800 of the country's nuclear warheads were in Ukraine. Newly independent Ukraine had suddenly turned into the world's third-ranking nuclear power, after Russia and the United States. Russian and U.S. leaders quickly set to work to persuade the Ukrainians to give up the nuclear weapons.

But many Ukrainians had different ideas. For one thing, they were deeply suspicious of Russia. How could Ukraine protect itself if Russia tried to build up a new Russian empire? Moreover, Ukrainian nationalists wanted Ukraine to be a powerful state in its own right. What better way than to keep the weapons the country had inherited from the Soviet Union?

The start of the post-Soviet era was a time of political and economic turmoil in Ukraine. Russia sharply increased the prices of its gas and oil exports, which Ukraine desperately needed. Coal miners went on strike in a region critical to the

Ukrainian economy. Prices soared out of sight, rising three times as fast as in Russia. Many Ukrainians blamed Russia, their main energy supplier, for both the strikes and the inflation. Adding further strain was a dispute between Ukraine and Russia over who now owned the Black Sea fleet of the former Soviet navy.

The issue of Ukraine-based nuclear weapons, therefore, was linked to worries about Ukrainian security and to Ukraine's political and economic future. The United States and other Western powers assured Ukrainian leaders of their support for Ukrainian independence. They sweetened the pot with economic aid. Then, the United States, Russia, and Britain jointly promised that they would respect Ukraine's borders. They also pledged that they would not twist Ukraine's arm through economic means. In exchange, they asked Ukraine to give up its nuclear weapons and sign two major disarmament treaties—the START I arms-reduction treaty and the Nuclear Nonproliferation Treaty.

Ukrainian President Leonid Kuchma—a former rocket engineer—accepted the bargain. In November 1994, Kuchma went before his nation's parliament and urged it to ratify the NNT. He suggested that by signing the treaty, Ukraine could win increased respect from the rest of the world. "The process of

Peace Work

world disarmament depends on our decision today," Kuchma said. The treaty passed by a vote of 301 to 8.

Before the end of 1994, Ukraine had started dismantling its nuclear missiles. The warheads went to Russia to be destroyed. The missiles stayed in Ukraine to be cut apart. Later, the resulting cylinders would be used as farm silos or fuel tanks. In Ukraine, at least, the turning of "swords" into "plowshares" had begun.

1. *Explain how relations between Russia and Ukraine affected the efforts of the United States to reduce the nuclear arsenal of the former Soviet Union.*
2. *Which of the following statements are true and which are false?*
   a. *Ukrainians fear possible aggression by Russia.*
   b. *Russia supplies most of the oil and gas needed by Ukraine.*
   c. *The United States gave economic aid to Ukraine to try to persuade it to give up nuclear weapons.*
   d. *Ukraine's President Kuchma insisted that his country remain a nuclear power.*
   e. *Today, Ukraine has the world's third largest stockpile of nuclear weapons.*

Crisis in Korea

In March 1993, North Korea touched off an international crisis by announcing its intention to withdraw from the Nuclear Nonproliferation Treaty. Never in the 23 years the treaty had been in effect had a nation backed out. Would North Korea become the first to do so?

North Korea had signed the treaty in 1985 and had begun allowing IAEA inspectors to check on its civilian nuclear power program. That worked fine for a while. But then the IAEA proposed a special inspection of two sites where it expected to find spent, or used, nuclear fuel. An inspection might determine whether North Korea had diverted any nuclear materials to military use. North Korea refused. When the IAEA insisted, North Korea said it would withdraw from the pact.

That set alarm bells ringing in Washington and other world capitals. American intelligence specialists worried in particular about a North Korean plant designed to reprocess spent nuclear fuel so it could be used again. Normally, such a plant would turn out fuel for civilian nuclear power plants. However, it might also turn the spent fuel into weapons-grade plutonium. The specialists warned that North Korea might have produced enough plutonium to make one or two nuclear weapons. Such a possibility was regarded as a serious threat to stability in Asia and the world. The potential threat was highlighted two months later when North Korea tested its first medium-range missile. Specialists said the missile was capable of carrying a small nuclear device. Japanese officials expressed fears that such a missile might reach some of their most heavily populated cities.

The Korean crisis raised questions about the nonproliferation system itself. The treaty acknowledges the right of every nation to use nuclear materials for peaceful purposes. Inspections are supposed to ensure that materials intended for civilian development are not misused. Japan, like other nations, has strongly supported the inspection system. Like the North Koreans, the Japanese have extracted plutonium from nuclear waste as part of a civilian nuclear power program. Unlike the North Koreans, however, the Japanese have not tried to block IAEA inspectors from doing their jobs.

The North Koreans claimed that their nuclear weapons program was solely for defense and that Japan and South Korea had been secretly arming themselves with nuclear weapons with the approval of the IAEA. Japanese and South Korean officials denied this. In fact, Japan has always rejected nuclear weapons. An attempt by South Korea to develop them was stopped by the United States in the late 1970s. Both nations have indicated a willingness to do without nuclear weapons as long as they have the military support of the United States and its "nuclear umbrella."

Legally, North Korea had a right to withdraw from the nonproliferation treaty after a three-month waiting period. But world reaction was so strong that North Korean leader Kim Il Sung had second thoughts. The crisis dragged on for a year and a half, with the United States threatening economic sanctions unless North Korea allowed the inspections. North Korea warned that it would view sanctions as an act of war. A military confrontation seemed possible, although U.S. and North Korean diplomats held round after round of meetings to work something out.

In October 1994, shortly after Kim Il Sung's death, the two sides arrived at a resolution. It was a plan of extreme complexity that would take ten years to complete. The bottom line was that North Korea would agree not to pursue a nuclear weapons program. It would also shut down its existing nuclear power stations and close its reprocessing plant. In return, the Western nations would provide North Korea with two new nuclear power reactors and other economic aid. South Korea and Japan would pay for most of the aid. The new reactors—for producing electric power—would be of a type that produced much less plutonium than the older type.

In the following months, U.S. and North Korean negotiators fleshed out the details of the agreement. The United States insisted that the new power plants be built in South Korea, since the South Koreans were bearing most of the cost. Reluctantly, the North Koreans agreed.

While U.S. officials hailed the agreement as a significant step toward preventing North Korea from acquiring nuclear arms, the agreement drew criticism in Congress. The Republican majority raised such points as these: (1) North Korea was being rewarded for raising a nuclear threat. (2) Several years would pass before North Korea had to allow full inspections of its nuclear waste sites. (3) The North Koreans could not be trusted. Defense Secretary William J. Perry replied: "This agreement is not based on trust." Instead, he said, North Korea would have to take step-by-step measures before receiving anything at all. President Clinton too defended the agreement. He said: "It's a crucial step toward drawing North Korea into the global community."

1. *Explain why the North Korean nuclear crisis of 1993–94 alarmed the United States and some of its Asian allies.*
2. *Match the item in Column A with an appropriate phrase from Column B.*

Column A	Column B
1. *Kim Il Sung*	a. *U.S. Secretary of Defense*
2. *plutonium*	b. *former President of North Korea*
3. *nuclear umbrella*	c. *nuclear material*
4. *William J. Perry*	d. *protection given by the U.S. to non-nuclear allies*

An End to Nuclear Testing?

When the Nuclear Nonproliferation Treaty came up for renewal in 1995, the nations that had signed the treaty met to discuss what to do. Should they extend the treaty indefinitely? That was what the United States and other nuclear powers wanted. Or should they limit the extension to 25 years? That was what many nonaligned nations proposed. The smaller nations did not want an indefinite extension until they felt confident that the nuclear nations would someday keep their promise to give up their own nuclear arms. That vague promise was part of the original treaty. After a four-week conference in New York, the signatory nations accepted the U.S. position and extended the treaty indefinitely. In order to win the extension, the nuclear powers had to repeat their old promise. They also made new promises—including a pledge to conclude a comprehensive ban on nuclear testing by the end of 1996.

Efforts to halt nuclear testing have been under way since the 1950s. At the time, a major concern was the health threat posed by radiation that was released into the atmosphere by aboveground nuclear tests. In 1963, the United States, Britain, and the Soviet Union signed the Limited Nuclear Test-Ban Treaty. The treaty pledged those nations not to test nuclear weapons in the atmosphere, underwater, or in space. It allowed underground tests to continue. In recent years, the other two declared nuclear powers, China and France, have observed the same restrictions.

In October 1992, a *moratorium*, or temporary halt, in nuclear weapons testing went into effect. It was the result of an agreement among the United States, Russia, France, and Britain. Meanwhile, representatives of 38 nations began meetings in Geneva, Switzerland, to hammer out an agreement on a comprehensive test-ban treaty. A comprehensive treaty would be one that banned all types of tests, including those underground.

A key issue at the Geneva talks was whether or not to continue to allow very small underground nuclear tests. The United States and Russia said they needed such tests in order to be sure of the safety and reliability of their weapons. Nonnuclear states strongly opposed any such loopholes. In August 1995, President Clinton dropped the U.S. request for small tests and said a new test ban should be both comprehensive and complete. That put pressure on Russia to go along.

Support for a comprehensive test-ban treaty seemed to be strong. Many nations strongly condemned China and France for staging new underground tests while discussions over the test-ban treaty were under way. China began new tests in 1993, France in 1995. Both nations said they intended to conduct a limited number of tests that would be finished before the end of 1996. Both said they would sign a comprehensive test-ban treaty.

1. *Explain how the Geneva talks on a comprehensive test-ban treaty were related to the extension of the Nuclear Nonproliferation Treaty.*
2. *How did President Clinton's 1995 decision on small underground tests affect the prospects for a comprehensive test-ban treaty?*

Chapter 7 Review

A. *On your answer sheet, write the letter of the correct response.*

1. *The nuclear age began in 1945, when (a) the United States used atomic bombs to end World War II (b) the Soviet Union used nuclear weapons on Japan (c) the United States and the Soviet Union fought a nuclear war.*
2. *During the cold war, the role assigned to nuclear weapons by the superpowers was that of (a) a means of dominating non-nuclear nations (b) a deterrent to nuclear war (c) a stimulus to economic and scientific progress.*
3. *During the 1980s, the effort to stop the development and testing of nuclear weapons was called (a) the nuclear-freeze movement (b) the nine-test program (c) the no-first-test alternative.*
4. *The purpose of the Nuclear Nonproliferation Treaty is (a) to ensure the destruction of all nuclear weapons (b) to prevent nuclear weapons testing (c) to prevent the development of nuclear weapons by nations that do not possess them.*
5. *The purpose of the International Atomic Energy Agency is (a) to see that nations with nuclear technology use it for civilian, rather than military, purposes (b) to prevent accidents in nuclear power plants (c) to fund the research and development of nuclear weapons.*

6. *After the Persian Gulf War, a problem was revealed by the effort to halt the Iraqi nuclear weapons program.* (a) *Other Middle Eastern nations supported the development of nuclear weapons by Iraq.* (b) *The export of nuclear weapons technology to Iraq by Western business firms had not been controlled.* (c) *Iraq was under the protection of Western nations.*

7. *In 1994, Ukraine agreed* (a) *to destroy its nuclear arsenal* (b) *to surrender all of its nuclear weapons to Russia* (c) *to join Russia in a combined nuclear weapons development program.*

8. *North Korea caused a crisis, in 1993, when it* (a) *threatened to invade South Korea and Japan* (b) *offered to share its nuclear technology with China* (c) *refused to allow further inspections of its nuclear facilities and announced its intention to withdraw from the Nuclear Nonproliferation Treaty.*

9. *Republican members of the U.S. Congress responded to the U.S.-North Korean agreement of 1994 by* (a) *praising it* (b) *raising questions about its wisdom* (c) *impeaching the officials who negotiated it.*

10. *The global effort to prevent nuclear proliferation is made difficult by many problems, including* (a) *the ease with which plutonium can be diverted from civilian to military use* (b) *a lack of interest by the United Nations* (c) *U.S. support of the nuclear weapons programs of its Asian allies.*

B. *Use the information found in the chapter to explain each of the following newspaper headlines.*

YELTSIN, CLINTON OFFER
SECURITY GUARANTEES TO UKRAINE

U.S. AND NORTH KOREA DISCUSS NUCLEAR DISPUTE

CHINESE, FRENCH N-TESTS MAY BE THE LAST

C. *Which statements are supported by the information in the graph on page 158 (Figure 7.1) and in the chapter?*

1. *The decision by Ukraine to give up nuclear weapons will result in the rapid elimination of Russia's nuclear arsenal as well.*

2. *At the beginning of the 21st century, the United States and Russia will still possess thousands of nuclear warheads.*

	U.S.	C.I.S
Warhead Totals in 1993	10,563	10,301
Warhead Totals by 2000 under S.T.A.R.T.	6000	6000
Warhead Totals by 2000 under S.T.A.R.T. II	3000-3500	3000-3500

Figure 7.1 Strategic Weapons Reduction

3. *Under START II, the United States and Russia will be entitled to equal numbers of nuclear warheads.*
4. *Tension between Ukraine and Russia will prevent ratification of the START treaties.*
5. *The United States had little direct role in the negotiations to persuade Ukraine to give up its nuclear weapons.*

Chapter 8

The Struggle to Keep the Peace

At the end of World War II, the United Nations was the hope of the world for global peace. That hope was frustrated during the long decades of the cold war.

During that era, the U.N. was not able to prevent destructive wars between Communists and anticommunists in Korea, Vietnam, and Afghanistan. Nor was it able to prevent violent struggles between Communists and anticommunists in Cuba, El Salvador, Nicaragua, and elsewhere in the developing nations—the so-called Third World. When the cold war ended in the 1990s, the big powers turned from confrontation to cooperation. New peacekeeping efforts in Latin America, Asia, Africa, and Europe expanded the role and responsibilities of the U.N. However, the continuing crises in Bosnia, Somalia, Rwanda, and elsewhere have given rise to doubts about the ability of the U.N. to achieve international peace and security.

Regional organizations have also worked for peace in the 1990s. Following the collapse of communism in Europe, the *North Atlantic Treaty Organization* (NATO) developed a new mission. In Latin America, the *Organization of American States* (OAS) cooperated with the U.N. in dealing with crises in Haiti and Peru. The *Organization of African Unity* (OAU) encouraged the independence of Namibia and the building of a multiracial society in South Africa. The *Arab League* mediated disputes among member nations in the Middle East and North Africa.

In addition to the upheavals caused by nationalistic, religious, and other competing groups, peacekeeping efforts were made more difficult by the growing international trade in weapons and military equipment.

The United Nations After the Cold War

In the 1990s, the United Nations sent tens of thousands of soldiers on peacekeeping missions to all parts of the world. In Africa, they helped to smooth Namibia's transition to independence after a long struggle against South Africa's colonial rule. In Mozambique (Africa), El Salvador (Central America), and Cambodia (Southeast Asia), U.N. peacekeepers helped put an end to devastating civil wars. In Haiti (Caribbean), they helped maintain peace after President Jean-Bertrand Aristide regained power from a military government. Those were the successes. In other cases, however, the U.N.'s peacekeeping forces stumbled. They looked on helplessly in Rwanda (Africa) as Rwandans slaughtered one another in 1994. They withdrew from Somalia (Africa) in 1995 while that country's civil war still raged. They struggled for years to bring order to Bosnia in the Balkans (Europe), after the former Yugoslavia dissolved into chaos. As one U.N. officer in Bosnia observed, "It's much easier to come in and keep peace when there's some peace around."

Indeed, one of the problems of peacekeeping forces is that people expect them to be more than peacekeepers. Ideally, the peacekeepers move in only after warring factions have settled their differences. Then their job is straightforward. They make sure all sides in a dispute observe peace settlements or truces. They run free elections and bring relief supplies to civilian populations. But in Rwanda, Somalia, and in Bosnia—and in other places as well—the peacekeepers found themselves in the midst of ongoing wars. At times, they themselves took part in the fighting.

Somalia. Somalia's civil war was one example. U.N. peacekeepers became embroiled in a quarrel with General Muhammad Farah Aydid, one of Somalia's many warlords. In June 1993, Aydid's forces ambushed and killed 24 Pakistani soldiers of the U.N. force. U.N. and allied American forces responded by launching a manhunt for Aydid. They shelled the clan leader's weapons depots and raided Aydid's headquarters. U.N. officials even offered a reward for Aydid's arrest. But they never captured him.

Casualties among the U.N. and American forces rose as they took an increasing part in the war. In October 1993, 18 U.S. Rangers died in a battle against Aydid's forces. Four days later, President Clinton announced he was withdrawing U.S. troops. Finally, in March 1995, the U.N. too gave up and withdrew its peacekeeping units. The Somali warlords kept on fighting.

The U.N. intervention in Somalia was not a total fiasco. One of the main goals at the beginning was to protect food deliveries to starving civilians. In the early 1990s, famine had taken the lives of at least 300,000 Somalis. The arrival of U.N. and U.S. troops in 1992 allowed much greater amounts of food to be distributed. The intervention also allowed Somali farmers to boost their output, and may have saved 100,000 lives. However, the U.N. made little headway in getting the warlords to negotiate a peace settlement. And the U.N. force's clashes with Aydid turned U.N. soldiers from neutral peacekeepers into partisan warriors.

1. *Identify Muhammad Farah Aydid.*
2. *State the two major U.N. goals in Somalia.*

The U.N.'s peacekeeping role expanded greatly in the early 1990s. In 1988, the U.N. had only five active peacekeeping operations. By 1993 it had 28. By the mid-1990s, however, the number had dropped into the mid-teens.

In earlier years, most U.N. peacekeeping forces were positioned between the armies of rival nations—for example, Israel and its Arab neighbors. More recently, the U.N. has also sent peacekeepers into domestic conflicts. Of a string of nine recent peacekeeping operations authorized by the Security Council, seven involved internal wars.

The U.N.'s peacekeeping soldiers are loaned to the world body by individual nations. They come from dozens of countries—from Venezuela and Canada, from Ukraine and Bangladesh, from Egypt and Nepal. The soldiers are usually lightly armed and are instructed to return fire only if attacked. However, the soldiers do not always heed their instructions. Military experts see a need for more professionalism and discipline.

As a result of the U.N.'s expanding role, the troops under U.N. command increased from 9,500 in 1988 to 70,000 in the mid-1990s. With an eye to future needs, U.N. Secretary-General

Boutros Boutros-Ghali requested standby arrangements under which member nations would provide specially trained units for peacekeeping service. However, the U.S. government was wary of giving the U.N. the role of "international police officer." The United States gave little support to Boutros-Ghali's proposal, and it was not implemented.

Bosnia. One of the greatest tests of the United Nations peacekeeping role came in the former Yugoslavia, and especially in Bosnia. Initially, U.N. troops there concentrated on protecting deliveries of food aid. However, their mandate quickly expanded. Soon it included protecting "safe havens" (areas that were supposed to be immune to attack). The U.N. also monitored a "no-fly zone" (where the Security Council barred all military flights other than those permitted by the United Nations). U.N. forces in Bosnia were at various times shot at, shelled, arrested, and held hostage. More than 120 died in the first four years of the operation.

In Bosnia, as in Somalia, U.N. peacekeepers risked taking sides. Hostility developed between U.N. forces and the Bosnian Serbs, who defied many of the Security Council's orders. Aiding the U.N. in its confrontation with the Bosnian Serbs was NATO, the Western military alliance. NATO airplanes and missiles attacked Bosnian Serb military targets on numerous occasions. At the end of 1995, 60,000 NATO troops (including 20,000 Americans) replaced the U.N. peacekeepers in Bosnia. Their job was to enforce a peace treaty signed by the leaders of Bosnia, Serbia, and Croatia after lengthy negotiations at a U.S. military base in Dayton, Ohio.

Rwanda. In Rwanda, the U.N. started by sending military observers to patrol the nation's borders in 1993. When a cease-fire went into effect later that year between rebels and the Rwandan government, the U.N. sent peacekeepers to monitor compliance. The 2,200 troops could do nothing to stop the genocidal slaughter that erupted in Rwanda in 1994. Indeed, those murdered included ten U.N. peacekeeping soldiers from Belgium, Rwanda's former colonial ruler.

1. *List three nations in which U.N. forces were involved in peacekeeping in the 1990s.*

2. *Explain the military problems connected with peacekeeping.*

Peacekeeping operations do not come cheap. In 1994 alone, the U.N. committed some $3.6 billion for peacekeeping (far more than its general budget of $1 billion). Like the expenses of the general budget, peacekeeping expenses are paid from assessments on U.N. member nations. However, the United States is among many nations that have balked at paying. Congress wants to cut the U.S. share from 33 percent to 25 percent of the total. The U.S. has become the U.N.'s biggest debtor, owing more than $1 billion. Stabilizing the U.N.'s financial situation has been a key issue facing its members in recent years.

Debate has also focused on the way the United Nations makes its decisions. Although the U.N.'s membership grew from 53 countries in 1945 to 185 in the 1990s, most peacekeeping decisions are made by the 15-member Security Council. Each of the council's five permanent members—the United States, Russia (which inherited the seat of the Soviet Union), Britain, France, and China—has veto power. They are the nations that won World War II and established the world order of the cold war period. In the post-cold war era, Japan and Germany pressed their case for admission to the Security Council. India, Egypt, Brazil, and other large developing nations also sought seats. Such nations wanted a voice in the

Members Only

decision-making process long dominated by the traditional big powers.

In 1992, Secretary-General Boutros-Ghali issued an Agenda for Peace. It was an expression of belief that the major powers, in the post-cold war era, were more eager than ever before to use the United Nations to achieve international security. However, the wide range of new problems faced by U.N. peacekeepers poses a challenge that will require greater military and financial support from member nations if the goal of world peace is to be achieved.

1. *Explain how the role of the United Nations changed following the end of the cold war.*
2. *List three reasons why critics of the U.N. doubt its ability to achieve international security or world peace.*
3. *Determine the error in each of the following sentences and, on your answer sheet, rewrite each as a correct sentence.*
    a. *From 1945 to 1990, the U.N. prevented cold war military conflicts.*
    b. *U.N. military forces accomplished their missions in the early 1990s.*
    c. *Financial support has not been a problem for U.N. peacekeepers in the 1990s.*
    d. *The present method of representation on the Security Council is satisfactory to all U.N. members.*

NATO: The Search for a New Mission

In November 1991, U.S. President George Bush met in Rome with the leaders of other member nations of the North Atlantic Treaty Organization (NATO) to set the alliance's future course. Their goal was to reorganize NATO's military forces and give the alliance a new purpose in Europe and elsewhere. The purpose for which NATO had been created in 1949—to defend Western Europe and North America from attack by the Soviet Union—had disappeared with the end of the cold war. The Soviet Union and the Warsaw Pact had been disbanded. Therefore, NATO needed a new mission.

The alliance's 16 member nations focused on three problem areas—Eastern Europe, the Balkans, and the Middle East. In Eastern Europe, the former satellite nations were eager to join

NATO in order to gain protection against any future threat from Russia. NATO promised to help defend those former "enemies." NATO also recognized that future threats to peace might come from the Balkans, where national and ethnic rivalries were simmering in the former Yugoslavia. The Middle East represented yet another potential threat. The danger there took the form of increased terrorism and disruption of Europe's oil supplies.

New Strategies and Organization. To deal with those issues, NATO leaders took a number of steps. They developed a new "southern strategy." They abandoned the alliance's forward-defense strategy of massing forces in Germany to meet a threat from the east. In its place, they adopted a more flexible military strategy, based on smaller but more modern forces backed by highly mobile reserves. As part of this streamlining, NATO reorganized the forces in its central region into three main groups:

- A Rapid-Reaction Corps of up to 70,000 soldiers capable of responding quickly anywhere within NATO's borders. The corps is commanded by a British general and has its headquarters in the United Kingdom.
- A Main Defense Force of seven heavily armored corps totaling 400,000 to 500,000 troops. Six of the units are multinational and are based in Western and Central Europe. The seventh is stationed in what used to be eastern Germany and is composed exclusively of German soldiers.
- An auxiliary force of unspecified size that could reinforce the main force during a prolonged crisis.

An American general continued to be NATO's supreme commander. However, the overall effect of the new design was to diminish U.S. domination of the alliance. Europeans now make up a larger proportion of the force than in the past.

Indeed, a key question of the post-cold war planning was how best to keep American troops committed to Europe's defense. Both the U.S. government and the NATO allies agreed on the continuing importance of an American military presence. U.S. leaders noted that bases in Germany are closer to potential troublespots in the Middle East and elsewhere than are military centers in the United States. In 1994, President Clinton said he would keep 100,000 U.S. troops in Europe.

Waiting for Admission

While the East European nations were eager to join NATO, NATO members were not quite ready to let them in. For one thing, the newly democratic countries of Eastern Europe had untested political systems, transitional economies, and weak armies. If they joined NATO, all NATO members would be obligated to go to their defense in case they came under attack. Were Americans ready to "die for Bratislava" (the capital of the new Slovak Republic)? NATO leaders were not sure. Moreover, Russia adamantly opposed any extension of NATO into Eastern Europe. It saw such an extension as a potential threat to its own security.

On the other hand, NATO leaders believed that some sort of link to NATO was necessary to promote stability in Eastern Europe. In 1994, they came up with a sort of "junior membership," inviting interested countries to cooperate with NATO in what was called a Partnership for Peace. The idea was to promote increased political and military cooperation (joint exercises, for example) without the burdens or opportunities of full membership. After first rejecting the idea, Russia signed on in 1995. It was one of 26 NATO "partners," stretching from Poland to Kazakhstan. NATO leaders allowed the main East

European nations to hope that they could eventually become full NATO members.

♦ *How does NATO's post-cold war strategy differ from its former forward-defense strategy?*

Another concern was NATO's nuclear strategy. The alliance decided at the 1991 Rome conference to continue the policy of threatening potential enemies with the first use of nuclear weapons in the event of a conventional war. However, NATO leaders also agreed to a 90 percent reduction in nuclear weapons based in Europe.

Strong supporters of NATO, especially in the United States and Britain, were disturbed by French and German proposals to form a joint army unit of 50,000 troops as the nucleus of an independent European defense force. The "Euro Army" concept reflected the long-standing desire of France to play a leading role in European defense without placing its forces under NATO command. The German government has also wanted to assume a greater leadership role in military affairs.

Because of Germany's Nazi past, many people, in Germany and elsewhere, fear any military role for Germany outside its own borders. West Germany's 1949 constitution, adopted while the country was under Allied occupation, limited the scope of the nation's military operations. Later amendments restricted the German military to a single goal: protecting German territory. Thus, during the Persian Gulf War, Germany took no direct part in the invasion of Iraq.

During and after the Gulf War, Germans debated whether it would be necessary to change the constitution before German forces could take part in an international military operation outside Germany. As a test, the government sent 150 military medics on the U.N. peacekeeping mission to Cambodia. Then it contributed soldiers to the U.N. force in Somalia. In response to a legal challenge, Germany's highest court ruled in 1994 that the government had violated the constitution by not seeking parliament's approval in advance. However, the court said the constitution did permit German troops to serve in international military actions abroad. Thereafter, Germany took a more active part in international operations. In 1995, Germany's parliament approved sending 4,000 ground troops as part of NATO's peacekeeping mission in Bosnia.

NATO's role in the crisis in Bosnia has grown over the years. At first, NATO ships merely kept watch to see that nations were observing U.N. sanctions against Yugoslavia. Later, NATO airplanes monitored a U.N. ban on military flights over Bosnia. Eventually, NATO planes bombed and U.S. ships fired cruise missiles at Bosnian Serb targets. After the peace agreement of 1995, NATO troops moved in to replace U.N. peacekeepers altogether.

Some people thought NATO was assuming too large a role. They wanted a further reduction in NATO military strength and the adoption of less ambitious goals. Critics claimed that NATO forces could do little about ethnic conflicts in Eastern Europe. They also argued that military threats from the Middle East would be lessened if the industrial nations, including NATO members, would stop selling weapons to that region and concentrate instead on solving environmental and economic problems in the Third World.

1. *Summarize the decisions made about NATO since 1991.*
2. *Explain why you AGREE or DISAGREE with each of the following statements:*
   a. *Following the end of the cold war, NATO should have been disbanded.*
   b. *NATO's military reorganization has increased its ability to keep the peace.*
   c. *NATO's nuclear policy will make the world safer.*
   d. *Germany should be prevented from playing a larger military role in NATO.*

Beyond Europe: Peacekeeping by Regional Bodies

Organization of American States. During the crisis over Haiti in the 1990s, the *Organization of American States* (OAS) played a major role. In 1991, two days after a military coup ousted the elected president, Jean-Bertrand Aristide, the OAS began applying economic sanctions. Soon after, the organization stiffened the sanctions. It ordered a cutoff of almost all trade between Haiti and Western Hemisphere nations. With the OAS leading the way, the United Nations later applied sanctions of its own against Haiti. Eventually, the sanctions caused great distress in Haiti and helped to weaken the military government. The Haitian junta stepped down in October 1994 under threat of a U.S. invasion.

Haiti was the first test of an OAS policy adopted earlier in 1991 to bolster democracy in the Western Hemisphere. Ever since its creation 43 years before, the OAS had worked to promote democracy. Its work bore fruit in the 1980s, as several Latin American military regimes gave way to elected governments. Never before had democracy been so widespread in the Americas. OAS leaders wanted to make sure the fragile new democracies did not slide back into military rule. So, in June 1991, the OAS authorized its foreign ministers to "adopt any measures deemed appropriate" to restore constitutional rule in any member country that experienced a military coup. In October 1991, the OAS leaders used that authority to place an embargo on Haiti.

The OAS was formed in Bogota, Colombia, in 1948, at the urging of the United States. Its headquarters are in Washington, D.C. The purposes of the OAS are to prevent military conflict within the Western Hemisphere, to protect the independence of the nations of the Americas from outside aggressors, and to improve the social and political systems of its member states. All 35 nations in the Americas, including Cuba, belong to the OAS.

The success of the OAS has depended on U.S. support for its policies and goals. During the cold war, U.S. efforts to transform the organization into an anticommunist alliance aroused Latin American resentment. Also resented were unilateral actions taken by the United States to contain communism in Cuba and to oppose leftist governments or movements in Guatemala, the Dominican Republic, Chile, El Salvador, and Nicaragua. Actions such as the U.S. invasion of the island of Grenada in 1983 and the intervention in Panama in 1989 completely ignored the OAS charter and reduced the effectiveness of the organization. In addition, many Latin Americans resented the U.S. position during the Falkland Islands War of 1982. U.S. leaders did nothing to prevent British military forces from entering the Western Hemisphere to fight Argentina over the disputed islands.

After the cold war, U.S. policy shifted in favor of stronger cooperation with the OAS. President Bush made the encouragement of democracy and human rights the focus of this policy.

To further improve the security and unity of the hemisphere, he negotiated a free trade agreement with Mexico and Canada, the North American Free Trade Agreement (NAFTA).

These policies were continued by President Clinton. The United States consulted with the OAS about its actions in the Haiti crisis. It supported OAS initiatives in Peru that pressured President Alberto Fujimori to restore democratic rule.

Today, the OAS is recognized as having the ability to organize inter-American action to safeguard democracy. The extent to which this is done will depend on the future willingness of the United States to strengthen and support the OAS.

- *Describe the relationship between the United States and the Organization of American States.*

Organization of African Unity. The *Organization of African Unity* (OAU) was formed in May 1963 by 32 African countries to coordinate cultural, scientific, political, and economic policies; to end colonialism in Africa; and to promote a common defense of its members' independence. Its membership has since risen to 53 nations. Annual meetings are held in Addis Ababa, Ethiopia.

With civil wars raging throughout the African continent, the OAU has been regarded as a weak and ineffectual organization. Problems such as human rights violations by several dictators have not been addressed for fear of splitting the organization. For the same reason, controversial issues have often been postponed.

Nevertheless, the OAU successfully mediated a territorial dispute between Algeria and Morocco and engaged in similar efforts in Zaire and Nigeria in the 1960s. The OAU played a major role in financing and supporting the efforts of the African National Congress to end apartheid and white-minority rule in South Africa. It also assisted the Southwest African People's Organization to achieve the independence of Namibia. And it supported the Zimbabwe African National Union-Patriotic Front to end white colonialism in that country. The diplomatic campaigns conducted by the OAU in behalf of those movements have been among the organization's best achievements.

However, the OAU was unable to mediate between the warring factions in Somalia, Sudan, or Angola. It did respond to the request of Western Saharans for independence from

Morocco by admitting the Sahrawi Arab Democratic Republic to OAU membership. That decision resulted in Morocco's withdrawal from the OAU. The OAU also helped the Economic Community of West African States in working for a solution to the civil war in Liberia.

Although the OAU has settled some African conflicts, it remains a financially weak organization. It cannot compel members to pay their dues. It has no armed forces or other means of enforcing its decisions. However, it continues to be the only African organization with even a limited capability to seek solutions to the massive problems of the continent.

Arab League. The *Arab League,* founded with British encouragement in March 1945, started with seven members. Eventually, its membership grew to 21 countries. In 1979, the league moved its headquarters from Cairo to Tunis after expelling Egypt for violating Arab solidarity and making peace with Israel. The league readmitted Egypt in 1988, returning its headquarters to Cairo.

The league encourages cultural, economic, and communication ties among members. It mediates disputes between Arab nations and represents them in certain international negotiations. It also has coordinated a military, diplomatic, and economic offensive against Israel, with whom several of the league members have been at war since 1948.

Immediately after Iraq invaded Kuwait in August 1990, Egypt and Saudi Arabia sponsored a resolution authorizing the military forces of the Arab League to cooperate with U.S. and British troops in the Persian Gulf War. A minority of league members objected to this decision. In early 1991, Iraq, Jordan, Yemen, Tunisia, Algeria, and the Palestine Liberation Organization accused Egypt of abandoning the principles of the league. Although a majority of Arab League members supported the U.S.-led coalition that drove Iraqi forces out of Kuwait, postwar divisions within the league limited its effectiveness in the area of peacekeeping.

1. *List regional organizations and assess how effective each one is at peacekeeping.*
2. *Complete each sentence.*
   a. *After the cold war, the United States changed its policy in the Western Hemisphere by ____.*

b. Peacekeeping in Africa, in the 1990s, has been made difficult by ____.

c. In response to Iraq's 1990 invasion of Kuwait, the Arab League ____.

The International Trade in Weapons

When Rwandan rebels and government forces clashed in the early 1990s, each side had a sizable stash of weapons for its troops. There were mortars from France, Kalashnikov assault rifles from Romania and Russia, and machine guns and grenades from South Africa. Each year, buyers spend tens of billions of dollars for weapons sold on the world arms market.

Many of the world's nations have busy arms-exporting industries. China leads in the production of light arms, such as rifles and hand grenades; it also sells missiles. Sweden sells aircraft. The Czech Republic sells jet trainers. France sells everything from fighter planes to submarines. But the United States outsells almost everyone. Among the large deals by U.S. armaments makers in the 1990s were McDonnell Douglas' sale of F-15 fighter planes (made in Missouri) to Israel and Saudi Arabia, and General Dynamics' sale of M1-A2 battle tanks (made in Ohio) to Kuwait.

While the world's leaders often denounce the trade in arms, they also encourage it. For years, U.S. administrations have actively assisted U.S. corporations in winning arms contracts from allied nations. After the cold war ended, with the U.S. government scaling back its own arms purchases, efforts to boost U.S. arms sales abroad took on a new urgency. U.S. arms manufacturers had to lay off workers, cut back research, and consolidate operations. In order to keep the arms industry from collapsing, government officials stepped up the promotion of sales to other countries.

The major nations do try to put limits on the sale of certain weapons, especially such modern ones as missiles. They also try to control sales of technology that might have military applications. Two main agreements help to coordinate those controls. The *Missile Technology Control Regime* (MTCR) was started in 1987 by the United States, Canada, France, Germany, Italy, Japan, the United Kingdom. Several other nations have signed on since. The MTCR seeks to restrict exports of all but the shortest-range ballistic and cruise missiles. A separate multilateral agreement deals with exports in general, especially exports of military technology and machinery that serve military purposes. This agreement targets sales to such "troublesome" states as Iraq, Iran, North Korea, and Libya.

In 1993, the United States imposed sanctions on Russian enterprises that sold missile technology to India and dangerous chemicals (which could be used in weapons) to Libya. In an effort to stem the spread of weapons of mass destruction, the Clinton administration barred American businesses from dealing with Russian firms that violate international guidelines concerning missile exports. That issue was also linked to cooperation with Russia on projects in space. The U.S., for example, would not allow Russia to share in the launching of commercial satellites or participate in the construction of a multibillion-dollar space station until Moscow agreed to abide by the multilateral controls. Russia later announced it would do so.

Although China did not sign the MTCR, it did agree to observe the controls. Nevertheless, Beijing sold sensitive missile technology to Pakistan in the 1990s. China also purchased advanced military technology from Israel. In its efforts to prod China into cooperation, the United States has from time to time cut off China's purchases of high-tech American goods.

Other limitations in the sales of arms have been decreed by the United Nations. For example, the U.N. placed an embargo on arms sales to the former Yugoslavia, hoping to limit the fighting in Croatia and Bosnia. Supporters of Bosnia criticized the embargo as one-sided, saying it hurt the Bosnian government forces more than it hurt the Bosnian Serbs. The United Nations ended the embargo when it turned Bosnian peacekeeping over to NATO at the end of 1995.

Overall, sales of weapons to Third World nations have declined since the end of the cold war. From a peak of $61 billion in 1988, arms sales dropped to around $25 billion a year in the mid-1990s.

- *State the contradiction in U.S. policy governing weapons sales.*

Some of the strongest competition for arms sales has occurred in Asia. The United States, Russia, France, Germany, and other suppliers have waged sharp rivalry for business there. Thailand and Malaysia, for example, weighed the merits of both Russian and U.S. fighter aircraft after sales presentations by the vice president of Russia and the chairperson of America's

McDonnell Douglas Corporation. Indonesia bought from Germany most of the ships and equipment of the former East German navy.

Starting in 1988, China steadily increased its military spending. It purchased sophisticated fighter aircraft from Russia and expressed interest in buying Russian aircraft carriers. China's military and naval buildup worries its neighbors, especially those with competing claims to certain strategic islands in the South China Sea. The buildup also bothers Japan, with which China competes economically for markets, investments, and resources. Taiwan, determined to maintain its independence from China, is also concerned by that nation's displays of its military might.

The Asian nation that posed the most serious threat to peace in the 1990s was North Korea. In addition to its growing nuclear capability, that Communist nation had also developed considerable conventional forces. It had more than one million troops, of which 65 percent were deployed close to the *demilitarized zone* along the border with South Korea. Military analysts predicted that any hostile actions by North Korea would force Japan to increase its military forces, thus touching off a similar response by China.

Concern about the growing military power of China,

Arms for Sale

North Korea, and other Asian nations caused the United States to seek new defense arrangements. In 1993, the United States, for the first time, engaged in multinational talks about Asian security. The talks were arranged by the *Association of Southeast Asian Nations* (ASEAN). That organization was formed in 1967 to promote economic, social, and cultural cooperation among the noncommunist states of the region. The purpose of the 1993 talks was to develop an understanding about mutual security that could lead to a slowdown of weapons purchasing. The members of ASEAN are Singapore, Indonesia, Thailand, Malaysia, Brunei, the Philippines, and (since 1995) Vietnam.

1. *Explain how the international arms trade has increased the difficulty of global peacekeeping.*
2. *Indicate which statements are* true *and which are* false.
    a. *The United States tries to block weapons sales to Iran.*
    b. *Russia and China were among the nations that set up the Missile Technology Control Regime (MTCR).*
    c. *North Korea's army of more than one million soldiers worried both South Korea and Japan.*
    d. *China was among the customers for Israeli armaments.*
    e. *A U.N. arms embargo prevented the United States from selling weapons to the government of Bosnia.*

Chapter 8 Review

A. *On your answer sheet, write the letter of the correct response.*

1. *Critics of the peacekeeping efforts of the United Nations in the 1990s raised doubts about (a) the training and funding of troops sent on peacekeeping missions (b) the domination of the Security Council by the United States, Britain, and France (c) both of the preceding.*
2. *Following the end of the cold war, U.N. peacekeeping efforts were expanded to include (a) internal conflicts, such as civil wars (b) the defense of entire continents (c) the restructuring of the governments of member nations.*
3. *In the 1990s, the most prominent U.N. peacekeeping operations were in (a) South Africa and Rwanda (b) Bosnia and Somalia (c) China and Taiwan.*

4. *In the new world order, nations that have argued for seats on the Security Council include (a) Japan and Germany (b) Armenia and Azerbaijan (c) Bosnia and Macedonia (d) Iraq and Iran.*

5. *At the Rome Conference of 1991, the NATO allies agreed (a) to remove all military forces from Central Europe (b) to cut back on nuclear weapons in Europe (c) to invite the nations of Eastern Europe and the republics of the former Soviet Union to join NATO.*

6. *NATO's new southern strategy is designed to enable the alliance to meet threats to peace from (a) the Balkans and the Middle East (b) Central and South America (c) Southeast Asia.*

7. *The regional organization that led the way for U.N. efforts to bring an end to the crisis in Haiti was the (a) Organization of African Unity (b) Arab League (c) Organization of American States.*

8. *The regional organization that supported the U.N. effort to liberate Kuwait from Iraq, in 1991, was the (a) Organization of African Unity (b) Arab League (c) Organization of American States.*

9. *Major suppliers of arms that are traded on the world market include (a) Venezuela and Colombia (b) France and the United States (c) Japan and Vietnam.*

10. *Two nations that the United States wants to prevent from acquiring modern weapons are (a) Saudi Arabia and Kuwait (b) Italy and Canada (c) Libya and North Korea.*

B. *Reread "The United Nations After the Cold War" on pages 160–164. Then write a sentence or two to define or identify each of the following:*

1. *Former Yugoslavia*
2. *Muhammad Farah Aydid*
3. *Boutros Boutros-Ghali*
4. *Security Council*
5. *Agenda for Peace*

C. *Reread "The International Trade in Weapons," on pages 172–175. Then complete each of the following sentences:*

1. *To help keep the peace, the United States and other powers have attempted to limit ____.*
2. *After the cold war, the U.S. government urgently supported arms sales by U.S. companies in order ____.*
3. *When Russian enterprises sold missile technology to India and dangerous chemicals to Libya, the United States ____.*
4. *In an attempt to get China to observe international missile controls, the United States has ____.*
5. *Neighboring nations worry about North Korea because ____.*

D. *Use information in the chapter to explain why you AGREE or DISAGREE with each of the following statements:*

1. *The United States should support global peacekeeping efforts by giving more financial and military support to the United Nations.*
2. *Regional organizations such as NATO should be authorized to use force to halt all internal disputes and conflicts between nations.*

Chapter 9

Human Rights: Issues and Problems

In June 1993, the first World Conference on Human Rights in a quarter century was held in Vienna, the capital of Austria. Convened by the United Nations, it was attended by 5,000 delegates from 160 countries and by representatives of more than 1,000 nongovernmental organizations. During a two-week period, the participants debated human rights in connection with the rights of women, minority groups, native peoples, migrant workers, the handicapped, and other groups. They also discussed political and economic rights.

Disagreement arose between the Western nations, which favored strengthening the United Nations' authority to defend human rights, and other countries. Several Asian nations wished to keep Westerners from interfering in their internal affairs in the name of human rights. The Western delegates tried to rally support for the principle that human rights should be guaranteed to the people of all nations. They rejected the idea that such rights can be withheld by the governments of some countries for historical, cultural, or religious reasons.

The developing nations demanded that economic development be considered a human right and attempted to set aside the Western requirement that financial aid be linked to respect for human rights. Western officials identified a small group of countries—China, Cuba, Syria, Iran, Vietnam, Pakistan, Malaysia, Singapore, Yemen, Indonesia, and a few others—as leaders in the fight to classify some human rights as "Western." Those nations, for example, did not consider the establishment of democratic government to be a human right.

U.N. Secretary-General Boutros Boutros-Ghali ruled that the

debates should not be "country-specific." His ruling drew protests from human rights activists, many of whom had come to the conference with charges of human rights violations in Bosnia, Tibet, Guatemala, and other countries.

The conference ended with the adoption of an agenda for international action on human rights and liberties. Nigeria, Uganda, and Gambia endorsed an American proposal that a new United Nations High Commissioner for Human Rights be appointed. Critics of the World Conference, including *Amnesty International*, the most prominent of the nongovernmental human rights organizations, claimed that little had been accomplished other than to confirm earlier United Nations human rights declarations. Others felt that the conference had identified the global issues and problems related to human rights in the 1990s.

Human Rights: The Historical Background

The idea that governments' practices and treatment of their own citizens should matter to the rest of the world gained acceptance in the period following World War II. As the world became aware of the cruelties that had been practiced by the Nazis, a concern for human rights became a mandate for the founders of the United Nations. The U.N. Charter, adopted in 1945, stated that the organization "shall promote . . . universal respect for, and observance of, human rights and fundamental freedoms for all without distinction as to race, sex, language, or religion." In 1948, the U.N. explained what was meant by "human rights" in the Universal Declaration of Human Rights. This statement of commitment was adopted by the U.N. General Assembly, with no votes against. However, the Soviet Union, the East European nations, South Africa, and Saudi Arabia abstained from voting on the declaration. In subsequent years, the nations of the world further committed themselves to respect human rights through a number of international agreements. These included the European Convention on Human Rights (1950), the International Covenant on Civil and Political Rights (1966), the American Convention on Human Rights (1969), the Helsinki Accords (1975), and the African Charter on People's and Human Rights (1981).

Citizens in many countries formed organizations (called nongovernmental organizations, or NGO's) to seek compliance with the provisions of those agreements. NGO's became a force in shaping international public opinion by speaking out against nations that violated human rights. Nevertheless, most governments did not react strongly to abuses of human rights by other governments until the 1980s.

During the 1980s, a number of governments joined in making human rights a goal of their foreign policies. The Scandinavian countries and the Netherlands began issuing reports on the human rights practices of governments to which they were giving economic aid. Canada and Australia made the promotion of human rights an important part of their participation in international affairs. The Council of Europe made Turkey's application for membership conditional on improving its human rights practices. The European Community made human rights practices an important part of its economic relations with several countries.

- *Explain how and why a concern for human rights developed after World War II.*

In the United States, President Ronald Reagan believed that free elections were a key human right. Thus, a focus on elections dominated U.S. policy on human rights during the 1980s. It led the United States to help remove from power anticommunist dictators and military rulers to whom the Reagan administration had initially been friendly. For example, the U.S. played a role in the departure of President Ferdinand Marcos from the Philippines in 1986 and in ending the dictatorship of General Augusto Pinochet in Chile in 1989. Nonetheless, the United States continued to maintain close relations with other anticommunist governments (in Paraguay, for example) that held no free elections and abused human rights.

The greater stress on human rights in international affairs made it more difficult for many governments to crush domestic critics, especially when their protests were about human rights violations and the denial of democratic procedures. A desire to avoid condemnation by other nations and a fear of losing Western economic aid played a part in the installation of democratic governments in a number of countries, such as Argentina in 1983 and Uruguay in 1985. In addition, popular revolts that removed dictators in Haiti and the Philippines in 1986 and forced the military to permit democratic elections in South Korea in 1987 were also due to the international community's growing sensitivity toward human rights. This concern also touched off worldwide condemnation when the government of China violently repressed the demands of Chinese students for democracy and human rights in 1989. Events in China did not prevent a peaceful transition from communism to multiparty democracy in neighboring Mongolia and a movement toward democracy in Nepal.

In the 1990s, the rights revolution has continued. Public awareness of human rights issues and problems has combined with the increased activities of well-organized nongovernmental organizations. This has generated pressure on governments to make human rights a key factor in international policy.

1. *List three international agreements about human rights.*
2. *Evaluate the U.S. policy on human rights during the 1980s.*
3. *Identify one human rights victory in Latin America and one in Asia.*

Immigrants and Aliens in Europe

During the 1990s, world disorder resulted in a dramatic increase in the number of people fleeing their homelands to avoid war or persecution. Turmoil in the former Yugoslav republics and in some Central Asian republics of the former Soviet Union, as well as in Iraq and in such African countries as Rwanda, Somalia, Ethiopia, Mozambique, and Liberia, created millions of refugees. The civil war in Bosnia and Croatia alone produced 3½ million refugees by 1995.

For many of those poor, dispossessed, and war-ravaged refugees, Western Europe was the preferred destination. More than 750,000 people seeking political asylum crowded into European countries in the peak year of 1992. The region's population of legal immigrants soared to nearly 20 million, plus an estimated 2 million illegal immigrants. In later years, the flow of aliens eased somewhat. (*Aliens* are people who do not have citizenship in the country in which they are living. Thus, all immigrants are aliens until they can become citizens.)

Almost all of the new arrivals required economic support from their host nations. Since the influx of immigrants came at a time of economic downturn throughout Western Europe, funding for United Nations refugee-assistance programs was tight. In addition, high levels of unemployment and shortages of housing caused increased resentment of the new arrivals.

Refugees

Some local people expressed their hostility by attacking immigrants, even killing them. Others demanded governmental action to restrict immigration. Many West Europeans seemed overwhelmed by the arrival of so many newcomers who were poor, lacked marketable skills, and were different in language, culture, religion, and sometimes race.

♦ *From which countries did refugees flee in the 1990s?*

Approximately half the immigrants to Europe in the 1990s were Muslims. The majority of those were North Africans. Among other Muslims were Bosnians, Turks, Pakistanis, and Somalis. In France, where most people are Roman Catholics, Islam replaced Protestantism as the second largest religion.

In Belgium, Austria, and Italy, antiimmigrant political parties gained new public support. In Spain, nationalist gangs killed immigrants and called for the expulsion of Arabs and Africans. Britain experienced an increase in antiforeigner demonstrations, as did Sweden.

Violence against foreigners was most extreme in Germany, which had nearly 7 million foreign residents, more than any other West European country. (Foreigners made up 7 percent of Germany's population.) Immigrants were widely accused of adding to the economic and social problems that arose from the unification of East and West Germany. "Skinheads," neo-Nazis, and other ultranationalists committed 1,500 or more attacks on foreigners each year from 1992 to 1994, killing several and injuring many. Most Germans were opposed to the attacks and criticized their government for not doing more to prevent them. In response, the government of Chancellor Helmut Kohl cracked down on the neo-Nazis. At the same time, the government pushed through parliament a law to restrict the entry of asylum seekers into Germany. The law drew broad support from voters and helped to undercut the appeal of far-right political parties that tried to exploit the immigration issue. However, human rights groups sharply protested the law.

♦ *How did emigration to Europe lead to violence in the 1990s?*

Italy experienced an economic expansion in the 1980s. As a result, approximately one million immigrants entered the country, many of them from Morocco and other African nations. Even after ten years, many of the immigrants were still living in poverty, doing work that native Italians did not wish to do. In the economic hard times of the 1990s, immigrants were no longer welcome. But 25,000 Albanians were allowed to enter Italy in 1991.

During the 1990s, most European nations took steps to restrict illegal immigrants. Governments introduced rigorous checks to identify and expel foreign students and foreign residents who took jobs illegally. They set up new methods of monitoring short-stay visitors and people who came to be reunited with their families or to marry a legal resident.

In France, 4 million foreigners made up some 7 percent of the population of 57 million. Immigration questions became hot issues in French political campaigns. At the urging of conservative Premier Édouard Balladur, parliament in 1993 toughened laws on immigration. One measure reversed a policy of automatically granting French citizenship to anyone born on French soil (even a child born to a couple from outside France). Another made it easier for the government to expel illegal aliens. Still another made it harder for foreigners to acquire residency papers. Human rights supporters called the changes discriminatory and unwise. However, with France in an economic slump and nearly 11 percent of the workforce unemployed, the antiimmigration measures had broad public support. In France's 1995 presidential election, Jean-Marie Le Pen, leader of the far-right National Front Party, won more than 15 percent of the vote on a "French-first" platform. Le Pen proposed closing France's borders, expelling immigrants, cutting off welfare payments to aliens, and withdrawing from the European Union.

The measures taken by the West European governments drew an appeal from the United Nations High Commissioner for Refugees and protests from refugee organizations. Among those most affected by the new restrictions were victims of the war in the former Yugoslavia. Many people seeking to flee the war zone were unable to rejoin family members already in West European countries.

The governments of the Czech Republic, Poland, and Hungary expressed fears that the restrictions on immigration into Western Europe would leave them with large refugee populations, causing ethnic unrest and economic hardship. In return for German economic aid, Poland agreed to accept refugees barred from Germany. However, the agreement was unpopular. All three countries began to develop stiffer deportation procedures and stronger border controls.

For supporters of human rights, such antiimmigration actions reflected a dangerous "Fortress Europe" attitude and a desire to keep out those in need of safety, political security, and economic opportunity. For the European leaders who sponsored them, the new laws were a way of protecting the economic status and political stability of their countries in a time of global economic difficulty.

1. *Explain why immigration became a major political issue in Germany and France in the 1990s.*
2. *Tell which of the following statements are true and which are false. Rewrite incorrect statements to make them true.*
    a. *The number of illegal aliens in Western Europe in the 1990s exceeded the number of legal immigrants.*
    b. *Germany had more foreign residents than any other European country.*
    c. *Violence against foreigners occurred only in Germany.*
    d. *Many West European nations passed laws to restrict immigration.*
    e. *Poland, Hungary, and the Czech Republic indicated a willingness to receive unlimited numbers of refugees.*

Immigrants and Aliens in America

The United States has long been considered a nation of immigrants and a haven for refugees. Although people from all corners of the globe populated and built America, for much of the nation's history, entry into the United States has been regulated by immigration *quotas* (numerical limits on the number of new arrivals from each country). During the 19th and early 20th centuries, quotas were designed to favor immigrants from Western Europe. In 1965, this discriminatory system was changed to provide applicants from all nations a chance to qualify for permanent residence. By the 1990s, new regulations set an annual limit of 20,000 entry visas for each country.

Recent law has given preference to people with family members who are United States citizens or already reside legally in the United States. Also given preference are workers whose skills are in demand and refugees fleeing war or persecution. Under this system, 600,000 to 850,000 legal immigrants entered the country annually during the first half of the 1990s. Among the latest arrivals, Asians, Africans, and Latin Americans outnumbered Europeans. Around the world, the number of people hoping to settle in the United States continually increases. In the mid-1990s, nearly 2½ million people were on lists awaiting admission. But many others did not wait. Illegal immigrants entered the United States at double the rate of legal entrants.

The treatment of immigrants has been a concern of human rights organizations. Many encounter discrimination when seeking jobs. It is against the law to hire an alien who lacks proper immigration documents, so employers who hire illegal aliens risk fines and other penalties. Some employers refuse to hire any job applicants who "look foreign," for fear they might turn out to have forged papers. Others freely hire illegal immigrants but force them to work under unhealthy or dangerous conditions for low wages. If undocumented workers protest, their bosses can report them to the Immigration and Naturalization Service (INS). Discovery by the INS usually results in deportation.

Smuggling of Immigrants. In August 1995, immigration officials cut through barbed wire to stage a predawn raid on a seedy garment factory sweatshop in El Monte, California. They said 72 immigrants from Thailand had been kept at the fenced-in compound in conditions close to slavery. Here is how officials described the operation: Some of the immigrants had arrived by airplane and been bused directly to the factory from the airport. They were kept there while they worked off their debt to those who had smuggled them into the country. Their pay was about half the legal minimum wage. Each night, guards locked the doors and patrolled the area, to prevent escapes. The workers sewed clothing that later appeared in stores under well-known American brand names. Officials did not immediately send the immigrants back to Thailand. Instead, they released the Thais and arranged for them to testify against the sweatshop operators.

The smuggling of immigrants into the United States by criminal organizations had become common by the 1990s. Those who pay the smugglers in full are free to seek work on their own. Those who do not pay may be subject to forced labor and physical mistreatment. Some of the immigrants are recruited by gangs for criminal activities. Thai immigrants are not the only ones to be subjected to forced labor upon arrival in the United States. Latin Americans, Chinese, and people from other parts of the world have suffered the same fate at the hands of criminal smugglers.

Seeking a New Homeland

1. *Give two possible reasons for someone to emigrate to the U.S. illegally.*
2. *State some of the problems faced by illegal immigrants.*

Immigration during the 1980s was higher than in any decade since 1900–1909, and the flow increased in the first half of the 1990s. By 1994, the foreign-born population of the United States numbered 22.6 million, or 8.7 percent of the total population. That was the highest proportion of foreign-born since 1940—although it paled in comparison to the modern record of 14.7 percent set in 1910. By some estimates, almost 40 percent of America's population growth over the next decade will come from immigrants.

Reactions Against Immigration. Fear of the consequences of sustained immigration led to a surge of modern nativism. *Nativism* is the belief that one's society cannot assimilate, or absorb, more outsiders. Nativism was also stimulated by other movements, such as zero population growth, environmentalism, and "English-first." Some Americans carried nativism to extremes. "Skinheads," white supremacists, and others committed acts of violence against foreigners, much as Europe's neo-Nazis did.

The rise in immigration and reaction against it spurred a national debate about immigration policy. Some political leaders at the state and national level described the rise in immigration as a threat. They said immigrants were adding to the cost of education, health services, police, and other public functions. The influx of immigrants, they argued, unfairly burdened taxpayers while contributing to unemployment and other social problems. Politicians from both major parties proposed sweeping measures to limit immigration, legal and illegal. In 1994, voters in California adopted by a three-to-two margin an initiative called Proposition 187. It changed state law to block illegal aliens from using public services like schools, colleges, and health care. (Court challenges prevented parts of the new law from being put into immediate effect.) Congress too took up bills to limit immigration and set stricter rules for those seeking political asylum.

Other political leaders, along with human rights groups, deplored the hostility to immigrants and urged caution in changing immigration laws. They said immigrants had contributed greatly to America in the past and should be encouraged to do so in the future. Supporters of this point of view argued that immigrants took jobs most Americans did not want, that they paid their fair share of taxes, and that many would suffer political persecution or even physical harm if they were sent home.

Human rights advocates also voiced concern over a 1993 decision of the U.S. Supreme Court upholding the forcible return to their country of Haitians intercepted at sea while attempting illegally to enter the United States. The U.S. Coast Guard began to stop Haitians at sea in May 1992. Without being allowed to claim political asylum, the Haitians were returned to the authority of the military dictatorship they were seeking to flee. In 1994, President Clinton modified the policy by ordering that Haitians stopped at sea be screened to determine their political status. International law requires that no refugees be returned to a place where they could suffer persecution. The flow of Haitians had tapered off by the time civilian government was reestablished in Haiti later in 1994.

Human rights and immigration experts worried, however, that the decision of the Supreme Court to uphold the repatriation of the Haitians would set a precedent for other national groups. Also, the United Nations High Commissioner for Refugees criticized the Supreme Court decision as a major setback to international refugee law. The decision seemed to place protection of borders above U.S. responsibilities under international law. Earlier, the United States had criticized Hong Kong for returning Vietnamese boat people without proper screening.

1. *Explain why human rights organizations became alarmed by changing American attitudes toward immigration and asylum in the 1990s.*
2. *Explain why you AGREE or DISAGREE with the following statement: European and American responses to immigration differed greatly in the 1990s.*
3. *Complete the following sentences:*
   a. *Under current U.S. law, 20,000 ____.*
   b. *Illegal aliens are often mistreated by ____.*
   c. *In 1994, California voters decided to ____.*

The Struggle for Women's Rights

At the Fourth World Conference on Women, held in Beijing in 1995, delegates found much to celebrate. Female literacy was on the rise, for example. And governments were paying greater attention than in the past to women's rights. But the delegates also found much to protest—from systematic rape during the wars in Bosnia and Rwanda to deeply entrenched social, economic, and legal discrimination against women. During the conference, the delegates drew up a "platform for action." They urged the governments they represented to use the document as a guideline for guaranteeing the "full enjoyment by women of their human rights."

One of the lessons of the Beijing conference, and of earlier U.N. conferences, was that women of very different cultures could unite to pursue common goals. Representatives of women's groups flocked to China from all over the world. The nongovernmental organizations held their own, separate conference in a Beijing suburb. They wanted to make themselves heard by government delegates at the official conference.

Of course, the women's groups didn't always agree. And often they emphasized different issues. In some Third World countries, key issues include the selling of women as slaves and the ritual mutilation of young women. In the United States, women's groups typically focus on such issues as reproductive rights and sex discrimination. Issues of sex discrimination include unequal employment and promotion opportunities, salary differences, and sexual harassment. Many issues were common to all the women's groups, however—from sex discrimination to domestic violence (the physical abuse of women within family situations).

Women World Leaders. In the 1990s, women's rights groups were encouraged by the achievement of leadership positions by women in several nations. At the start of 1995, ten of the world's 191 nations were headed by women. However, the proportion of women in legislatures and other political bodies was lower than it had been in the 1980s, largely because of the collapse of European communism. Communist nations had set quotas of up to 30 percent for women in office.

President Mary Robinson of the Republic of Ireland, in office since 1990, was one of Europe's most popular heads of state. On one occasion, a poll of Irish voters gave President Robinson a 93 percent approval rating, compared to the 28 percent rating of the Irish prime minister of the time.

In 1993, Kim Campbell became the first woman to serve as Canada's prime minister. She was chosen by fellow members of the Conservative Party to take over as party leader and prime minister after the resignation of Brian Mulroney, whose popularity had sunk to desperately low levels. However, Ms. Campbell served only briefly, as the Conservatives were defeated in national elections later in 1993. Several other women have reached high office in Canada, holding such positions as premier of Prince Edward Island, mayor of Ontario, leader of the New Democratic Party, and deputy leader of the Liberal Party.

President Vigdis Finnbogadottir was Iceland's head of state from 1980 to 1996. Gro Harlem Brundtland has served as prime minister of Norway.

Muslim societies are traditionally *patriarchal* (run by men). In 1993, however, Tansu Ciller, a former economics professor and economics minister, became the first woman to hold the office of prime minister of Turkey. Her election reflected the desire of many Turks to be regarded by Europe and America as modern and secular. She aimed, in addition, to lower Turkey's huge inflation rate and to privatize state-owned business enterprises, which had been losing money. When her party was defeated by an Islamic party in 1995 general elections, Mrs. Ciller was forced to resign.

In South Asia, three of the seven national leaders who gathered for regional summits in the mid-1990s were women. They were Prime Minister Benazir Bhutto of Pakistan, Prime Minister Khaleda Zia of Bangladesh, and President Chandrika Kumaratunga of Sri Lanka. All were members of political dynasties started by fathers or husbands.

Both Bangladesh and Pakistan are mainly Muslim countries. Ms. Bhutto became prime minister of Pakistan in 1989, lost an election, then returned to power in 1993. She opened Pakistan's first all-women police station and started a women's bank. Ms. Zia became prime minister of Bangladesh in 1991. She aggressively promoted the education and economic self-sufficiency of women. The leader of the country's political opposition, Sheik Hasina Wazed, was also a woman. So were at least 10 percent of the members of Parliament.

In Sri Lanka, a majority of the people are Buddhists. Ms. Kumaratunga won a 1994 election that was called "the battle of the widows." Her rival was the widow of an opposition leader killed two weeks before the election by a suicide bomber. Ms. Kumaratunga's father served as Sri Lanka's prime minister in the 1950s and was assassinated in 1959, when she

Looking for the Big Jobs

was 14. Her husband too was a political figure who was assassinated. Immediately after her election as president, Ms. Kumaratunga appointed her 78-year-old mother as prime minister. (The mother, Sirimavo Bandaranaike, had been the first woman in the world to serve as prime minister, in 1960. She led her political party to an election victory a year after her husband's assassination.)

Women Leaders in the United States. In the United States, women experienced political gains with the appointments of Janet Reno as the first woman U.S. attorney general and Ruth Bader Ginsburg as the second woman Supreme Court justice. (Sandra Day O'Connor, appointed in 1981, was the first.) As director of the Women's Rights Project of the American Civil Liberties Union, Ruth Bader Ginsburg had earlier argued six cases before the Supreme Court, winning five of them. By convincing the justices that laws that discriminated between men and women were unconstitutional, she succeeded in changing U.S. law as it affects women.

American women gained high office in larger numbers in 1992 than in any previous year. In the House of Representatives, the number of seats held by women increased from 28 to 47, and in the Senate from 2 to 5. Consequently, 1992 was called the "Year of the Woman." By 1995, 48 women were serving as representatives and 8 as senators. Nonetheless, the United States ranked forty-third in the proportion of women in its national legislative body, among 106 nations with freely elected parliaments. In the United States, women held 11 percent of seats. In Sweden, in contrast, the proportion was 40 percent.

The economic and political gains made by women in Communist and Western nations were not equaled by women in other societies, especially those in the Islamic nations and Africa. The traditional subordination of women to men in those regions of the world led to inequality and abuse.

1. *Compare and contrast the agendas of women's groups in Third World countries and in industrialized countries.*
2. *Match each person in Column A with the correct identification from Column B.*

Column A	Column B
1. *Mary Robinson*	a. *U.S. Attorney General*
2. *Khaleda Zia*	b. *Prime Minister of Norway*
3. *Vigdis Finnbogadottir*	c. *U.S. Supreme Court Justice*
4. *Gro Harlem Brundtland*	d. *President of Ireland*
5. *Janet Reno*	e. *President of Iceland*
6. *Ruth Bader Ginsburg*	f. *Prime Minister of Bangladesh*

Poverty and Health Care

For many people, the right to primary health care has become one of the most important of human rights. The availability and quality of health care has varied greatly in global regions and nations.

Between 1960 and 1993, life expectancy at birth in *developing countries*—countries with little or no technology, low income for the majority of the people, and few or poorly developed resources—increased from 46 years to 63 years. Also, the number of children in these countries who die before their fifth birthday dropped by two thirds during the same period of time. Those gains were made possible by the increased availability of basic public health services. Standard immunizations, for example, saved approximately 3 million lives each year. Although the gap between rich and poor countries did not narrow in terms of income, it did in the area of health.

Nevertheless, enormous health problems remain. Much of the $2 trillion spent globally on health services each year is used ineffectively. Also, growing numbers of older people are creating new demands on health systems in developing countries. Seniors require care for heart attacks, cancer, and a wide range of diseases of the elderly.

The World Bank, which funds economic development programs in the poorer nations, has drawn a direct connection between economic progress and health. By increasing its expenditures on health services to $1 billion in the mid-1990s, the World Bank became the largest single source of funding for health. The bank identified expanded immunization programs and increased distribution of vitamin A and iodine supplements to the world's one billion impoverished people as the most effective way to improve health in developing countries.

Another priority identified by the World Bank concerned the responsibility of governments to provide inexpensive and effective drugs for school-age children suffering from certain microbe infections and from deficiencies of vitamins and other essential nutrients.

Global threats to health identified by experts, in the 1990s, include drug-resistant forms of malaria and tuberculosis, growing consumption of tobacco in Third World nations, and acquired immune deficiency syndrome (AIDS). It is feared that the death rate from malaria might double to 2 million people a year in the next decade. Tobacco-related deaths from heart disease and cancer might double to 2 million people a year by 2010. Government-sponsored educational programs to reduce smoking will be urgently needed to prevent tobacco-related deaths in the developing countries from exceeding the number of deaths caused by AIDS, tuberculosis, and childbirth complications combined.

In developing countries, death rates among children have been ten times higher than in more developed nations. In some nations, improvements have been dramatic. In Indonesia, for example, the child death rate dropped by half from 1960 to 1990. In Ghana, however, the child death rate over the same period dropped only slightly. Almost half of the preventable deaths of children, in recent years, have been due to diarrhea and respiratory illness combined with malnutrition. If, through expanded health care programs, the child death rate in poorer countries could be reduced to the levels found in wealthy nations, 11 million fewer children would die each year.

It has been estimated that 7 million adults die each year of illnesses that could be cured or prevented at low cost. Tuberculosis alone causes 2 million deaths a year. About 400,000 women a year die from pregnancy and childbirth complications. Maternal death rates are 30 times higher in developing countries than in wealthier nations.

♦ *List some of the major health problems in the world today.*

Health care experts have urged governments to double or triple the funds spent on basic public health programs such as immunizations, AIDS prevention, treatment of sexually transmitted diseases, and essential clinical services. Governments have been advised that cost-effective health services do not require sophisticated hospitals and specialized physicians. Lower level health centers in larger numbers have been recommended as better ways to provide services to more people.

In low-income countries, public spending has often been concentrated on high-cost hospitals in urban centers. Meanwhile, poor people in outlying areas remain desperately in need of health services. In Peru, for example, more than 60 percent of the poor must travel more than an hour to receive basic health care.

The unavailability of medicines has also been a problem for poverty-stricken populations. The World Health Organization has compiled lists of essential low-cost drugs that address the important health problems of whole populations. However, only a few nations have used those lists when selecting drugs for government purchase and public use.

The World Bank has urged governments to promote family planning to help couples lower their fertility and to lengthen the intervals between births. In Egypt, an infant born within 18 months of an older sibling is three times as likely to die as are those born after a longer interval. Experts claim that improved access to family-planning services might save 850,000 children from dying each year and eliminate 100,000 maternal deaths.

To secure for citizens their right to basic health care, several nations have developed government-funded and -regulated national health services. National health plans are common in most industrialized countries of the West, although lately countries like Britain, Sweden, and Canada have been cutting back services. In Canada, for example, a highly praised universal health insurance program is supported by provincial governments and community service agencies. Canadians pay high taxes for health and other social services. In the 1990s, many Canadians questioned whether they were getting their money's worth. Prime Minister Jean Chrétien of the Liberal Party, who took office in 1993, pledged to cut annual health spending by $7 billion (U.S.), from 10 percent to 8.5 percent of the GDP.

In the United States, most people receive medical and health services through insurance plans funded jointly by employers and employees. Coverage varies greatly, however, while health-related costs have risen rapidly. Millions of Americans have only limited access to services, while the unemployed, the elderly, and other segments of the population obtain basic services only with difficulty—or not at all. Congress turned down a proposed national health care plan submitted in 1993 by President Clinton. Republicans who gained control of Congress the following year set out to trim rather than expand public health programs in their drive to control soaring federal budget deficits.

1. *Explain whether you AGREE or DISAGREE with the following statement:*
   Access to basic health care is a fundamental human right.

2. *State the reason why the World Bank has urged governments to improve health services in developing countries.*

3. *Which statements are recommendations made by health experts to the governments of underdeveloped nations?*

   a. *Increase the distribution of immunizations and vitamin A and iodine.*
   b. *Provide inexpensive drugs for children suffering from microbe infections and nutritional deficiencies.*
   c. *Build more sophisticated hospitals.*
   d. *Educate people about tobacco, AIDS, and sexually transmitted diseases.*
   e. *Promote family-planning services.*

Chapter 9 Review

A. *Write the letter of the correct response.*

1. *At the World Conference on Human Rights, in 1993, disagreement arose between the Western nations and some Asian and African countries over (a) the definition of human rights (b) the funding of human rights programs (c) the authority of the U.N. to intervene in human rights issues.*
2. *Nongovernmental human rights organizations at the Vienna Conference criticized the decision of the U.N. secretary-general to (a) confine presentations to government representatives only (b) ensure that debates were not country-specific (c) prevent discussion of political rights.*
3. *Historically, the belief in the obligation of nations to secure for their citizens basic human rights began after World War II because (a) Western nations needed a justification for interference in the internal affairs of Third World nations (b) the United States found human rights to be a useful way to embarrass the Soviet Union during the cold war (c) governments and populations were shocked by the cruelties practiced by the Nazis during the World War II era.*
4. *During the 1980s, the United States (a) identified human rights with free elections (b) identified human rights with social and economic progress (c) pursued human rights only in Communist nations.*
5. *In the 1990s, refugees pouring into Western Europe as a result of world discord came in large numbers from (a) Southeast Asia (b) Eastern Europe, the Middle East, and North Africa (c) Latin America and Southern Africa.*
6. *Resentment of immigrants in Western Europe, in the 1990s, has been strongly related to (a) distrust of communism (b) rising oil prices (c) global economic difficulties and shortages of jobs and housing.*
7. *A major human rights problem in the United States, in recent years, has been (a) the abuse of illegal aliens by criminal organizations (b) the deportation of all newly arrived immigrants by the Immigration and Naturalization Service (c) the passage of laws barring immigration from the Middle East, Africa, and Asia.*
8. *The "platform for action" of the Fourth World Conference on Women was adopted by (a) government delegates (b) nongovernmental organizations (c) both of the previous.*

9. *Women's groups around the world have been concerned with ending violence and other forms of abuse against women. American women's rights organizations, however, have focused upon (a) assisting Third World women to emigrate to the United States (b) ending unequal job opportunities and salaries, and other forms of discrimination (c) helping women to escape discrimination in the United States by emigrating to other countries.*

10. *Human rights organizations concerned with basic health services for all people have emphasized the need for (a) immunization and nutritional programs (b) sex education and family planning (c) both of the previous.*

B. *Reread "Immigrants and Aliens in Europe," on pages 181–184. Then write an essay on immigration issues in Western Europe by answering the following questions:*

1. *Why are so many immigrants moving into Western Europe?*

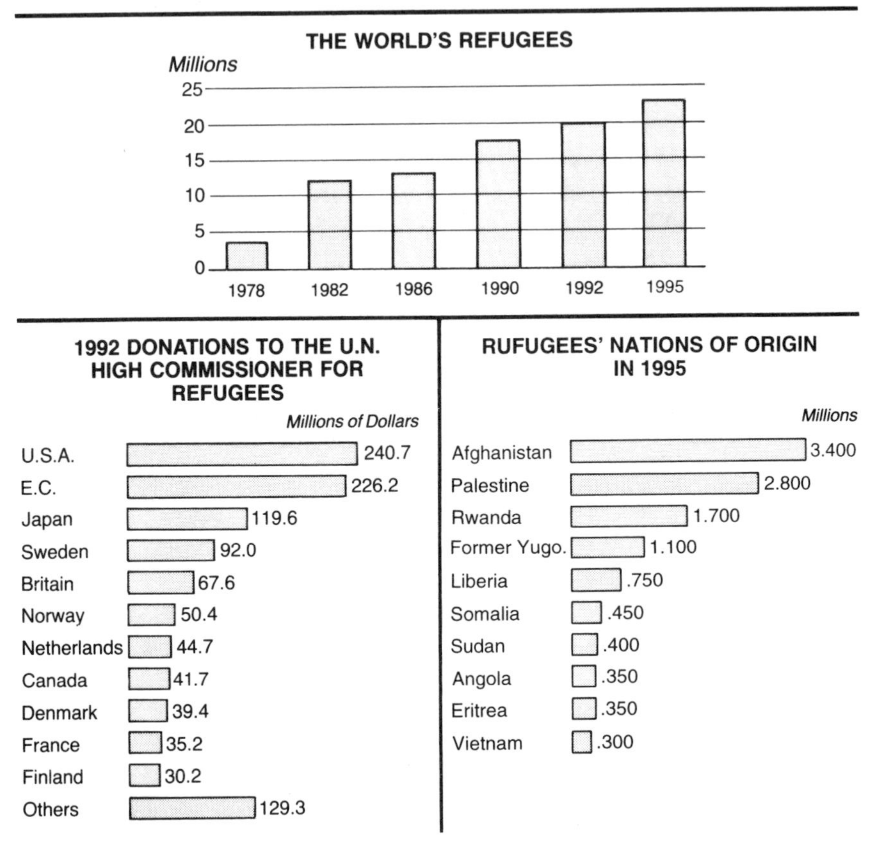

Figure 9.1 The Global Refugee Crisis

2. *How have France and Germany been affected by immigration in comparison to other European nations?*
3. *How does immigration's effect on the nations of Western Europe compare to its effect on the United States?*

C. *Examine the graphs (Figure 9.1) on page 197 and indicate which statements are true and which are false.*

1. *In 1992, the United States contributed more money to United Nations refugee assistance programs than did any other nation.*
2. *In 1992, the number of refugees in the world was higher than in 1995.*
3. *In 1978, the number of refugees in the world was fewer than 5 million.*
4. *As of 1995, more refugees originated in Afghanistan than in any other single country.*
5. *At least one African country in 1995 had more than a million refugees living outside its borders.*

D. *Reread "The Struggle for Women's Rights," on pages 188–192, and "Poverty and Health Care," on pages 192–195. Then write one or two paragraphs on each of the following topics.*

1. *Women as national leaders.*
2. *Health services in developing nations.*

Chapter 10

Terrorists and Ultranationalists Threaten International Security

Terrorism has been defined as the systematic use of violence against society in general and innocent people in particular to express beliefs and achieve political goals. In modern times, terrorism has largely been an instrument of the weak (individuals or small groups of commandos) against the strong (dominant majorities and governments). Terrorism brings injury, death, and destruction to innocent bystanders, as well as to religious and political opponents in every region of the world. Terrorism has come to be regarded as a major threat to domestic and international security. Governments, as well as regional and international organizations, have been compelled to apply more and more of their resources to combat this menace.

Ultranationalists assert the right of a particular national or ethnic group to be the dominant force in their country. Their aggressive behavior toward other ethnic groups and cultures residing in their midst marks them as racists. Since they organize and use violence in much the same way as do terrorists, such right-wing extremists also threaten domestic tranquility and world peace.

Recent Events Around the World

Bombings in the United States. In the 1990s, the United States experienced a kind of terrorism familiar to other countries. A powerful car bomb exploded in a garage under the World Trade Center in New York City in 1993, causing extensive damage and six deaths. Two years later, a truck bomb demolished the Alfred P. Murrah Federal Building in Oklahoma City. That bomb killed 168 people, including 15 children at a day care center. Other than their destructiveness, the two incidents had little in common. One was attributed to international terrorists, the other, to homegrown extremists.

U.S. authorities blamed the World Trade Center bombing on Islamic militants from the Middle East. Officials linked the bombing to an alleged plot—uncovered later in 1993—to blow up a United Nations building in New York City and the Holland Tunnel (a major transportation link between that city and New Jersey); and to assassinate such prominent political leaders as U.N. Secretary-General Boutros Boutros-Ghali. A key figure in both events, investigators claimed, was an Egyptian fundamentalist Muslim leader named Sheik Omar Abdel Rahman, who lived in the United States. Four militant Islamists (an Egyptian and three Palestinians) were convicted of the trade center bombing in 1994. The sheik and nine other defendants (including two U.S.-born Muslims) were found guilty in the broader plot the following year.

In sharp contrast, the main suspect in the Oklahoma City bombing was a former U.S. soldier named Timothy J. McVeigh, born near Buffalo, New York. Prosecutors charged that he and one or more Army buddies committed the crime out of revulsion against the U.S. government. Reports suggested that McVeigh had been enraged by a 1993 raid by federal agents on a compound near Waco, Texas, occupied by Branch Davidian religious cultists. A long siege of the compound ended in a fast-spreading fire that killed about 80 of the cultists. That holocaust took place two years to the day before the bomb destroyed the Murrah Building.

- *Compare and contrast the World Trade Center and Oklahoma City bombings.*

Terrorism. The Middle East has long been a hotbed of terrorism. While Arab-Israeli differences have spawned much of

Terrorist Attack

the violence, other terrorist movements were also active in the 1990s. In Algeria, tens of thousands of people died in terrorist attacks that started in 1992. Militant Algerian Islamists struggled to overthrow a government that they felt cheated them out of an electoral triumph. In Egypt, another set of militant Islamists made terrorist attacks against tourists and officials in an attempt to bring down President Hosni Mubarak. The militants considered Mubarak to be hostile to Islam and overly friendly to the United States and Israel.

Outside the Middle East, terrorism was also on the march. In 1995, a series of bombs exploded in subway cars and garbage cans in French cities. Authorities blamed the Islamist opponents of the Algerian government, angry at French cooperation with Algerian leaders. In South America, a bomb attributed to either drug gangs or leftist guerrillas killed 30 people at a festival in Bogotá, the Colombian capital. In Asia, terrorists released a nerve gas called sarin in five Tokyo subway cars during rush hour, killing 12 people. Japanese officials charged members and leaders of a religious cult called Aum Shinrikyo.

In many areas of the world, terrorist campaigns drag on for years. In Spain, a terrorist organization known by the initials

ETA began carrying out attacks in the 1960s. The organization demands the separation from Spain of the northern provinces inhabited by Basques. Throughout Europe, Kurdish rebels mounted a wave of coordinated assaults on Turkish diplomatic missions and businesses. They have been struggling for more than a decade to gain independence from or autonomy within Turkey. In Sri Lanka (South Asia), rebels from the minority Tamil community used terror in a war for autonomy or independence that began in 1983. In the southern Philippines, Muslim rebels in the Moro Front waged a war of terrorist and guerrilla attacks for autonomy for more than two decades. And that is just a sampling.

Terrorist campaigns do not necessarily go on forever. They have tapered off or been suspended in some parts of the world. This happened in Canada, where Quebec separatists resorted to terrorism in the 1960s and 1970s, then turned to more peaceful methods. It also happened in Northern Ireland, where the Irish Republican Army (IRA) began a campaign of terror in the 1970s. In 1994, the Roman Catholic-led IRA and its Protestant extremist opponents declared a halt to violence so political negotiations over the province's future could begin.

- *Describe how terrorism has been used in three world regions.*

Ultranationalist Violence. Another threat to world peace has come from ultranationalist, or right-wing, violence. In 1993, a shadowy group calling itself the Bavarian Liberation Army was blamed for a series of terrorist attacks in Austria. Many of the attacks used letter bombs. In 1995, in the Austrian town of Oberwart, someone hid a pipe bomb in a placard that said, "Gypsies go back to India." The bomb killed four men early on a Sunday morning. The following day, another pipe bomb, disguised as an aerosol can, wounded a municipal garbage worker in a nearby town. Near the bomb was a sign: "Go back to Dalmatia." Many residents of the town are Austrians of Croatian descent. Dalmatia is a region in Croatia.

Ultranationalist violence has been a concern elsewhere in Europe, and in countries around the world. Typically, ultranationalist violence is directed against ethnic or religious groups. It may also be aimed at governments seen as hostile to ultranationalist goals.

Recognition of the global threat of terrorism and ultranationalism has caused governments to develop strategies to combat them. In the United States, more than 200 Pentagon officials and counterterrorism experts met in 1993 to consider future problems. They concluded that the increase of ethnic and regional conflicts would give rise to new radical movements, leading to new forms of terrorism. One expert predicted a "global increase in anarchy" (lawlessness and disorder). Some at the meeting worried about what they called mass terrorism, such as the ethnic cleansing carried out in Bosnia. Others were more concerned about single-issue terrorism—attacks by extremists who share no ideology, only hatred for a particular enemy. There was general agreement that increased border controls and strengthened counterterrorist organization would be necessary. It was also recognized that free societies, by their very openness, are especially vulnerable to terrorism.

1. *PROVE or DISPROVE: Terrorism is a global threat to world peace.*
2. *Explain why terrorism and ultranationalist violence are similar.*
3. *Tell which of the following statements are true, and which are false. Rewrite the incorrect ones to make them true.*
   a. *Militant Islamists bombed the Alfred P. Murrah Building in Oklahoma City.*
   b. *Tamil rebels have used terror in a drive to win self-rule in Sri Lanka.*
   c. *The ETA is a Basque terrorist organization.*
   d. *The Irish Republican Army called a halt to its campaign of violence.*
   e. *Austrian authorities suspect left-wing revolutionaries of pipe bomb attacks on minorities.*

Terrorism: The Historical Background

As a political tool, terrorism came to prominence during the French Revolution (1789–99). Radical revolutionaries, called Jacobins, began a reign of terror by sending supporters of the monarchy and other suspected political enemies to the guillotine for beheading. This kind of terrorism used the instruments of state power against political enemies. Similar methods were used by the Bolsheviks after they seized power in Russia in 1917. In the United States, groups like the Ku Klux Klan used terror as a means of enforcing white supremacy in the South after the Civil War.

In recent years, the term *terrorism* has been applied most often to acts of violence by guerrillas or militant organizations rather than to actions taken by governments. In this connection, four main types of activity have emerged: assassinations, bombings, seizures of hostages, and hijackings of airplanes and ships. In the 1970s, the term *international terrorism* began to be used to describe acts of violence committed by political groups outside their own country. Another term that became common in this period was *state-sponsored terrorism*. It refers to acts of violence encouraged by governments or states for political purposes.

After World War II, a number of uprisings by nationalist groups occurred in the Third World. In Kenya, Cyprus, South Yemen, Algeria, and other places, officials and citizens of the ruling colonial government were attacked in the course of campaigns for national independence. This happened also in Israel, where Zionist leaders Menachim Begin and Yitzhak Shamir led two terrorist groups, Irgun and Stern. The groups assassinated Arabs and British officials in a drive to bring about Israeli independence.

Political groups seeking various forms of political and social change within independent countries also resorted to acts of terror. This was a widespread practice by Latin American urban guerrillas in Argentina, Brazil, Uruguay, and elsewhere, and by rural guerrillas in Peru, Colombia, El Salvador, and Nicaragua. Terror was also practiced by groups demanding radical change in the more developed democracies. The Red Army Faction in West Germany, the Red Brigades in Italy, and the Weathermen in the United States used acts of violence in attempts to force those in authority to make the changes they demanded. During the 1960s and early 1970s, a goal of many of those groups was to force the United States to pull its soldiers out of Vietnam. Most such movements aimed to promote social revolution and were regarded as left wing. Many were sympathetic to communism. During the 1970s and 1980s, however, there were also campaigns of terror by right-wing groups (ultranationalists), especially those active in France and Italy.

Governments too used terrorist acts to advance their goals in this period. In one famous incident, a Communist agent killed an anticommunist Bulgarian dissident in a London subway by pricking his leg with a poison-tipped umbrella. During the 1960s, U.S. officials plotted ways of assassinating Cuban

Premier Fidel Castro. They considered a range of methods, from poisons to explosives. They even went so far as to hire Mafia assassins. When news of such acts became public in the 1970s, Congress clamped tighter restrictions on U.S. intelligence agencies.

In the late 1970s, the U.S. government made the fight against terrorism a major part of its foreign policy. Officials drew up a list of countries believed to support terrorism. The government set up special military units to prevent terrorist acts and to retaliate against terrorism, when appropriate.

1. *List some standard terrorist activities.*
2. *Explain the difference between left-wing and right-wing terrorists.*

After the 1979 Islamic revolution in Iran, which brought to power the fundamentalist government of the Ayatollah Khomeini, international terrorism increased. Iranian militants held 52 Americans hostage in Iran for 444 days, until early 1981. A terrorist on a suicide mission blew up the U.S. Marine headquarters in Lebanon, in 1983, killing 241 Americans. At the same time, a suicide bomber destroyed a French paratroop barracks in Beirut, killing 58. Also, terrorists kidnapped, tortured, and killed the chief of the U.S. Central Intelligence Agency (the U.S. spy agency) station in Beirut. According to the 1987 book *Veil*, by investigative reporter Bob Woodward, the CIA's director retaliated by ordering an attack on a Muslim cleric who headed a terrorist organization. The 1985 attack, using a truck bomb in a Beirut courtyard, killed 80 people but left the cleric unhurt.

More incidents followed. A passenger ship, the *Achille Lauro*, was hijacked in 1985 and an American was killed. The number of terrorist incidents rose above one thousand in 1988. In addition, several Americans and Europeans were kidnapped and held hostage for years by terrorists based in Lebanon. In 1989, the Pentagon reported the existence of 52 terrorist groups in various parts of the world.

Among the most prominent victims of political assassination in the 1980s were Egypt's President Anwar Sadat in 1981, India's Prime Minister Indira Gandhi in 1984, Sweden's Premier Olaf Palme in 1986, Lebanon's Premier Rashid Karami in 1987, and Pakistan's President Muhammad Zia ul-Haq in 1988.

A Terrorist's View

There were also destructive incidents of terrorism within local communities. Largely in Third World countries, they involved problems between people of different ethnic or religious groups. Conflicts pitted Christians against Muslims in Lebanon, Tamils against Sinhalese in Sri Lanka, Hindus against Sikhs in Punjab, and Jews against Palestinian Muslims and Christians in the Middle East. They led to massacres, mass kidnappings, forcible displacements, systematic rapes, and other acts of violence. Such situations also occurred in Europe. Greeks and Turks terrorized one another on Cyprus, as did Catholics and Protestants in Northern Ireland. Following the breakdown of Communist authority in the former Soviet Union and Eastern Europe, ethnic rivalries led to communal conflicts in many parts of the region.

In the 1990s, terrorism frequently stemmed from the efforts of militant Islamists to replace secular governments with Islamic rule. Terrorist attacks were directed also at Western nations that maintained supportive relationships with those secular regimes.

- *In your opinion, would the United States be justified in using terrorism to respond to terrorism? Explain.*

In the United States, Europe, and South Africa, right-wing ultranationalists have become another source of terrorist activity. Prominent among them have been the neo-Nazis. Their violence stems from racism and a desire to achieve the domination of white Christians over all other ethnic and religious groups. In philosophy and action, some of them identify with Nazi Germany's Third Reich (1933–45) of the World War II era. Hate crimes, including murder, assault, and vandalism, are their specialty. Their victims are immigrants, blacks, Hispanics, Asians, Jews, and others. Neo-Nazis and other right-wingers have alarmed law enforcement authorities and terrorism specialists because many are well armed and militaristic in training and organization. Some far-right groups have formed political parties in an attempt to gain power through democratic elections.

1. *Summarize some major examples of terrorism before 1945.*
2. *Match each victim of political assassination with his or her country.*

Column A	Column B
1. *Anwar Sadat*	a. *Lebanon*
2. *Indira Gandhi*	b. *Pakistan*
3. *Rashid Karami*	c. *Egypt*
4. *Muhammad Zia ul-Haq*	d. *India*

3. *Complete each sentence.*
   a. *In the early 1980s, 52 Americans were held hostage in ____.*
   b. *Militant Islamists seek to ____.*
   c. *Ultranationalists are often racists who seek the supremacy of ____.*
   d. *Neo-Nazis identify with the German ____ ____.*

A Case Study in Terrorism: The PLO

During the period of the Arab-Israeli wars, dozens of terrorist organizations stalked the Middle East. Chief among them was the *Palestine Liberation Organization* (PLO). The PLO was an umbrella organization, uniting many separate groups. It was formed at a summit conference of Arab leaders in January

1964. Its purpose was to direct the renewed nationalism of the Palestinians. They had been displaced as a result of the first Arab-Israeli war, which broke out upon the formation of the state of Israel in 1948, and of later wars between Israel and its Arab neighbors. The PLO's goal was to destroy Israel and gain political control of Palestine. In the attacks that it organized against Israel, terrorism played a large part.

During the Six-Day War of June 1967, Israel defeated the armies of Egypt, Syria, and Jordan. Conquest of the West Bank region and the Gaza Strip brought 1½ million Palestinians under Israeli rule. The PLO responded with a campaign of bombings inside Israel.

In February 1969, Yasir Arafat was elected chairman of the PLO. Arafat was the head of Fatah, the largest Palestinian guerrilla group. He brought Fatah and many other groups together under the Palestinian Armed Struggle Command. By 1970, this unified command included Fatah, the Popular Front for the Liberation of Palestine (PFLP), the Popular Front-General Command (PF-GC), the Democratic Front for the Liberation of Palestine (DFLP), Saiqa, and the Arab Liberation Front (ALF). Saiqa was sponsored by the government of Syria, while ALF was controlled by Iraq. These and other groups not connected to the PLO attacked all those they considered to be enemies of their cause. Such "enemies" included moderate Palestinians who favored a political solution to the Arab-Israeli conflict.

In 1972, PLO-backed terrorists killed 28 people and injured 72 at Lod International Airport in Tel Aviv. In the same year, the PLO's radical Black September faction sent a terrorist team to the summer Olympic games in Munich, Germany. Storming the Olympic Village, they murdered 11 Israeli athletes.

The PLO also established a representative body to discuss policy. At a 1974 conference in Morocco, leaders from across the Arab world declared the PLO to be "the sole legitimate representative of the Palestinian people." The leaders pledged to support the PLO in the struggle against Israel. That pledge was confirmed at another Arab summit conference in 1982. In that year, however, the PLO was driven out of its key bases in Lebanon by a massive invasion of Israeli forces. The PLO guerrillas scattered to North Yemen, Algeria, Sudan, Iraq, and Tunisia. Yasir Arafat established a new headquarters in Tunisia and vowed to continue the struggle against Israel.

In 1985, gunmen from a PLO-backed terrorist organization

attacked the ticket counters of El Al (Israel's airline) at the Rome and Vienna airports, murdering 18 people and injuring 111 more.

♦ *Describe the growth of the PLO as a terrorist organization.*

The PLO was weakened by its retreat from Lebanon; by the Israeli bombing of its headquarters in Tunisia in 1985; by the *intifada,* or uprising, of young Palestinians in Gaza and the West Bank, which began in 1987 without PLO support; and by the 1987 killing, by Israeli commandos, of Abu Jihad, Arafat's deputy and the chief planner of PLO terror attacks. Most of all, Arafat's approval of the 1990 Iraqi invasion of Kuwait cost the PLO the financial backing of Saudi Arabia and a number of other Arab states.

Before the Persian Gulf War, the PLO was able to fund medical services, educational activities, and welfare payments for the Palestinians in Gaza and the West Bank. The cutoff of aid from the wealthy Arab states forced the PLO to discontinue many of those services and caused it to lose support. A number of young Palestinians turned instead to the leadership of Hamas, a militant Islamist resistance movement.

The PLO also lost the support of other militant groups. The Fatah Revolutionary Command was suspected of killing Abu Iyad, another of Arafat's chief lieutenants, in 1991. The loss of allies was the result of a PLO decision, in 1988, to change tactics. In that year, Arafat promised that the PLO would no longer engage in terrorism and would accept the right of Israel to exist. The goal of the PLO became the establishment of a Palestinian state in the West Bank and Gaza, alongside Israel.

Since 1964, therefore, the PLO has evolved from an umbrella organization coordinating terrorist attacks on Israel into a political party with which most governments, including those of Israel and the United States, are willing to negotiate. Arafat signed important peace agreements with the Israeli government in 1993 and 1995. (See Chapter 4.) His reputation as a terrorist slowly faded. In 1994, Arafat shared the Nobel Peace Prize with Israeli Prime Minister Yitzhak Rabin and Israeli Foreign Minister Shimon Peres.

The transformation of the PLO in some ways reflected the changed nature of Middle Eastern terrorism in the 1990s. Groups like Hamas still staged terrorist attacks within Israel.

Indeed, the years 1994 and 1995 saw many suicide bombings that killed dozens of Israeli civilians. But terrorist groups were changing their goals and choosing new targets.

Some organizations, such as the PFLP, which long directed violence against Israel, concluded that terrorism would not work. Other groups grew extremely weak. They no longer had the support of Libya, Syria, and other Arab nations that were now seeking to improve their global image. More importantly, Arab leaders were concerned about the threat of militant Islamists to their own governments. Many terrorist groups of the 1990s focused on replacing secular Arab governments with Muslim fundamentalist regimes. In pursuit of this objective, militant Islamists struck at targets in the Arab world, Europe, and the United States. The fundamentalist regimes of Iran and Sudan were regarded as the key sponsors of the new terrorism.

1. *Explain how the development of the PLO, from 1964 to the present, reflected changes in the practice of terrorism in the Middle East.*
2. *PROVE or DISPROVE: In the 1990s, Hamas threatened the political base of the PLO and its claim as the "sole, legitimate representative of the Palestinian people."*
3. *For each year, state a development or event in the history of Middle Eastern terrorism:*

   1964, 1974, 1982, 1987, 1990, 1995

A Case Study in Ultranationalism: Germany's Extreme Right Wing

As the 1990s began, newly unified Germany faced great problems. High among them was the threat that neo-Nazis and other right-wingers posed to democracy. In 1992, officials of Chancellor Helmut Kohl's conservative government began branding the rightists as terrorists, to be treated as seriously as were the leftist assassins who had targeted industrialists and politicians in the 1970s and 1980s. Germany's federal prosecutor expressed the belief that the aim of the right-wingers was to reestablish a National Socialist (that is, Nazi) dictatorship.

During 1992, more than 2,000 right-wing extremist acts of

Sellers of Hate

violence were committed in Germany, including beatings of foreigners and firebombings of the homes of asylum seekers. Seventeen were murders. Of the dead, nine were Germans and eight foreigners. One of the victims was a ship's captain in the port city of Hamburg who was beaten to death after he stated that Adolf Hitler (Nazi dictator of Germany from 1933 to 1945) was a criminal.

According to German authorities, the initiators of those attacks were young men between the ages of 14 and 30. Some were unemployed. Others were apprentices or unskilled workers. Some were members of right-wing parties or cliques; others supported the beliefs of those groups. Many were skinheads, sharing a liking for shaved heads and heavy boots. And almost all were male. Although right-wing groups had female supporters, they were kept in the background. Right-wing extremists stressed the biological inequality of peoples, races, and the sexes.

Authorities believe that approximately 65,000 people in Germany have extreme right-wing beliefs. About 55,000 of those belong to the major parties of the extreme right. The largest far-right party is the German People's Union (DVU), with about 26,000 members. The oldest is the National Democratic Party of Germany (NPD), with about 5,000 members.

The NPD has existed for many years. The DVU, which is closely connected to the NPD, was founded in 1987 by Gerhard Frey, the publisher of the NPD newspaper. The most successful vote-getter on the far right is the Republican Party, with about 23,000 members. Founded in 1983, the Republican Party is led by Franz Schönhuber, a former member of the Nazi S.S. (The S.S. was the private army of Adolf Hitler and the most powerful organization in Hitler's Third Reich.)

Although far-right party leaders claim they are not Nazis, they support some of the basic ideas of Nazism. They are ultranationalistic and advocate subordination of individual rights to those of the nation. Many deny the crimes of the Nazis, claiming that the Holocaust (the murder of 6 million Jews and 3 million other Europeans during World War II) did not happen. They claim that Germans are racially superior. They make antiforeign and anti-Semitic statements. Although the party leaders do not advocate violence, critics accuse them of feeding an atmosphere of fear, hatred, and intolerance that encourages violence.

In addition to the political parties, Germany has several other neo-Nazi groups, some with fewer than 100 members. The estimated 6,400 militant ultranationalists in Germany who are prone to violence are to be found in those groups. Since the country's unification, in 1990, the violence-prone groups have grown.

Both the DVU and the Republican Party had some electoral success in the late 1980s and early 1990s. In 1989, the Republicans placed six deputies in the European Parliament, winning 7.1 percent of the German vote. However, support for the far-right parties shrank in the 1990s, partly out of revulsion against neo-Nazi violence. In the 1994 election of a new German Parliament, the Republicans received just 1.9 percent of the vote, far below the 5 percent that are necessary to qualify for seats.

1. *Discuss the role of ultranationalism in Germany in the 1990s.*
2. *State possible reasons for the increase in neo-Nazi activity after the 1990 unification of East and West Germany.*
3. *Identify each of the following:*
    a. *Helmut Kohl*
    b. *Gerhard Frey*
    c. *Franz Schönhuber*

Beyond Germany

Belgium. Ultranationalists are a threat to democracy and to international security—and not in Germany alone. Belgium has long been an international meeting place for right-wing extremists. Such groups are most active in the city of Antwerp. There, skinheads and neo-Nazis from all over Europe and the United States can purchase racist and Fascist literature, much of it outlawed in nations like Germany.

In Antwerp's city council elections of 1994, the ultranationalist Vlaams Blok (Flemish Bloc) got one third of the vote, leading all other parties. (The population of Belgium is divided into two main ethnic groups—Flemings and Walloons. Some Flemings, who are Germanic in origin, would like to separate from the more Latin Walloons and establish a country of their own. Should that happen, Belgium would cease to exist.) The ultranationalists were frozen out of the Antwerp city government, however, when other parties formed a coalition against the extremists. In Belgium's 1995 parliamentary elections, the Vlaams Blok won about 8 percent of the vote.

A leading Flemish ultranationalist is Filip De Winter, who has served in the Belgian parliament. De Winter's goal is to create a "Greater Netherlands" of Flanders (the Flemish part of Belgium) and Holland. To this end, he formed an alliance between Belgian right-wingers and two far-right groups in Holland. For years, De Winter's followers have interacted with Europe's most extreme right-wing organizations, including certain neo-Nazi groups banned in Germany. Under pressure from the Dutch and German governments, Belgium has begun to strengthen its antiracism laws.

In recent years, the Flemish ultranationalists have been guided in their political development by Jean-Marie Le Pen, leader of the right-wing National Front in neighboring France. During the 1980s and 1990s, the National Front built up a following by promoting antiforeign sentiment. In 1995, the National Front won control of its first local government, the city of Marignane in southern France. The new National Front mayor promised to give preference to French citizens in housing, municipal jobs, and social assistance.

Ultranationalism is also to be found beyond Europe. Neo-Nazi groups in the United States have committed a number of racially motivated murders in recent years, as well as acts of vandalism against synagogues and other targets. Members of organizations such as the Aryan Brotherhood and the Nation have been arrested by the FBI in connection with a variety of hate crimes directed against minority group members in government and the arts.

♦ *Explain why ultranationalists endanger democratic societies.*

Yugoslavia. Ultranationalism and racism played a part in the disintegration of Yugoslavia in the 1990s. Ethnic and religious hatreds in the Balkan region date back many centuries, to a time when the area was a battleground between the Muslim sultans of the Ottoman Empire and the Christian rulers of Europe. Atrocities committed in the 1400s are still fresh in memory—as are the more recent wrongs suffered during World War II. After Bosnian Serbs overran the U.N.-protected city of Srebrenica in 1995, 4,000 to 6,000 Bosnian Muslims were reported missing. Satellite photos showed large mounds of freshly turned soil nearby, and U.S. leaders suggested that Bosnian Serbs had shot and buried many of the missing. Bosnian Serbs made their own accusations of mass murder against their Croatian and Muslim enemies.

South Africa. In South Africa, white ultranationalists sowed terror during the transition to black rule—and could do so again. F. W. De Klerk was president of South Africa and head of the National Party during the early 1990s. He put an end to apartheid and negotiated an end to white rule. To some white South Africans, that made De Klerk a traitor. Other whites, including members of the National Party and of the Afrikaner-based Conservative Party, cooperated in the transition.

Fighting tooth and nail against such cooperation was the Afrikaner Resistance Movement (AWB). Led by Eugene Terre-'Blanche, the AWB is a racist, neo-Nazi organization that now demands an Afrikaner state within the new South Africa. In July 1993, members of the AWB staged an armed assault on a multiparty conference at the Johannesburg World Trade Center. Conservative Party leaders apologized to the black delegates who were brutalized and insulted by the white intruders. AWB members were also blamed for a series of terrorist bombings that killed at least 20 people in the run-up to the 1994 election that confirmed the transition to majority rule. Shortly before that election, the AWB had an estimated 18,000 members. However, membership later dropped. After Nelson Mandela took over as South Africa's president, mainstream right-wing leaders began to shun Terre'Blanche and his extremist movement.

1. *State two examples of ultranationalism in areas beyond Germany.*
2. *Identify each of the following:*
   a. *Filip De Winter*
   b. *Jean-Marie Le Pen*
   c. *Eugene Terre'Blanche*
3. *Explain why you AGREE or DISAGREE with each of the following statements.*
   a. *The neo-Nazis of today threaten world peace, as did the Nazis of the World War II era.*
   b. *Germany is the only country in which neo-Nazism exists.*
   c. *The hate generated by neo-Nazis and other ultranationalists leads to violence and threatens international security.*
   d. *The neo-Nazis of today have no resemblance to the Nazis of the World War II era.*
   e. *Neo-Nazis share many of the beliefs of the original Nazis.*

Chapter 10 Review

A. *On your answer sheet, write the letter of the correct response.*

1. *Terrorism and ultranationalism are similar in that both (a) use violence to pursue their goals (b) lead to the formation of political parties (c) are always successful in achieving their goals.*
2. *The 1995 bombing of a building in Oklahoma City led to the arrest of (a) members of the Afrikaner Resistance Movement (b) followers of Sheik Omar Abdel Rahman (c) a former U.S. soldier.*
3. *A movement that gave up a campaign of terrorism was run by (a) Tamils in Sri Lanka (b) Quebec separatists in Canada (c) Basque separatists in Spain.*
4. *A national leader assassinated by terrorists was (a) Chancellor Helmut Kohl of Germany (b) President F. W. De Klerk of South Africa (c) Prime Minister Indira Gandhi of India.*
5. *Militant Islamists have attempted to overthrow the governments of (a) Egypt and Algeria (b) Libya and Sudan (c) Sri Lanka and Japan.*

6. *Two nations whose governments have been accused of supporting Islamist terrorism are (a) Algeria and Liberia (b) Jordan and Lebanon (c) Iran and Sudan.*

7. *Until 1988, the goal of the PLO was (a) to become the dominant power in the Middle East (b) the destruction of Israel (c) support of Islamic fundamentalism.*

8. *A problem faced by Yasir Arafat in the 1990s was (a) loss of financial support from several Arab governments (b) a challenge to PLO leadership by Hamas (c) both of the previous.*

9. *European neo-Nazis and other ultranationalists were responsible for violence against (a) immigrants and asylum seekers (b) former officials of the Third Reich (c) Red Army Faction terrorists.*

10. *The goal of some Flemish ultranationalists is (a) formation of a closer union between Flemish and Walloon sections of Belgium (b) union between Flanders and France (c) union between Flanders and Holland.*

B. *Reread "Recent Events Around the World," on pages 200–203. Then write an essay on terrorism in Europe by answering the following questions:*

1. *Why were these terrorist attacks carried out and by whom?*
2. *How did these attacks differ in location, method, and purpose?*
3. *Why did these terrorist actions lead to demands for government action?*

C. *Review "Recent Events Around the World" on pages 200–203. Then indicate on your answer sheet which statements are* true *and which are* false.

1. *In 1993, the kind of terrorism practiced elsewhere in the world was brought to the United States.*
2. *European neo-Nazis bombed the World Trade Center and planned to bomb the United Nations in New York City.*
3. *Among those arrested by the FBI was Sheik Omar Abdel Rahman, a Muslim cleric.*
4. *The events of the 1990s prove that terrorists are no threat to American cities.*
5. *Recent events indicate that terrorists have the ability to strike even in the heart of a nation that is at peace.*

Unit II Review

A. *Use information from this unit to explain the problems of peace-keeping in each of the following areas:*

1. *former Yugoslavia*
2. *the Middle East*
3. *Africa*
4. *Asia*

B. *Review Chapter 8, ''The Struggle to Keep the Peace,'' on pages 159–175. Then indicate whether the statements below are true or false.*

1. *Countries that contribute soldiers to U.N. peacekeeping missions run the risk of subjecting those soldiers to combat.*
2. *By 1995, Poland, Hungary, and the Czech Republic had been granted full NATO membership.*
3. *The Organization of American States supported efforts to restore Jean-Bertrand Aristide to power in Haiti.*
4. *The Organization of African Unity successfully negotiated solutions to conflicts in Somalia, Sudan, and Angola.*
5. *The Arab League coordinated military, diplomatic, and economic actions against Israel.*

C. *Review Chapter 9, ''Human Rights: Issues and Problems,'' on pages 178–195. Then write an essay of two or three paragraphs about ONE of the following:*

1. *The 1993 World Conference on Human Rights*
2. *Immigrants in Europe and America*
3. *Advances in Women's Rights*
4. *Is Basic Health Care a Human Right?*

D. *Review Chapter 10, ''Terrorists and Ultranationalists Threaten International Security,'' on pages 199-215. Then PROVE or DISPROVE the following statements:*

1. *Terrorism and ultranationalism are equally dangerous to world peace.*
2. *Neo-Nazism is a force which operates only in Germany.*
3. *In the 1990s, terrorism has been mainly a Middle Eastern problem.*

4. *Concerns about ethnicity and religion have been causes of both terrorism and ultranationalism.*
5. *Terrorism and ultranationalism have never affected the United States.*

UNIT III

THE GLOBAL ECONOMY

Next time you buy something, check the label. You may be surprised to see the name of a small and faraway land. Many of the products on U.S. store shelves come from nations that have only recently entered the world economy. Many once-obscure nations now sell their products all over the world.

The economy of the 1990s is increasingly a global one. Nations are coming together in alliances to build economic strength. They are coordinating their policies and sharing their resources. By doing this, they find they can stimulate investment and compete more effectively with nations from other regions.

Chapter 11

Economic Organization: Global and Regional

The Group of Seven

"There's a world economic crisis looming? Who's in charge?"

"Try calling the G-7."

No, G-7 is not an intelligence agency or a private detective's office. It is an organization of the world's seven leading industrial nations: "the Group of Seven," to be exact. Member nations are Britain, Canada, France, Germany, Italy, Japan, and the United States. Those nations' top leaders have been holding annual meetings every year since 1975 in an attempt to keep the global economy humming and to coordinate actions on other matters. They have had successes and they have had failures. Says Robert D. Putnam, a professor of government at Harvard: "If the Seven don't talk, it's a more dangerous world."

At recent meetings, the G-7 has grappled with issues raised by rapid changes in the way money moves around the world. On a weekday evening when people in San Francisco are getting ready for bed, businesses in Tokyo are well into their next workday. Before going to bed, a San Franciscan in pajamas can sit down at a computer, check the prices on the Tokyo stock market, and instruct a broker to buy shares in a Japanese company. Before dawn in San Francisco, the transaction will be completed. Likewise, someone in Japan or Hong Kong can place overnight orders on U.S. stock or currency markets. (Currency markets are where, for example, U.S. dollars are traded for Japanese yen.) Like your neighborhood convenience store, some of the world's financial markets stay open 24 hours a day.

All this means that a financial crisis in one country can make waves around the world in hours, if not minutes. Every 24 hours, $1 trillion changes hands on the world's currency markets. That total is four times greater than it was in the 1980s. A trillion dollars is a lot of money to be moving back and forth. Sometimes it moves too fast and turns a small crisis into a big one, or a big crisis into an even bigger one.

That's what happened in December 1994, when Mexico ran out of places to borrow money to meet its debt payments. News of Mexico's dilemma sent the value of the Mexican peso into a nosedive. Eager to sell before the price fell any lower, investors and banks that held Mexican pesos dumped them onto the currency market. But of course that just forced the price down even more. When institutions like the International Monetary Fund (IMF) could not raise enough money to rescue the Mexican government, the United States helped to arrange a multibillion-dollar loan. But that addressed only Mexico's immediate crisis, not a future one that might be just as bad, or worse.

At the next G-7 summit in Halifax, Canada, in June 1995, leaders tried to work out better ways of dealing with such crises. The G-7 leaders issued a statement that said, in part:

> The world economy has changed beyond all recognition over the last fifty years. The process of globalization, driven by technological change, has led to increased economic interdependence. . . . The prevention of crisis . . . requires an improved early-warning system, so that we can act more quickly to prevent or handle economic shocks.

The leaders proposed creating a new emergency source of funds so that the IMF could act quickly in any future crisis.

The issues addressed by the G-7 reflect the key global concerns of the 1990s. Foremost among them are efforts to lower tariffs in order to stimulate world trade, prevent recessions (or at least keep their effects from spreading), reduce chronic unemployment, promote human rights, limit nuclear proliferation, and find solutions to political crises, such as the war in Bosnia.

Although Russia is not a member of the Group of Seven, its president has been invited to sit in on some of the group's discussions. During the early 1990s, the G-7 took on the task of rescuing the Russian economy. In pursuit of that goal, G-7 members chipped in billions of dollars in aid to Russia. At other sessions, the G-7 put pressure on Japan and the United States to change some of their policies. The issue with Japan was trade. Japan was running up huge trade surpluses with Europe and North America. Other G-7 members urged it to buy more from those regions to restore a balance. The issue with the United States was its huge federal budget deficits. Other G-7 members pressed the U.S. to balance its budget.

The discussions held at the G-7's annual conferences reflect the economic interdependence of nations in the 1990s. To achieve prosperity, countries must cooperate and coordinate their policies through a variety of international and regional organizations.

1. *What sorts of changes have led the G-7 to say that the world is more interdependent than ever before?*
2. *Explain why you AGREE or DISAGREE: The G-7 is needed to help resolve problems in the world economy.*
3. *Research the Group of Seven in your school library. Find its strengths and weaknesses. List ways in which the G-7 could be made better at solving problems.*

The World Bank

Stimulating economic growth in developing nations by means of loans and advice is the function of the *World Bank*. Created after World War II, the World Bank became the largest single source of lending for development. Between 1947 and 1990, the funds lent to nations in Asia, Latin America, the Middle East, and Africa totaled $186 billion. Those loans were granted mainly to higher-income developing countries, because such borrowers are regarded as more creditworthy.

Three other organizations work with the World Bank. Collectively they are known as the World Bank Group.

- The *International Development Association* (IDA) was set up in 1960. It provides loans for up to 40 years, with a ten-year grace period and no interest, to the poorest countries. The IDA gets its capital from the World Bank and from periodic donations from wealthy countries.

- The *International Finance Corporation* (IFC), founded in 1956, has the mission of spreading private enterprise across the world. It assists developing countries in attracting investors. The IFC uses its own funds to mobilize the financing of projects by other investors and lenders.
- The *Multilateral Investment Guarantee Agency* (MIGA) was established in 1988. Its job is to stimulate the flow of foreign investment to developing nations by providing guarantees against political risk such as armed conflict and civil war, nationalization and expropriation, restrictions on currency transfer, and breaches of contract by host governments.

The World Bank is owned by its 180 member nations. They provide its basic financing. All powers of the World Bank are vested in a board of governors, consisting of one governor from each member country. As that body meets only once a year, most of its authority is delegated to a 22-member board of executive directors who meet in permanent session at the headquarters of the bank in Washington, D.C. Shares in the bank determine voting power. With 45 percent of the shares, the G-7 nations control the World Bank.

The United States has enjoyed a dominant role in the leadership of the World Bank. All presidents of the bank have been Americans selected by the U.S. president. That has not prevented the bank from making loans to nations regarded by the United States as unsuitable or for projects not favored by the United States. However, the bank has undertaken no major programs or initiatives without American approval.

Lately, the World Bank has supplemented its own lending by helping nations to find private sources of capital. As recently as 1990, World Bank and other official development aid exceeded private investment in developing countries. By the mid-1990s, private investment was more than three times larger than official aid.

1. *Explain the purpose of the World Bank.*
2. *PROVE or DISPROVE: The programs of the World Bank are totally controlled by the United States.*
3. *Examine the table and answer the questions that follow.*

Table 11.1. The World Bank's Largest Borrowers: Cumulative Lending through June 1990 (Amounts in US $ billions)

Loans		IDA Credits		Total Financing	
1. India	$18.32	1. India	$16.96	1. India	$35.27
2. Brazil	17.98	2. Bangladesh	5.25	2. Brazil	17.98
3. Mexico	17.36	3. China	3.93	3. Mexico	17.36
4. Indonesia	14.83	4. Pakistan	3.24	4. Indonesia	15.76
5. Turkey	10.16	5. Tanzania	1.77	5. Turkey	10.34
6. South Korea	7.15	6. Ghana	1.45	6. Pakistan	7.41
7. Philippines	6.75	7. Kenya	1.40	7. South Korea	7.26
8. Colombia	6.53	8. Sudan	1.34	8. Philippines	6.87
9. Yugoslavia	5.81	9. Sri Lanka	1.32	9. Colombia	6.55
10. Nigeria	5.59	10. Ethiopia	1.26	10. Nigeria	5.85
11. China	5.28	11. Uganda	1.09	11. Yugoslavia	5.81
12. Morocco	5.18	12. Zaire	1.06	12. Morocco	5.23
13. Argentina	5.12	13. Nepal	1.06	13. Argentina	5.12
14. Thailand	4.19	14. Madagascar	1.00	14. Thailand	4.31
15. Pakistan	4.18	15. Egypt	0.98	15. Egypt	4.10

a. Between 1947, when lending began, and 1990, the Asian nation that benefited most from World Bank loans was ____.

b. The African nation that got the most total financing from the World Bank through 1990 was ____.

c. In Latin America, ____ borrowed $6.53 billion from the World Bank.

d. The African nation that received $1.06 billion in IDA credits was ____.

The International Monetary Fund

The work of the *International Monetary Fund* (IMF) has been closely connected to that of the World Bank. Established in 1944, the IMF was designed to oversee the global rules governing money and to ensure orderly currency arrangements among the industrial nations. It also was intended to be a lender of last resort for rich and poor nations alike. Through the years, however, the role of the IMF has changed. Today, its primary mission is to assist faltering economies in the Third World. Its aid comes with conditions, though, since the IMF requires that nations first open their economies to free market forces. Also, it insists on cutting budget deficits, which often means sharp cuts in social programs.

The IMF's policies are highly controversial. Critics call the IMF a tool of the industrial and capitalist nations. They say the IMF's insistence on strict free market policies exposes Third World economies to greedy international corporations, corruption, social unrest, and political instability. Supporters of the IMF admit that free market remedies can cause pain at first. However, they argue that developing nations will benefit in the long run by building healthier, more competitive economies.

In the 1990s, the IMF supervised economic reform programs in more than 50 countries. The countries included Russia, other former Soviet republics, and the nations of Eastern Europe. The IMF guided the development of capitalism in those countries as they moved away from Communist-style central planning to free market economic systems.

In Russia, a conflict developed between IMF officials and the government of President Boris Yeltsin over the decontrol of energy prices and the reduction of subsidies to state-owned businesses. The IMF wanted a faster rate of progress than the Russians were willing to provide at first. Finally, to control inflation and qualify for a large IMF loan, President Yeltsin's government raised interest rates by 170 percent in 1993. In

Strict Teacher

another effort to increase foreign aid from the IMF and Western investors, the Russians reduced the amount of money in circulation by declaring pre-1993 rubles invalid. By the mid-1990s, those and other measures seemed to be having the desired effect. After Russian economic output shrank to half its former size from 1991 to 1995, it began to grow again. A government minister predicted a yearly growth rate of 10 to 12 percent by the end of the decade.

The strict conditions set by the IMF for loans and the closeness with which the conditions are monitored have created tensions between the IMF and the developing nations. To qualify for an IMF loan, a borrower must agree to IMF requirements for economic reform and restructuring. Failure to carry out such measures usually results in suspension of the loan. A $10.2 billion IMF loan to Russia was made dependent on continuing economic reform.

In the 1980s, recessions in industrial countries left many Third World nations unable to pay their debts to foreign investors. That was the case in Latin America and sub-Saharan Africa. By the 1990s, the task of financing debt-reduction schemes and managing the global debt crisis involved the IMF in many complex problems and resulted in record amounts owed to the IMF by debtor nations in the Third World.

Like the World Bank, the IMF is controlled by the wealthy nations, especially the United States, France, Britain, Germany, Japan, and Saudi Arabia. Those and other nations provide the financial resources of the IMF in accordance with a quota assigned to each member country. Each member government is represented on the board of governors. The board delegates many of its powers to 22 executive directors in Washington. The managing director is usually a European.

1. *List the purposes of the International Monetary Fund.*
2. *What conditions does the IMF attach to its assistance?*

World Trade Groups

From 1948 to 1995, the main international framework for organizing world trade was the *General Agreement on Tariffs and Trade* (GATT). It gave way in 1995 to a new body called the *World Trade Organization* (WTO).

General Agreement on Tariffs and Trade. GATT was created at a time when tariff barriers erected during the Great Depression of the 1930s were limiting world trade. It aimed to expand world trade by reducing such barriers. The WTO serves a similar purpose. However, it goes beyond GATT in trying to open up trade in services (for example, banking and insurance) as well as trade in goods.

How did GATT work? First of all, it set rules governing certain aspects of global trade. For example, GATT required each member nation to treat all other members equally. This rule was known as the most-favored-nation clause. Under this clause, if Country A granted a trade benefit to Country B, it had to extend the same benefit automatically to all other member countries. In other words, each nation had the same benefits as the most-favored nation. The same rule is applied by the WTO. It aims to level the trading field and make global trade freer for all.

Second, GATT provided its 125 member nations with a forum for striking deals and settling disputes on trade. The last and most far-reaching achievement of GATT was a seven-year period of trade negotiations known as the *Uruguay Round.* The Uruguay Round ended in 1994 with the signing of an agreement to chop tariffs on imports by an average of 40 percent. The 1994 pact was the first GATT agreement to cover such areas as agriculture, textiles, and financial services. The agreement was so full of details and footnotes that it filled the equivalent of four big-city phone books.

Although GATT was a global organization, it had a small secretarial staff and a tiny budget. One of its major functions was to settle disputes. To do this, it relied upon expert panels to handle complaints about rule violations. The process was slow, and the findings of the panels were not binding. The WTO is more powerful. It can assess trade penalties against member nations found to have broken its rules.

GATT specialized in conference diplomacy. It staged eight successive rounds of multilateral trade negotiations. The first six rounds, held between the late 1940s and the 1960s, led to a dramatic decline in tariff barriers and a major increase in world trade. In the 1970s and 1980s, however, the industrial nations practiced a greater degree of protectionism. The causes of this trend were rising energy costs, periodic recessions, and increasing competition from newly industrialized nations. The United States, Japan, and other nations used tariffs and other means to protect endangered industries. Evasion of the most-favored-nation rule for a wide range of industries and products placed a growing amount of world trade beyond the authority of GATT.

The Uruguay Round, which was the eighth and last, turned back the tide of protectionism. It also opened the subject of trade in services. Services represent the fastest growing area of world trade. They include banking, insurance, telecommunications, construction, aviation, shipping, tourism, advertising, and broadcasting. Setting up global rules for them is expected to go on for decades. Negotiators in the Uruguay Round failed to reach agreement on free trade rules involving movies, television programs, and music; civil aircraft; and shipping and financial services like stock brokerage and banking. Talks continued on those subjects.

Developing nations, which had only limited involvement in previous GATT discussions, participated fully in the Uruguay Round. However, many of them were unhappy with the results. By one estimate, African nations stood to lose $2.6 billion a year under the 1994 agreement. In part, that was because the Uruguay agreement required Europe and the United States to cut subsidies (government aid) to farmers. That was expected to lead to higher prices for foods like wheat and corn that African nations import. At the same time, however, the liberalized trade rules were expected to result in stiffer competition (and thus lower prices) for income-producing African crops such as coffee and cocoa.

The World Trade Organization. The World Trade Organization opened with a staff of 450 people. Its headquarters are in Geneva, Switzerland. Most GATT members joined the new organization, but some key nations were not on the initial membership list. Both Russia and China, for example, were absent, although they applied for membership and began negotiating terms.

The WTO's underlying principles are essentially the same as GATT's. Beyond the equal-treatment (or most-favored-nation) clause, key principles are:

- **Encouraging development.** The WTO has looser rules for developing nations than for industrial nations.
- **Opening greater access to markets.** The WTO continues GATT's emphasis on negotiating lower tariffs. Most forms of *quotas* (specific limits or targets for imports or exports) are forbidden.

Taking Down Barriers

- **Promoting fair competition.** Dumping and subsidies are considered unfair forms of competition. *Dumping* is selling a product or service at below its actual cost. If a nation violates a rule against dumping or subsidies, other nations can impose special "compensating tariffs" on that nation's exports.

One of the WTO's first accomplishments was a 1995 agreement to further liberalize trade in financial services. The WTO has also promised to address the environmental impact of trade liberalization.

1. *Explain the purpose of GATT.*
2. *How does the WTO differ from GATT?*
3. *How did the Uruguay Round change world trade?*
4. *How was the 1994 GATT agreement different from earlier ones?*

The European Union

So far we have discussed organizations that are more or less global in scope. But the interdependence of nations has led to the rise of regional economic bodies as well. One of the oldest and most successful of these bodies is the 15-nation European Union (EU).

The European Union traces its roots to 1957, when six nations organized the *European Community* (EC), or *Common Market*. From the first, the goal was to encourage economic cooperation among the industrial countries of the region by eliminating trade barriers to form a single market. The EC expanded over the years and became a major world economic force. By 1986 it had 12 members—Belgium, Denmark, France, Germany, Greece, Ireland, Italy, Luxembourg, the Netherlands, Portugal, Spain, and the United Kingdom. In 1995, Austria, Sweden, and Finland joined, boosting membership to 15.

The EC became the European Union when it adopted measures that carried it beyond the status of a common market. The biggest changes resulted from a treaty that the community's member nations signed in 1992 in the Dutch city of Maastricht. The *Maastricht Treaty* (or Treaty on European Union) provided for an economic union, to be achieved by the removal of almost all barriers to the free movement across borders of people, goods, and services. The treaty also committed members to establish a single European currency by 1999, and to coordinate foreign and defense policies. Creation of a single market, with provision for admitting new member nations, was intended to continue the process of strengthening

Figure 11.1 The European Union

Western Europe economically, while creating more political unity. A key goal was increased ability to compete with the United States and Japan, the commercial rivals of the European nations.

Many supporters of a strong union viewed the treaty as an important step toward a federal Europe. The treaty increased the powers of the community's institutions, especially the executive offices in Brussels, Belgium. However, many Europeans feared just such a development. They worried that stronger European institutions would undermine the sovereignty of individual nations. Britain was the leader of go-slow forces that did not want the European Union to gain too much power.

Lively debates over the treaty delayed ratification in some countries. A variety of problems complicated the national debates. Chief among them were economic recession and rising unemployment, growing intolerance of Third World immigrants, demands for greater trade protectionism, and polls showing low levels of popularity for many European leaders. Those problems made the pursuit of economic and political union more difficult. In the end, however, all member nations accepted the Maastricht Treaty.

- *List some of the obstacles to approval of the Maastricht Treaty.*

The decision to create a single European currency stirred strong feelings in many countries. Would it mean an end to the British pound, the French franc, the German mark, and other national currencies? That seemed likely, as EU bureaucrats began to make plans for printing the new European money. EU leaders debated what to call the new currency. "The Euro" was the most popular of the names suggested. Each nation might have its own version—the "Euro-Franc" and the "Euro-Mark," for example.

But putting a monetary union into effect posed a major challenge. First, the EU nations would have to meet strict rules on national debts and budget deficits. Only a handful of nations were expected to be ready to start using the new currency in 1999. Others would have to begin later.

Many nations have applied to join the EU. The union had expected Norway to come in with the three countries that entered in 1995. However, Norwegian voters rejected membership in a 1994 referendum. One of the EU's most persistent applicants has been Turkey, a predominantly Muslim country that straddles the border between Europe and Asia. Turkey first applied in 1987. For years the EU discouraged Turkey, saying that country was not yet ready economically and was not democratic enough. However, in 1995, EU leaders agreed to let Turkey move closer to membership by entering a customs union, allowing free trade between Turkey and the EU. Turkey's application for full membership remained on the agenda.

The EU has also offered greater market access for the Czech Republic, Slovakia, Poland, Hungary, Romania, and Bulgaria. But negotiations on a trade agreement between the EU and Russia became deadlocked. Several EU members felt threatened by competition from lower priced steel, textiles, and farm products produced in Eastern Europe. However, most believed that the EU had to grow if it was to develop the coordinated policies necessary to compete successfully with the United States and Japan. The European Union planned to conduct negotiations on full membership for several East European nations.

Whichever nations eventually join the EU, trade within Europe is likely to become freer. In January 1994, the EU and several neighboring nations formed a 19-nation *European Economic Area* (EEA). The EEA became the world's largest trading bloc. It sought to promote freer trade among its members without the commitment to political unity that was part of the EU.

The institutions of the European Union have become more democratic over the years. On major issues, the final say still rests with the governments of individual nations, and the larger nations have the most power. But the people of EU countries have a voice too, through the European Parliament, which meets in Strasbourg, France.

The European Parliament is the legislative body of the European Union. Its members are elected every five years. With the enlargement of the EU to 15 nations, there are now 626 members of the European Parliament. The number elected from each country depends on its population. However, in the legislative chamber, members are seated by party, not by nationality. In the European Parliament that was elected in 1994, the Socialists and the European People's Party (composed of conservatives and Christian Democrats) were the largest groups.

The parliament has authority over the budget of the EU. And it can pass laws that apply to all EU nations. A Council of Ministers, composed of ministers representing the governments of the member nations, must approve all laws and budgetary decisions. There is also a 20-member European Commission, which acts as the executive branch of the EU. It is responsible for carrying out the laws and decisions of the council and the parliament. Under the Maastricht Treaty, the parliament gained the power to approve or reject candidates nominated by the council as members of the European commission. The parliament must also approve the appointment of the commission's president.

Another EU organization, the *European Monetary Institute* (EMI), began operations in 1994. The EMI is eventually to become a European Central Bank. As the regulator of banks in the EU and the single European currency, it will be one of the most powerful of EU bodies. The EMI has its headquarters in Frankfurt, Germany.

1. *State the purpose of the European Union.*
2. *List the member nations of the EU.*
3. *Complete each sentence:*
   a. *The Maastricht Treaty is also called the_____.*
   b. *Among the difficult problems faced by the EU in the 1990s were _____.*
   c. *A member nation that does not want the EU to gain too much power is _____.*
   d. *In 1999, some EU countries are expected to introduce a common _____.*
   e. *Three functions of the European Parliament are to _____.*
4. *Jacques Delor, a Belgian diplomat, was one of the EU leaders in the early 1990s. Research Delor's life. Find out what role he played in the EU and why he was a controversial figure.*

The Organization of Petroleum Exporting Countries (OPEC)

The *Organization of Petroleum Exporting Countries* (OPEC) was founded in 1960. By the 1970s it included most major petroleum-exporting countries. OPEC was mostly concerned at first with trying to gain more profits for its members. To do this, it pressed foreign companies to give up control of oil production facilities to host countries, mainly in the Middle East and North Africa. As OPEC countries gained control of production, they also acquired the power to manipulate oil prices.

Rapid price increases during and after 1974 led to higher profits for the OPEC nations. Higher prices provided the oil producing nations an incentive to explore and develop new sources of oil. With new sources, the supply of oil increased. That drove down prices in the early 1980s. Since then, OPEC has used production quotas to limit the market supply and stabilize prices. Saudi Arabia, the largest and most influential oil producer, has encouraged this policy.

In the 1990s, changes in the oil market and in the Middle East began to affect the status of OPEC. The capacity of OPEC members to expand oil production, for example, is now largely confined to the nations surrounding the Persian Gulf. Also, the discovery of new, non-OPEC oil sources and the substitution of alternatives to oil (gas, coal, nuclear energy) have weakened OPEC's power. In addition, Iraq's possible reentry into the oil market had the potential to cause a new decline in oil prices.

OPEC members often argue about whether to reduce oil output to stabilize prices. The dilemma is this: While OPEC as a group wants to hold production steady in order to maintain the stability of prices, individual OPEC countries want to increase their own output in order to increase their revenues. OPEC sets quotas for its member nations, but the quotas are often violated.

1. *State the purpose of OPEC and explain its importance as an organization.*
2. *List two reasons why OPEC might not be as powerful in the 1990s as it was in the 1970s.*

The North American Free Trade Agreement (NAFTA)

As Europe moves toward economic unity and the establishment of a single market, similar efforts have started in the Americas. In 1991, the governments of Canada, the United States, and Mexico negotiated the *North American Free Trade Agreement* (NAFTA). This agreement aims to eliminate, within 15 years, tariffs and other trade barriers among the three nations. The

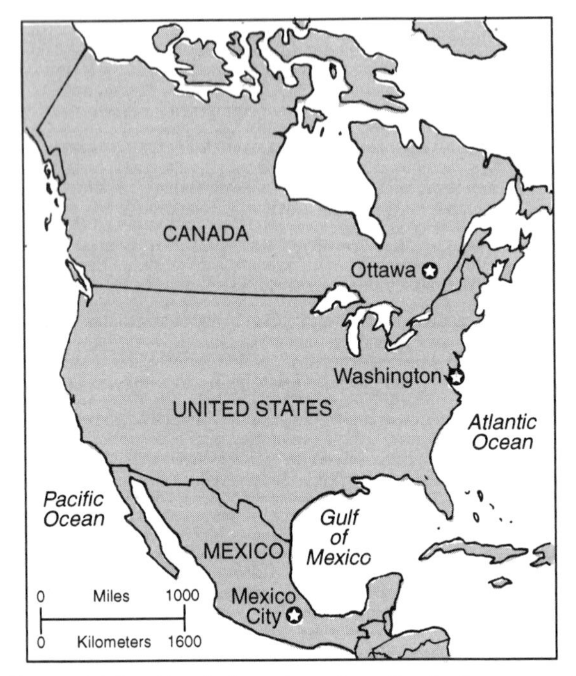

Figure 11.2 North American Free Trade Agreement

first tariff reductions went into effect in 1994. NAFTA will eventually create a single market of more than 380 million people.

In the United States, NAFTA stirred up a lively debate before Congress voted its approval in November 1993. Supporters said a North American free trade area was necessary if the region was to compete with the European Union and other regional economic blocs. They argued that free trade under NAFTA would enable the United States, Mexico, and Canada to make their economies more efficient. In each nation, the most competitive industries would grow, because they would have access to larger markets. Supporters also argued that NAFTA would expand U.S. exports, create high-technology jobs in the United States, promote democratic reforms (and thus political stability) in Mexico, and reduce illegal immigration from Mexico to the United States. The administrations of Presidents George Bush and Bill Clinton both strongly supported NAFTA.

Opposition to the pact came from several quarters. Labor unions argued that NAFTA would encourage U.S. companies to move factories to Mexico, where wages were much lower. (In a notable image, third-party presidential candidate H. Ross Perot spoke of "the giant sucking sound" of U.S. jobs going south.) Environmentalists argued that Mexico would lure away U.S. industries by offering an escape from U.S. antipollution laws. They also warned that Congress would weaken U.S. environmental laws in response. The legislatures of several states passed resolutions hostile to NAFTA. Claims were made that NAFTA would overturn state laws like a Minnesota program to promote local farm products, since such laws could be seen as interfering with free trade. Others said that the freedom of Congress to pass laws on environmental and consumer issues might be impeded by the need to conform to NAFTA's free trade rules.

Changes were added to NAFTA to meet some of the critics' concerns. One change created a U.S. "safety net" to help people who lost jobs as a result of the agreement. The safety net extended unemployment benefits for up to a year and provided training for new jobs. Another change aimed to enforce compliance with environmental standards.

In both Canada and Mexico, similar debates took place. Critics claimed that NAFTA would expose the two countries to invasion by U.S. multinational companies and undermine their political sovereignty. In reply, NAFTA supporters argued that the pact would sharpen the competitive edge of all three North American countries. Without NAFTA, it was argued, the region could not stand up to the fierce competition from Europe, Japan, and the industrializing nations of the Third World.

- *Describe the arguments made in the United States for and against NAFTA.*

Once NAFTA went into effect, the debate shifted to who had been right—supporters or critics. But answers were not immediately available. The Joint Economic Committee of Congress declared: "It will take at least five to ten years for the full effects of the agreement to [become clear]."

It was obvious, however, that NAFTA was making a mark. Just ask the workers who used to make Nintendo game machines in Redmond, Washington. Soon after NAFTA went into effect, Nintendo announced it was moving the factory to Mexico. However, NAFTA also got credit for creating new jobs. For example, a small company that made thermometers in Middlefield, Connecticut, hired more workers when it doubled its sales to Mexico during NAFTA's first year. The removal of

Fair Trade?

a 20 percent tariff on thermometers made the company's products cheaper to Mexican buyers, and sales went up.

The job of measuring the effects of NAFTA became more complicated when Mexico's economy took a nosedive in December 1994. Over a six-week period, the Mexican currency, the peso, dropped from a value of 29 U.S. cents to 17 U.S. cents for one peso. That meant that Mexican wages, already low by U.S. standards, became relatively even lower. It also meant that Mexicans' pesos would buy far fewer imported goods than before. During 1994, the U.S. sold $1.3 billion more to Mexico than it bought from Mexico. But the peso crisis reversed the flow. During most of 1995, U.S. exports to Mexico ran more than $1 billion lower *per month* than Mexican exports to the United States.

Almost before the ink was dry on the NAFTA accord, U.S. officials began talking about enlarging the free trade area. One proposal envisioned a Western Hemisphere free trade zone stretching from Canada to Chile and Argentina. Another proposal looked eastward, to link the United States, Canada, and Mexico with European nations. Still another would form closer economic ties between the United States and Asian and Pacific nations.

U.S. leaders put the greatest emphasis on Latin America. A

summit of Latin American leaders in Miami in December 1994 agreed to start negotiations immediately over the details of a hemispheric trade zone. The leaders set a target date of 2005 for signing a treaty. As the conference's host, President Clinton spoke out strongly in favor of a Western Hemisphere accord. "When our work is done," he said, "the free trade area of the Americas will stretch from Alaska to Argentina. In less than a decade, if current trends continue, this hemisphere will be the world's largest market." In anticipation of the wider accord, U.S. officials began negotiations with Chile, hoping it might become a fourth member of NAFTA. Chile underwent free market reforms in the 1970s and 1980s. It has had a booming economy for more than a decade.

1. *Tell why you AGREE or DISAGREE: The North American Free Trade Agreement has already begun to improve Americans' lives.*
2. *State one reason why Mexicans or Canadians might welcome NAFTA and one reason why they might fear it.*
3. *Indicate which of the following statements are true and which are false.*
   a. *NAFTA was first negotiated by the administration of U.S. President George Bush.*
   b. *Critics argued that NAFTA could have bad effects on the environment.*
   c. *The issue of state sovereignty caused some Americans to oppose NAFTA.*
   d. *Mexican workers earn lower average wages than U.S. workers.*
   e. *NAFTA gives Canadians increased access to Mexican and U.S. markets for their products.*

4. *Compare NAFTA to the EU. How are they similar? How are they different? How do both organizations reflect global economic trends in the 1990s?*

Chapter 11 Review

A. *On your answer sheet, write the letter of the correct response.*

1. *At the Halifax Conference of 1995, the Group of Seven agreed upon (a) tariff increases on selected products (b) greater*

protectionism for their industries (c) a new emergency source of funds for the IMF.

2. *A nation that is not a member of the G-7 is (a) Italy (b) Russia (c) Japan.*
3. *During the Uruguay Round, GATT attempted to (a) increase the pace at which capitalism developed in formerly Communist nations (b) encourage social welfare programs in the least developed nations (c) increase global trade through liberalized trading rules.*
4. *A concern of the World Bank in the 1990s has been (a) reducing the influence of the United States in determining its policies (b) helping nations to find private sources of capital (c) reducing tariffs among European nations.*
5. *A problem faced by the International Monetary Fund in the 1990s has been (a) persuading Saudi Arabia to support IMF activities (b) heavy debts owed by Third World nations (c) preventing a Communist revival in Eastern Europe.*
6. *The purpose of the Maastricht Treaty was to achieve for the European Union (a) more economic unity, including a single currency and a European central bank (b) increased political unity, including increased powers for the Europen Parliament and the European Commission (c) both of the preceding.*
7. *The countries that joined the European Union in 1995 were (a) Austria, Sweden, and Finland (b) Norway, Spain, and Denmark (c) Turkey, Hungary, and Poland.*
8. *The Organization of Petroleum Exporting Countries faced competition in the 1990s from (a) non-OPEC oil suppliers (b) alternative energy sources (c) both of the preceding.*
9. *The North American Free Trade Agreement was designed to (a) create a single trading area for Canada, the United States, and Mexico (b) protect U.S. industries from Canadian and Mexican competition (c) enable the United States to control North American economic affairs.*
10. *Objections to NAFTA were raised by (a) the Mexican government (b) the U.S. government (c) American environmental groups.*

B. *Reread* "The European Union," *on pages 230–234. Then write an essay on economic unity in Europe by answering the following questions:*

1. *What is meant by the term "single market"?*

2. *What is the Maastricht Treaty and what is its relationship to the EU?*

3. *Why is the European Union likely to add still more members?*

C. *Use information in Chapter 11 to explain the meaning of the following newspaper headlines:*

NEEDY NATIONS RESIST IMF RESTRAINTS

EUROPEANS PURSUE DREAM OF UNITY

OPEC TRIES TO PREVENT PRICE FALL

ENVIRONMENTALISTS FIND FAULT WITH NAFTA

Chapter 12

Global Business and Trade

In addition to major political changes, the 1990s brought significant economic developments as well. The abandonment of communism in the former Soviet Union and Eastern Europe sparked a movement toward private enterprise. The Communist leaders of China repressed demands for democracy but embraced free markets. The governments of Latin America turned toward both capitalism and democracy. Those trends were expected to stimulate worldwide economic expansion. Although the global economy faltered for a time in the 1990s, new markets and new economic opportunities appeared for the industrialized and the developing nations. For global business and trade, a new order began to emerge.

The New Economic Order

In the late 20th century, many nations began to develop capitalism. They began the process of building business connections with the wealthier countries and with one another. The struggling economies of Eastern Europe sold more farm products and manufactured goods to their former cold war rivals in Western Europe. Third World nations welcomed foreign companies and investors. As a result, their economies expanded. From 1991 to 1995, China claimed an average growth rate of 11.7 percent per year. Other countries that had high growth rates in recent years included Malaysia (9 percent), Indonesia (6.8 percent), and Chile (7 percent).

The industrial nations had relatively low rates of growth in the early 1990s. Britain, the United States, and Canada showed little growth. In France, unemployment soared. Japan's economy was weaker than it had been in the previous 40 years, with near zero growth for four straight years. However, signs of economic recovery appeared in the mid-1990s. As a group, the industrial countries were recording growth rates in the range of 2 to 3 percent per year.

The relatively poor performances of industrial nations' economies aroused much anxiety within those nations. People feared the long-term loss of jobs to developing nations—as when several American manufacturers were accused of shifting thousands of jobs to Mexico. Such job shifts stirred worries about long-term unemployment and poverty, along with declining living standards, in the industrial world.

The recent worries have resulted from a new, highly competitive world economic order that arose in the late 1980s and 1990s. The new order is largely the result of the integration into the global economy of the emerging capitalist nations and much of the developing world. With more than 3 billion inhabitants hungry for a better life, new free market countries in the Third World and elsewhere have begun competing, as never before, with the industrialized nations. Japan, for exam-

New Economic Order

ple, has taken notice of developing rivals in Asia. The *Chinese Economic Area* (CEA) (China, Hong Kong, and Taiwan) dramatically increased its exports, moving from eleventh place in world trade rankings in 1973, to fifth place in 1990, and more recently even higher.

Eastern Europe has been somewhat less successful in competing with the West. However, Eastern Europe's exports to the European Union have been on the rise. Poland, Hungary, the Czech Republic, and Slovakia have been the most successful at moving toward market economies and rebuilding trade with the West. Those nations have agreed to create a free trade area by 1999. In 1992, they signed trade agreements with the EU. About 40 percent of their exports to the EU are in "sensitive" competitive sectors, such as food, textiles, steel, and chemicals. Alarmed at the increasing inflow of East European goods, some unhappy competitors in the EU nations have called for more protectionism in the form of higher tariffs and other trade barriers.

1. *Explain how a new world economic order began to develop in the 1990s.*
2. *List three examples of rapidly expanding economies in the Third World.*
3. *Define the term "Chinese Economic Area."*

Changes in Global Trade and Investment

As hard times hit in the early 1990s, many in Western Europe began to reason that record levels of unemployment had a more worrisome cause than the region's economic slump. Behind many of the job losses were changes in global investment and employment practices. Attention focused on the high cost of employing people in Western Europe. Economists warned that investments were shifting to countries that offered a better combination of labor costs, productivity, and growing markets. In those categories, Europe found itself increasingly unable to compete with industries in Southeast Asia and other Third World regions.

As the developing nations increased their exports and a new global trading system emerged, the world's richest nations received a new wave of goods and people from the developing capitalist countries. To stay competitive, many business firms *restructured*, or *downsized*. That is, they trimmed costs by laying off production workers and cutting out layers of managers. Some firms opened new plants in the developing world. Investment in technology also moved abroad. As a result, the industrialized nations experienced a still greater loss of jobs. For example, Russia's aluminum companies increased their sales to world markets. Subsequently, the Aluminum Company of America laid off 750 of its workers. The Western world's aluminum industry reduced its output by 7.5 percent.

Free market economies developed in Southeast Asia and Latin America. In both regions, labor was plentiful and wages were low. Manufacturing moved from the industrialized nations to those regions because Western production workers earned five times as much as Taiwanese workers and ten times as much as Brazilian or Mexican workers.

Technology transfer from the industrialized nations is also part of the new economic order. South Korea, Taiwan, Hong Kong, and Singapore—the Four Tigers of Asia—are creating high-tech industries. Multinational corporations are building state-of-the-art manufacturing facilities there and in other developing countries. The economies of the world's developing countries have been growing more rapidly than those of the industrial countries.

Four Tigers of Asia

Investment in developing countries shot up during the 1990s. American and Japanese investors, for example, made India a center for the manufacture of computer microchips. Investors poured billions of dollars into the stock markets of India, Korea, Mexico, and other Third World nations.

Many countries in Eastern Europe and Latin America have been privatizing—selling government-owned businesses to foreign and domestic investors. After decades of attempting to be self-sufficient, many countries in those regions have seen the advantages of attracting foreign investment and being part of the new global economy. That, too, has drawn money away from the industrialized nations to the new capitalist countries.

1. *Describe the changes in global trade and investment in the 1990s.*
2. *Identify the Four Tigers of Asia.*
3. *PROVE or DISPROVE: The new capitalist nations have drawn jobs and money away from the older industrialized nations.*

Restructuring and Competitiveness

When the cold war ended, defense spending dropped and defense production declined. One million American defense workers lost their jobs. Companies in France and Britain also laid off workers. These cuts helped to boost unemployment in the United States and Europe.

The industrial world is attempting to adapt to the new economic order. Facing tougher competition at home and abroad, American companies have invested in new technologies and restructured their operations to improve efficiency, become more competitive, and regain lost markets. More than any other industrial country, the United States has cut back government regulation of financial services, airlines, telecommunications, and trucking industries.

Similar efforts have occurred in Europe. France has undertaken to privatize nearly two dozen state-owned companies, including Air France and Renault. Under private ownership, those companies could restructure to become more competitive. The German government made plans to sell to private investors its giant state-owned telecommunications firm, Deutsche Telekom. That sale would create one of the largest investor-owned corporations in Europe.

Japanese companies are also being hurt by increased global competition. In response, they are building more factories overseas. Nissan Motor's $800 million expansion of its auto plant in Mexico will enable it to produce cars not only for the Mexican market but also for export to Japan, Canada, and the rest of Latin America. In Mexico, lower production costs will provide Nissan a better opportunity to increase sales.

Economists say that freer trade will speed economic growth. The emerging capitalist countries are beginning to spend more money on roads, sewers, the environment, health care, and consumer goods. Over the next decade, Asia, excluding Japan, is expected to spend at least $1 trillion on telecommunications and power equipment. That investment will provide new market opportunities for the industrialized nations. Westinghouse Electric Corporation, for example, negotiated an agreement to modernize 400 power plants in China.

Consumer spending is also rising rapidly in the developing nations. The prospect of billions of new customers is expected to increase production and sales for American, European, and Japanese firms by the late 1990s.

Despite the prospect for future improvement, the new economic order has made things difficult for the industrialized nations. The combination of global competition and technological change has eliminated jobs and held down wages. Cheap labor in the emerging capitalist nations makes workers in the industrial world feel threatened. Many want their governments to curb imports and restrict immigration.

Nevertheless, the survival of the industrialized nations in the new global economy may depend on freer trade and freer markets to stimulate economic growth and employment. The nations that have enjoyed unchallenged economic power will have to learn to compete better in the changed marketplace created by the new economic order.

1. *Describe the efforts of the governments of France and the United States to make their industries more competitive.*

2. *Explain Japan's reaction to the new economic order.*

3. *Complete each sentence:*

   a. *Economists say that freer trade ____.*
   b. *In the developing world, consumer spending is ____.*
   c. *In the industrial nations, many people want their governments to ____.*

Giants of Global Industry and Trade

In the 1990s, changes in the worldwide economy led major corporations to restructure in order to remain competitive. Some firms have been more successful at this than others.

To reduce costs and improve efficiency, International Business Machines (IBM) eliminated 122,000 jobs from its American and overseas operations. It was one of the largest cutbacks of people, factories, and equipment in corporate history. At its peak in 1985, IBM had 405,000 workers. In the mid-1990s, the global giant was down to 225,000 employees. Such streamlining was IBM's response to the world economic slowdown and the growing intensity of competition in the computer industry.

Turmoil in the international computer market affected many major firms in the 1990s. Two well-known American computer companies, Apple and Dell, eliminated jobs and found other ways of reducing costs and increasing productivity. Tandy, another American manufacturer, dropped out of the personal computer market, selling its assets and production facilities to a research firm.

In the telecommunications industry, however, business earnings rose. Corporate restructurings and technological developments gave Japan's Nippon Telegraph & Telephone Corporation and the American Telephone & Telegraph Company increased shares of the market. NT&T impressed investors by its plans to cut personnel by more than 10,000 each year over several years. Analysts hailed that plan as one of the best examples of corporate restructuring. AT&T planned to cut 123,000 jobs.

Other Japanese firms did well, bolstered by Japan's close cooperation between government agencies and private industry. The Toyota Motor Company increased the value of its shares of stock by 30 percent over a two-year period. Some 36 Japanese firms rose in business activity, giving Japan a total market value increase of 51 percent. (*Market value* is the amount of capital a company can bring to the marketplace.) This was accomplished despite a recession and political uncertainty. However, many of Japan's biggest companies were not so lucky. They lost money during some periods before the economy began to revive in the mid-1990s.

In Europe, falling prices and shrinking markets hurt several of the business giants. Ferruzzi, Italy's second largest private company, developed a debt of $20 billion. Unable to pay its creditors, the huge conglomerate placed its management in the hands of the banks. Britain's Wellcome, producer of the AIDS drug AZT, lost 32 percent in market value as many governments pressured it to cut prices. France's LVMH (Louis Vuitton Moët Hennessy, seller of Christian Dior clothing, Louis Vuitton handbags, and Hennessy cognac) lost 10 percent of its market value. Hard times reduced consumers' interest in luxury goods. Firms dealing in lower priced products also had problems. British food retailers such as J. Sainsbury and Argyll Group experienced heavy competition from newly opened discount stores. The downturn hit Britain hard. However, British Telecommunications and British Airways held up well. British Airways, in particular, expanded its global operations.

Elsewhere in Europe, certain industries experienced a long-term slump. The automobile industry suffered. Germany's Mercedes-Benz, in the midst of costly restructuring, lost 30 percent of its market value. France's Peugeot declined by 33 percent. Fiat, Italy's giant automobile and industrial company, reported heavy losses. In the United States, however, Chrysler Corporation presented a successful line of sedans and increased its market value. General Motors also increased its profits. Such successes resulted from improved efficiency in automaking and an increased volume of business, especially in Latin America. Ford Motor Company also reported strong improvements in earnings. For the American Big Three automakers, the restructuring that made them more competitive followed a long period of falling sales and profits.

Food and tobacco companies had difficulties. Philip Morris Company, caught in a cigarette price war, lost 37 percent of its market value. Wal-Mart Stores, Inc., one of the largest American retailers, suffered from the slowdown in consumer spending. Its value, which had been rising by double-digit percentages each year, fell into the single digits in the early 1990s.

In contrast, industry and commerce boomed in Southeast Asia. Singapore's surging exports drove up the market value of its business firms sharply. In Hong Kong, real estate prices soared. In the developing economies, such as South Korea and Argentina, many corporations experienced huge gains in market value. That reflected the shift in investment to Latin America and Asia that has been a key part of the new economic order.

In the hard times of the early 1990s, the steps taken by some American and Japanese corporate giants to restructure and improve their competitiveness demonstrated an ability to adjust to the new global economy. Corporate leaders say their companies' success in upcoming years will depend upon the spread of government deregulation of industries throughout the world, the reduction of trade barriers, and the growth of new markets and investment opportunities in the developing countries.

1. *Explain the importance of corporate restructuring in the 1990s.*
2. *For each nation, list a corporate giant: U.S., Japan, Britain, France, Germany.*
3. *Explain why you AGREE or DISAGREE with the following statement: American and Japanese firms have had more success adjusting to the new economic order than have European companies.*

Economic Opportunities in the Emerging Third World

In 1960, Asian nations represented only 4 percent of the world's gross domestic product. Their share of GDP increased to 25 percent in 1993. By the year 2000, Asia will account for 33 percent of global GDP. The economies of China, South Korea, and Thailand are growing at faster rates than are those of the United States, Europe, and Japan. As Asian nations developed key industries, they accumulated sizable trade surpluses with the United States. They also attracted considerable foreign investment. In South Korea, for example, investment increased to such an extent that the government limited non-Korean shareholdings in any company to 15 percent. As a result, foreigners had to buy shares in South Korean firms from other foreigners, often paying 50 percent more than the market value of the shares.

Similar patterns developed in Latin America. The privatization of Argentina's state-owned oil company, YPF, in 1993, attracted so much attention from investors around the world that the government increased the proportion of shares to be sold from 33 percent of the total to 45 percent. The Argentine government earned $3 billion from the sale, and YPF became a public company with a market value of $6.7 billion. That made YPF one of the most valuable companies in the world's emerging financial markets.

Privatizations have become one of the main reasons for the flow of foreign investments into the developing countries. Investors from the industrialized nations have flocked to the Third World seeking higher profits than they can find at home. As a result, foreign holdings of corporate stocks have soared. U.S. investors alone poured $5.1 billion into enterprises in 13 countries in Latin America and Southeast Asia in 1992.

- *Explain the attraction of Asia and Latin America for American and other investors.*

Argentina and Brazil both hope to become economic success stories in Latin America. At a time when the region has been moving toward low inflation, balanced budgets, streamlined government employment, deregulation of industry, and lower tariff barriers, the two countries' changes have been fast and deep.

Argentina started first, launching its free market economic reform in 1991. The reform brought Argentina's inflation rate down from 1344 percent in 1990 to less than 5 percent in 1994. Argentina's debt dropped to 25 percent of its gross domestic product. The lowering of import barriers brought in foreign investment and foreign goods. The government sold almost all of its state-owned businesses. Tax collections rose sharply.

In the first half of the 1990s, Argentina had one of the highest rates of economic growth in Latin America, topping 6 percent for four years in a row. Its growth rate was among the best in the world. The International Monetary Fund used Argentina as a model from which other developing countries might learn.

Meanwhile, Brazil, Latin America's largest democracy, was biding its time. In the early 1990s it took few steps toward restructuring. All that changed, however, with the election of President Fernando Henrique Cardoso in October 1994. As you read in Chapter 6, President Cardoso persuaded Brazil's Congress to add a number of free market amendments to the constitution. He opened Brazil's economy to investment by foreigners, introduced a new currency, and curbed inflation. President Cardoso seemed in no hurry to privatize the state-owned telephone and electricity companies. Rather, he proposed ending their monopolies by allowing private firms to compete with them for business.

While Argentina and Brazil won praise from international investors and agencies like the IMF, their reforms were not without pain. Unemployment remained high in both countries.

Cuts in Argentina's social services sliced into the "safety net" for the poorest citizens. The Mexican peso crisis of December 1994 made investors skittish about pouring money into Latin America in general. During 1995, Argentina plunged into a deep recession, with the government raising taxes and borrowing money to try to make ends meet. Nonetheless, Argentina's voters reelected President Carlos Menem, and he vowed to carry on with the restructuring.

1. *State two economic differences between Argentina and Brazil in the 1990s.*
2. *Explain the relationship among these terms: privatization, investment, and economic growth in the Third World.*

Business Activity in the Third World

How to make exports profitable is a common concern of the countries in Central America. World prices for staple exports such as coffee, sugar, cotton, and beef often plunge because of oversupply.

The income of Central American countries is also threatened by the policies of some of their customers. In 1993, the European Union began applying quotas on banana imports, causing a drop in sales and income for Honduras and Costa Rica. The North American Free Trade Agreement (NAFTA) also represents a threat to Central America. NAFTA gives Mexican producers of manufactured and processed goods greater access to North American markets. This may reduce the flow of Central American products to those markets. In response to such problems, the Central American countries have begun to develop their own form of economic union.

Between 1986 and 1993, trade within Central America nearly doubled. Nicaragua, Guatemala, Honduras, and El Salvador have begun to eliminate barriers to the movement of goods, labor, and money across one another's borders. Unlike a previous common market scheme in the 1960s, this new plan opens Central America to trade with the rest of the world. The four countries set a low common tariff for most imports and negotiated free trade agreements with Mexico, Colombia, and Venezuela.

Costa Rica, the region's most stable and prosperous country, has also been cutting tariffs. Fearing an invasion of jobseekers from nearby countries with higher unemployment,

Costa Rica has been cautious about joining its neighbors' economic union. However, its government has been discussing trade agreements with Mexico and the United States.

Among the goals of the four Central American governments is monetary union and a single currency. Panama is expected to join the free trade plan, but may opt out of the common tariff arrangement.

Southeast Asia has also been the scene of bustling business activity in the 1990s. The single largest new real estate development in the world began in Kuala Lumpur, the capital of Malaysia, in 1993. It included an office complex with the world's two tallest skyscrapers, which exceed the height of the Sears Tower in Chicago by 22 feet. The Malaysian development also had a multistory shopping center, a luxury hotel, and a landscaped park. Plans called for adding hotels and office buildings, new roads, a theater, and condominiums over a 20-year period. A new railway for the city center was also planned. In addition to this multibillion-dollar operation, other developments were under consideration for Kuala Lumpur. Among them was the construction of a ten-story department store by Sogo, a Japanese commercial chain. This ambitious, long-range building program reflected Malaysia's status as one of the world's emerging economies.

Large business firms called *conglomerates* (combinations of two or more businesses in unrelated fields) have been rapidly increasing in Southeast Asia. Most are multinational companies, with business operations spanning a number of countries. Charoen Pokphand (CP) of Thailand, for example, does everything from brewing beer in China, to farming shrimp in Mexico, to installing telephones in Bangkok. It owns more than 300 companies and does $5 billion in yearly business. Approximately 50 percent of its assets are outside Thailand.

Until recently, the term *multinational* in Southeast Asia applied mainly to Western or Japanese companies. Investments from those sources transformed the economies of Thailand, Malaysia, and Indonesia. Now Southeast Asian conglomerates are reaching abroad. The growing economies of East Asia, especially that of China, are being guided by financial giants situated in Thailand, Singapore, Hong Kong, and Indonesia.

For the most part, the Southeast Asian conglomerates have preferred to do most of their investing in Asia. Despite its business ventures in North America and Europe, CP of Thailand is more heavily committed to Asia. More than 50 percent of its foreign business is done in China. CP has expanded vastly in recent years. One of its most ambitious projects has been construction of a $3 billion petrochemical plant outside Shanghai.

Most of the Southeast Asian multinational firms are management and investment companies, not manufacturers of specific products. Their procedure is to identify business opportunities, recruit managers, borrow the necessary money, and then buy the technology. Compared to the Western and Japanese conglomerates, the Southeast Asian firms are daring in their investment policies. They aim for rapid growth. So does the region in which they operate.

1. *PROVE or DISPROVE: Free trade among the Central American nations should increase economic growth in that region.*
2. *Define conglomerate and multinational.*
3. *Which of the following statements are true and which are false?*
   a. *The rise of multinational conglomerates in Southeast Asia is a sign of economic growth in the region.*
   b. *Southeast Asian firms have invested more heavily in Europe than in Asia.*
   c. *European and North American investment in Asia has been overshadowed by the economic activity of the Southeast Asian conglomerates.*
   d. *China has become a major field of investment for both Western and Asian firms.*
   e. *The Southeast Asian conglomerates are mainly management and investment companies.*

Economic Growth and the Quality of Life

Since 1990, the *United Nations Development Program* has been examining the extent to which global economic growth responds to human needs. It has asserted a need for measures to ensure that economic development benefits ordinary people, not just governments and powerful groups. In a report, it called for a "people-centered world order" in which security is redefined as security for people rather than for nations and is achieved through economic development. To reverse a trend in which economies expand without creating new jobs, the report recommends the conversion of defense industries to civilian production, more investment in education, deregulation of businesses, and aid to small enterprises.

In its human development reports, the U.N. Development Program has rated nations according to their ability to raise living standards and otherwise improve the quality of life for their citizens. Each nation's rating is based upon such criteria as life expectancy, educational standards, and individual purchasing power. Among the industrialized nations, for example, Japan received a high rating because of high personal income. The United States was in sixth place. The report noted a broad gap between the living standards of white Americans and Americans of other races.

Several developing countries scored higher on the human-development scale than did some more industrialized ones. Uruguay, for example, ranked above Poland. The lowest human-development scores were given to the poorest African nations. In Somalia, Mali, Sierra Leone, and other African countries, wealth is limited to a very few.

In the U.N. reports, a high per capita (per person) income or gross national product did not necessarily mean a high quality of life. The average Brazilian, for example, earned more than did the average Costa Rican. Costa Rica, however, received a higher human development rating than Brazil. The average Costa Rican lives longer, is better educated, and enjoys cleaner water and more sanitation than does a Brazilian.

Differences in quality of life between men and women were also noted. No country was credited with treating its female citizens as well as its males. Women in most nations, for example, had fewer job opportunities and lower earnings than men. In the developing countries, the greatest differences between men and women have been in the areas of employment, health care, nutrition, and education.

If nations all over the world can strengthen the link between economic growth and human development, they will improve the quality of life for their people.

1. *Define:*
   a. *people-centered world order*
   b. *human development scale*
2. *List some of the factors that have been linked to quality of life in developing and industrialized nations.*
3. *Explain why some developing countries scored higher on the human development scale than did some more industrialized countries.*

Chapter 12 Review

A. *On your answer sheet, write the letter of the correct response.*

1. *In the new economic order of the 1990s, new investment opportunities have developed especially in (a) Western Europe and North America (b) Southeast Asia and Latin America (c) Africa and the Middle East.*
2. *The developing country with the highest economic growth rate in the early 1990s was (a) China (b) Argentina (c) Slovakia.*
3. *As a trading bloc, the Chinese Economic Area consists of (a) China, Hong Kong, Taiwan (b) China, Singapore, Malaysia (c) China, Mongolia, Vietnam.*
4. *Three nations of Eastern Europe that plan to form a free trade area include (a) Russia, Ukraine, Belarus (b) Serbia, Macedonia, Greece (c) Poland, the Czech Republic, Slovakia.*
5. *To become more competitive, an American corporation that successfully restructured was (a) Nissan Motors (b) International Business Machines (c) Renault.*
6. *A company that quit manufacturing personal computers in the early 1990s was (a) Tandy (b) Apple (c) IBM.*
7. *The "Asian Tigers" of global trade are (a) Vietnam, Laos, Cambodia (b) Thailand, India, Pakistan, Nepal (c) South Korea, Hong Kong, Taiwan, Singapore.*
8. *Thailand's Charoen Pokphand (CP) is an example of a (a) conglomerate (b) multinational (c) both of the previous.*
9. *To compensate for the effects of NAFTA, a group of countries have made free trade agreements in (a) Central America (b) the Middle East (c) Africa.*
10. *A nation used as a model of economic restructuring by the International Monetary Fund was (a) Brazil (b) Argentina (c) Peru.*

B. *Reread "Business Activity in the Third World," starting on page 252. Then write an essay on international investment by answering the following questions.*

1. *How are some Central American countries responding to NAFTA?*
2. *What is one way in which business activity has expanded in Southeast Asia?*
3. *How have practices in Southeast Asia changed in the 1990s?*

C. *Reread "The New Economic Order," starting on page 242. Then read the statements below. Write a paragraph to explain how the four statements are related to the new economic order.*

1. *To stimulate business activity and investment, Britain cut interest rates and devalued (lowered the value of) its currency.*
2. *Italy, Spain, Finland, and Sweden increased their export sales by devaluing their currencies.*
3. *Business activity increased in East European nations like Poland.*
4. *An economic downturn in countries like Germany and France restrained the growth of Europe's economy.*

Chapter 13

Global Technology and Science

The Introduction of Smart Cards

Passengers on certain sections of the Paris Metro (subway) can sail through the turnstiles without reaching into their pockets for a token or a card. They carry a special *smart card* that stays in their pockets. The card contains a tiny built-in microchip. When the passenger buys the card, it is encoded with an amount of money to pay for subway fares. As the passenger passes through the turnstile, an electronic device reads the card and deducts the price of a subway fare. Every so often, the passenger pays more money, and the new value is recorded electronically on the card. There's no muss or fuss.

Similar cards have been introduced on U.S. toll roads and bridges. In Orange County, California, the cards allow drivers to avoid waiting in line to pay tolls. The driver places the card on the vehicle's dashboard. There's no need to wave the card in front of a beam. A radio receiver does the work automatically. As one driver told a reporter, "It's kind of fun to whiz by at 60 miles an hour while others are waiting in line."

In the Danish town of Naestved, residents tried out another scheme for using a smart card instead of cash. They bought the plastic cards, also called *plastic purses,* in shops, restaurants, banks, and gas stations. They could add bank credit to the card through an automated teller machine (ATM) using a personal identification number (PIN). Then they used the cards to pay for purchases in a variety of stores.

Smart Move

Is old-fashioned money on the way out? Some experts claim that the smart card or plastic purse revolution is making cash obsolete. Central banks will need to print or mint less money. They'll no longer need to transport and secure so many coins and banknotes.

Gemplus, a French manufacturer, produces an "intelligent," nonforgeable identity card containing a microchip. The card carries a photograph of its owner, as well as a range of personal details. The European Union has tested a health card capable of storing a person's medical history. Schools in France and in some U.S. cities are now using microchip cards that contain records of students' financial status, academic grades, and attendance.

Smart cards represent only one way in which advances in technology are affecting everyday life. Advances in transportation, space exploration, health and medical technology, telecommunications, computer technology, and environmental protection are also helping to reshape the global economy in the 1990s.

1. *Define the following terms:*

    a. *smart card*
    b. *plastic purse revolution*

2. *Explain why you AGREE or DISAGREE with the following statement: Smart cards are an improvement over traditional money.*

The Continuing Computer Revolution

Compact electronic computing machines, able to process and store information rapidly, have developed rapidly since the 1940s. The introduction of the microchip—storing thousands of transistors on a small silicon chip—in 1970 made it possible for computers to operate more quickly and store huge amounts of information, while taking up less space. By the 1990s, computers had become essential tools in every field of human activity.

Electronic Superhighways. The increasing commercial value of information has transformed the economies of the industrialized nations. By 1990, for example, the production and sale of information accounted for 50 percent of the gross domestic product of the United States. Approximately half of all workers in the United States have jobs in the information business. Today, information is the source of great wealth. And technology has made it possible for information of any kind to race along *electronic superhighways* at the speed of light.

Tiny strands of high-strength glass, called *fiber optic cable*, can transport pulses of light. Sound and text are examples of data that can be reduced to pulses of light and transmitted via glass cable within or between computers. Fiber optics have been linked to digital technology. Letters, numbers, sounds, and images are reduced to a sequence of zeros and ones. In computers, more data are processed faster. These developments help to propel the latest stage of the computer revolution, the development of interactive media.

Interactive media combine computer technology with telecommunications. They are providing consumers with new ways of obtaining and using information. New advances are announced almost daily. Television viewers, for example, will interact with a box in their living room, ordering any program they want, shopping, or checking bank balances. In the United States alone, there are 92 million households. Nearly all have televisions and telephones. And more than one third have personal computers. The growth of interactivity is linking

Information Superhighway

these to an *information superhighway.* A number of Japanese, European, and American computer and cable television firms have formed partnerships in order to develop interactive media and share in the huge profits this innovation in computers and telecommunications will generate.

Among multimedia products are interactive laser videodiscs based on television shows that can be viewed on a personal computer equipped with a CD-ROM player. Another product will be "smart" televisions equipped with microchips designed to receive signals from the broadcaster identifying certain types of programs. Viewers will be given increased ability to screen out programs with objectionable content and to monitor the hundreds of new channels that will become available.

Corporations have been competing frantically to offer commercial services over the worldwide Internet. The *Internet,* an existing form of information superhighway, is a web of electronic connections open to public access. It links computers in far-flung locations into what amounts to one giant network. Individuals in their homes or cars can reach the Internet by using telephone signals. All they need is a phone, a computer, and a *modem* (a device for converting digital computer signals into sounds that telephone equipment can deal with). Businesses and universities often connect to the Internet over higher speed direct lines. For years now, people have been using the Internet to exchange messages (electronic mail, or *e-mail*), to share files, and to search for information.

Lately, the fastest-growing segment of the Internet has been the World Wide Web. It delivers sound, still pictures, and moving video images, in addition to plain text. Many businesspeople hope to develop the World Wide Web as the world's shopping mall. They have introduced a variety of forms of electronic cash and online credit cards, which are competing for users. The big problem has been security—making sure that no one can counterfeit the cash or steal a credit card number.

New Technologies. Innovation in computer technology is giving rise to a variety of new products. In 1993, Apple Computer introduced a line of pen-based, handheld *personal digital assistants* (PDA's) called MessagePads, which used a special operating system known as Newton. Smaller than a VHS cassette, it was a pocket organizer that "talked" with telephones, faxes, and computers. Using a special pen, a person can write words onto the display. Those handwritten words can then be turned into typed electronic text. Competing pen-based communicators have been developed, such as the Zoomer from Tandy/Casio and the Wizard pocket organizer from Sharp. PDA's are used by drivers for package-delivery services, among others.

The IBM production center in Sindelfingen, Germany, has worked on a "virtual" keyboard to replace computer keyboards. With a flat-surface keypad and a video camera that watches the fingers, the computer decides which letter is required and displays it on a screen. The video camera takes 25 pictures a second to follow finger movements. These are interpreted by a program requiring only seven kilobytes of computer memory. Intended for use with IBM personal computers, this innovation aims to reduce the size and weight of computers and to eliminate a number of breakable mechanical parts.

MIPS Technologies, Silicon Graphics, and other American firms have taken the computer revolution another step forward by developing a form of computer processing called Reduced Instruction Set Computing (RISC). RISC is a rival to the Complex Instruction Set Computing (CISC) used in the so-called *x*86 series of microprocessors produced by Intel Corporation since 1978.

Intel chips are used in 85 percent of the world's personal computers. The *x*86 chip is typically found in computers running the Microsoft Corporation's DOS (Disk Operating System) and Windows 95, and those running IBM's OS/2 Warp. The latest *x*86 chips, such as Intel's Pentium and P6, use a modified form of CISC that incorporates some of the advantages of RISC.

RISC microprocessors run 50 percent faster than chips based on the CISC design. They also require less power, take up less space, generate less heat, and are easier to manufacture. RISC-based PowerPC chips are used in high-end computers produced by Macintosh, IBM, Motorola, and other companies. The growing impact of RISC chips on the PC market influenced Microsoft to make its network-oriented Windows NT operating system run on RISC as well as CISC processors. Also, RISC processors run such products as PDA's and digital television set-top controllers.

Supercomputers. Beyond the realm of personal computers, interactive media, and personal digital assistants is the world of supercomputers. These are used by large industrial firms and government agencies for major research and development operations.

One of the world's most powerful computers is located at the Los Alamos National Laboratory in New Mexico. The Thinking Machine CM-5 incorporates 1,024 processors that can perform 131 billion floating point calculations per second. It is used for calculations arising from fusion experiments.

Another powerful supercomputer is located in Britain. It is a 16-processor Cray Research Y-MPC916, used by the European Center for Medium-Range Weather Forecasting. Another supercomputer in Britain belongs to Grant Tensor, an oil exploration company. It processes data from surveys covering tens of thousands of miles in the North Sea.

Supercomputers that use *massively parallel processing* have been in great demand in the 1990s. By linking a number of small and relatively inexpensive processors together, designers can make the combination far more powerful than a mainframe computer. Programmers no longer need to work through a problem by dealing with each equation in sequence. Instead, they can split it into smaller, independent problems, assign each to a different processor, and obtain a faster solution.

Massively parallel processing has been especially popular

among researchers working with large-scale computations. For example, in 1995 the U.S. government ordered a supercomputer that could mimic nuclear bomb explosions. With such a machine, scientists can test designs for nuclear weapons without exploding actual devices. The government ordered an Intel supercomputer containing 9,000 separate microprocessors, each of them a P6 chip containing 5½ million transistors. The Intel supercomputer is designed to perform one trillion calculations per second—or 300 calculations for every person in the world every second. That's more than seven times the speed of the fastest previous supercomputer.

The United States and Japan lead the world in the possession of supercomputers. These machines are the proudest achievements to date of the continuing computer revolution.

1. *Define the following terms:*
   - a. *interactive media*
   - b. *information superhighway*
   - c. *fiber optics*
   - d. *digital electronics*
   - e. *smart televisions*
   - f. *Internet*
   - g. *World Wide Web*
   - h. *personal digital assistants*
   - i. *RISC*
   - j. *supercomputers*
2. *Select any two of the terms listed above. For each, write a paragraph explaining its importance in the continuing computer revolution.*

The Expanding World of Telecommunications

Consider this scenario: You're on a camping trip in some isolated region—high in the Rockies, perhaps, or deep in the Amazon jungle. Back home, a crisis arises. Your parents need to reach you. They pick up a phone, dial your number, and in your lonely camp you get their call. A communications company sent the call via satellite, direct to your handheld phone.

Global Communications. A number of companies have proposed global communications systems that would allow this scenario to become commonplace. One venture, called Iridium, is sponsored by a group of companies led by Motorola. It would send 66 small satellites into low orbits, about 100 miles above the earth. A rival venture, called Teledesic, is led by William H. Gates (of Microsoft) and Craig O. McCaw (a cellular communications executive). It would use 840 satellites, also in low orbit. Because of the large number of satellites involved, such systems would be expensive.

A cheaper system, but one that would work with fixed rather than mobile communications units, has been proposed by the AT&T Corporation. A user would set up a dish antenna about the size of a jumbo pizza. The system would use only 12 satellites in much higher orbits, 22,000 miles above the equator. AT&T sees its venture as a way of linking computers to the Internet without requiring local phone connections. The system would allow the transfer of data at much greater speeds than those reached by modems.

Those ventures are just a few of the corporate world's responses to the explosive growth in wireless communications. The field includes cellular telephones, two-way paging devices, handheld computers, and mobile fax machines. All such devices use radio waves to send and receive information.

Among the improved communications services under development by U.S. firms is a sort of computerized secretary. Your communications service would screen your messages and automatically route them to a pager or pocket phone wherever you might be.

Improvements in telephone technology have also been emerging outside the United States. Vodafone Group is the largest supplier of cellular phone service in Britain. The company has also established an extensive network of foreign operations.

Vodafone was one of two British companies that were authorized to build a cellular network in the United Kingdom in the 1980s. The other firm was Cellnet, partly owned by British Telecom. Vodafone had 2 million subscribers by 1995. At that time, an estimated 16 million people in the United States used cellular phones. Industry forecasts predicted that 15 percent of the population in Britain and the United States would use cellular phones by 1999.

Some of Vodafone's services use digital techniques. That is, conversations or data are carried as sequences of zeros and ones for rapid transmission. Such a system differs from the analog techniques used by traditional telephones. A digital transmission is like a blinking light, with only two states, zero or one, "on" or "off." An analog signal represents a continuous series of data, exactly representing the original data. It is more like a saxophone solo, sliding up and down across many possible notes, or states. Digital calls are clearer and more secure from eavesdropping than calls over analog systems.

The expansion of digital cellular services has been speeded by the development of a common standard, called Global System for Mobile Communications, or GSM. That standard allows Vodafone's subscribers to make calls to and from dozens of different countries. In the 1980s, each country had its own analog cellular system. Customers who traveled outside their own country usually found that their cellular phones would not work with the system of another country. So European governments agreed on a GSM standard for an all-digital telephone service. By the start of 1995, GSM networks were planned or operating in 60 countries in Europe, the Middle East, the Far East, Australia, Africa, and South America.

In a GSM cellular system, customers receive a smart card called a Subscriber Identity Module (SIM). It looks much like a thick credit card. Subscribers do not have to carry their cellular phone on trips. They can slide their cards into any digital phone, and the calls are charged automatically to their own accounts.

Computer-Displayed Newspapers. Another coming advance in telecommunications may be a computer-displayed newspaper. The idea is to replace or supplement printed newspapers with individual data systems. Special software will tailor a news report to a customer's interests. It will also search the world's libraries for information the user might need, according to a list of personal preferences provided in advance. The computerized newspaper will provide information without using paper.

The alternative to paper will look like a tablet. It will have a high-definition, touch-sensitive screen a little bigger and thicker than a magazine. Such a tablet will fit easily into a briefcase. It will have a number of built-in features, such as a wireless telephone and a voice synthesis chip. Once or twice a day, the owner would download the latest news. The tablet would display the main news items, as the front page of the newspaper does. At the user's touch, selected stories would fill the screen. All subjects—finance, science, technology, book reviews—would appear at a touch on a menu bar. The tablet would be able to read stories aloud. Attached to a printer, it could print out selected articles.

Banking Services. New developments are also changing the banking industry. The Maryland National Bank, in Baltimore, provided some of its customers with a special telephone. The phone had a miniature version of an automated teller machine's display. It talked to the same data network that served real ATM's. The phone could do anything an ATM can do, except dispense cash. The low cost of the special telephone and the low monthly charges make this type of home banking cheaper than paying bills by check. Online Resources and Communications Corporation developed the technology.

Meanwhile, banks all across the country have been urging customers to use ATM machines and other forms of on-line banking. They hope to save money by closing many of their traditional branches, as more and more customers do their banking from home.

Technological change in the telecommunications field involves television, radio, compact discs, and every other means of communication. Fierce competition has broken out among competing firms. The drive to eliminate distance as an obstacle to communication has become a key feature of the global economy in the 1990s.

1. *Explain why you AGREE or DISAGREE: Using a news tablet will be a much better way of getting the news than reading a traditional newspaper.*

2. *Match term or name listed in Column A with an accomplishment or goal in Column B.*

Column A	Column B
1. *AT&T*	a. *a common standard for digital cellular services*
2. *William H. Gates*	b. *operates Britain's largest digital cellphone service*
3. *Vodafone Group*	c. *company partly owned by British Telecom*
4. *Cellnet*	d. *handling a continuously variable series of data states*
5. *digital techniques*	e. *plans a global communications service using low-altitude satellites*
6. *GSM*	f. *handling data as a sequence of zeros and ones*
7. *analog*	g. *plans a global communications service using high-altitude satellites*

3. Complete the following sentences:

a. High-orbiting satellites make telecommunications cheaper than low-orbiting satellites because ____.
b. Compared to analog phone systems, digital systems provide connects that are ____.
c. A feature of the news tablet would be ____.
d. Electronic banking can help banks save money by ____.

The Technology of Environmental Protection

The United Nations Conference on Environment and Development (UNCED), held in Rio de Janeiro, Brazil, in 1992, was attended by delegates and diplomats from 178 countries. Thousands of representatives of nongovernmental organizations also participated. The conferees drew up a list of global policies for the protection of the environment. These included: (*1*) Agenda 21, a 40-chapter proposal for environmental development, (*2*) the Rio Declaration, a list of environmental and economic development concerns; and (*3*) statements about the prevention of global climatic changes and the protection of threatened forests.

Saving the Amazon Rain Forest. The Amazon rain forest heads the list of areas that scientists and environmentalists wish to protect. Its 5 million square kilometers comprise the largest continuous expanse of tropical rain forest remaining in the world. Although such forests cover only 7 percent of the planet's land surface, they contain approximately 50 percent of the plants and animals found on the globe. Of these, thousands of species face extinction each year as a result of forest destruction. (Trees are being felled at the rate of 4,500 acres every hour.) Because Brazil has the highest number of diverse species of plants and animals in the world, it is the center of efforts to stop global deforestation.

However, Brazil has a national debt of well over $100 billion. It has widespread poverty and an unequal distribution of wealth. Efforts to preserve the Amazon rain forest must be consistent with the human need for economic development. Scientists have been attempting to develop the methods and technology to accomplish both.

In the 1990s, scientists have been investigating ways to use the millions of acres of nonproductive land that lie abandoned throughout the Amazon. Once cut down by loggers, the rain forest becomes an open field or a second-growth forest. Some researchers have been urging the establishment of cattle ranches to make this land productive. Others propose replanting trees and controlled logging. Still others suggest planting farm crops. Scientists warn, however, that the soil underneath the tropical rain forests is easily eroded, and must be treated with care.

Researchers are also working with the people of the Amazon rain forest. They hope the people's knowledge of the forest will lead to new technologies for identifying and extracting medicinal plants, new crops, and ways of logging mahogany that will be less destructive to the environment. Methods of harvesting natural products—such as latex, palm hearts, and Brazil nuts—without damaging the rain forest are also being studied.

Economic development that preserves the environment and allows resources to be used over and over is called *sustainable development*. The patterns of sustainable development discovered in the Amazon may help to preserve threatened forest lands in other parts of the world.

- *Explain why environmentalists are so concerned about the Amazon rain forest.*

Air Pollution Controls. To slow the rate of global warming, the emission of carbon dioxide into the atmosphere must be reduced. Carbon dioxide is a gas that is released when such fuels as coal, gasoline, and wood are burned. In the atmosphere, it serves as a sort of a one-way window pane, like the glass in a greenhouse. The sun's radiation passes down through the window pane to warm the earth. But some of the heat from the earth's surface is radiated to the atmospheric window pane, and then is trapped on the earth, creating a "greenhouse effect."

In the United States, new laws and new technologies have helped to limit carbon dioxide emissions. But the United States is unlikely to be able to keep a pledge it and other nations made at the Rio de Janeiro conference of 1992. That pledge was to cut the emission of heat-trapping gases in the year 2000 back to the level of 1990.

The 1990 Clean Air Act stiffened antipollution laws that

Greenhouse Effect

applied to cars, trucks, and buses. Since motor vehicles account for more than half of all air pollutants, air quality improves as older cars go out of use. Models on sale in the mid-1990s emitted only one percent as much pollution as those made 20 years earlier. California and 12 other states were planning to introduce still tougher standards in the late 1990s.

The American automobile industry has been under pressure to develop a high-performance *zero-emission* car—one that offers the convenience of any other car but gives off no pollutants. General Motors announced plans to sell an electric car in fall 1996 in areas of the western United States. In Europe, an Environmental Concept Car (ECC) model has been developed by Volvo, the Swedish automobile manufacturer. The ECC is driven by a high-efficiency electric motor. The motor can operate on power supplied by on-board batteries, making the ECC a zero-emission vehicle for use in congested cities. When more range and performance are required, the driver can dial in a hybrid mode. This starts up a gas turbine engine that drives an ultra-efficient, high-speed generator. Even when the car is operating in the hybrid mode, emission levels are low. The ECC and other electric models may be the environmental cars of the future. In the United States, the Chrysler Corporation has displayed an electric race car. It combines a turbine and flywheel, providing 500 horsepower for quick acceleration. Will we all be driving electric cars in the future? Perhaps that won't be necessary. Automakers are finding new ways to cut the emissions from gasoline-powered engines. And they are also experimenting with other kinds of fuels.

During the past 200 years, the demand for energy in industrialized countries has soared. Large future increases in global energy demand are expected from developing countries. The ideal fuel should be domestically supplied, renewable, and nonpolluting. Ultimately, this need may be met by a combination of solar energy and nuclear fusion to supply electricity and hydrogen gas. Until such systems are developed, however, environmentalists are paying increased attention to natural gas, or methane.

Natural gas is abundant in North America, Europe, Asia, and elsewhere. It is the least polluting of the hydrocarbons. Currently, the United States relies primarily on coal for generating electricity and on petroleum for transportation. Because of declining U.S. petroleum production, the country has had to import more than half of its crude oil since 1994. The cost of that oil adds to U.S. trade deficits. It is argued, therefore, that increased use of natural gas would have both environmental and economic benefits.

In recent years, natural gas has gained ground in the transportation field. In some places it powers buses, mail delivery trucks, and other vehicles. Since 1992, a handful of natural gas-powered sanitation trucks have operated in New York City. In addition, gas furnaces heated 57 percent of American homes in the 1990s, and natural gas was used as a fuel to produce electrical energy more cleanly and efficiently than oil or coal.

♦ *Describe recent efforts to reduce reliance on petroleum.*

Recycling. Technology has made it possible to increase the use of recycled paper. Several major American business firms have joined with the Environmental Defense Fund in a long-range project to further improve the production of paper made from recycled trash. Their goal is to reduce the use of landfills. A similar effort by the EDF and the McDonald's Corporation led to McDonald's decision to replace its plastic foam hamburger boxes with a less bulky paper wrapper. Paper products make up one third of all municipal trash.

The appearance and strength of recycled paper have been

problems that scientists are attempting to overcome. Recycled paper is often not as bright as virgin paper because not all the ink is removed in reprocessing. It is sometimes weaker, causing rolls of paper to break in printing presses. However, paper containing 10 percent wood fiber recovered from trash is now available, thus enabling publishers to use more recycled paper.

Peaceful Uses of Military Technology. Environmentalists have been aided since the end of the cold war by the willingness of both American and Russian military authorities to assist with scientific investigation. For example, the U.S. National Reconnaissance Office (NRO), which operates the country's spy satellites, began conducting a series of experiments. Its satellites peer at environmental targets—such as rivers and polar ice sheets—instead of missile silos. These experiments are putting military satellites to work for environmental research.

The Integrated Undersea Sound Surveillance System of the U.S. Navy consists of hydrophones placed around the globe. During the cold war, the system was used to monitor Soviet nuclear submarines. More recently, the system has been used to record underwater sounds from earthquakes, volcanoes, and whales. The biological researchers want to study regional differences in whale song and track whales' migrations.

In another environmental project, a U.S. Navy nuclear attack submarine carried five scientists and their equipment beneath the Arctic icecap. The scientists studied the movement of the ice, measured pollution from coastal runoff, charted the seafloor, and mapped circulation in the Arctic Ocean.

Even spy planes and satellites are used in environmental projects. Russia let West European scientists use a Russian high-altitude spy plane to measure the ozone layer. The Central Intelligence Agency offered its spy satellites for research on global climate change.

1. *What problems have had to be overcome in promoting the use of recycled paper?*
2. *Examine the graph (Figure 13.1) on page 273 and state which of the following are correct statements.*
    a. *Hydroelectric power was the main energy source used by Americans in the 1990s.*
    b. *The generation of electricity depended most heavily on the burning of coal in the 1990s.*

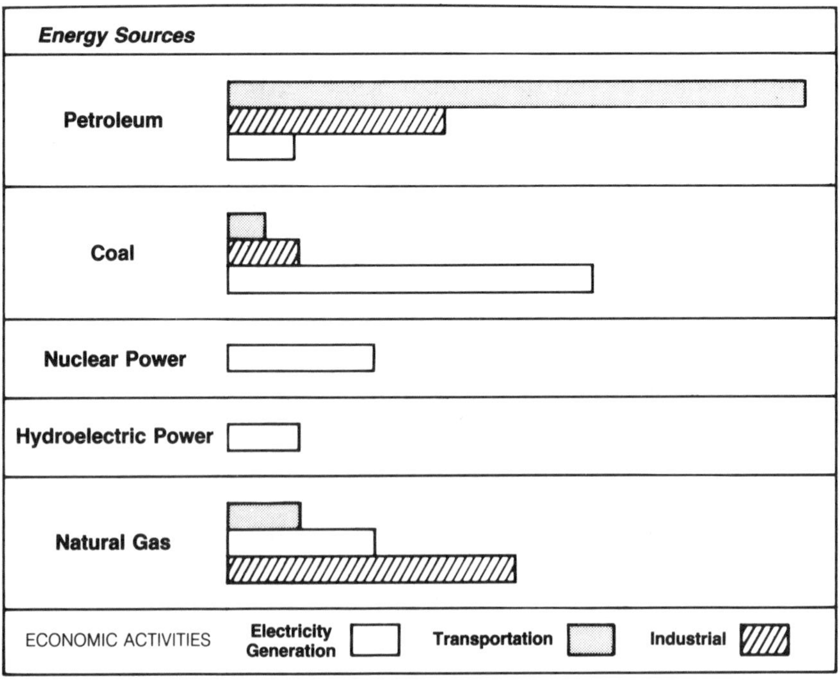

Energy Sources

Petroleum

Coal

Nuclear Power

Hydroelectric Power

Natural Gas

ECONOMIC ACTIVITIES Electricity Generation Transportation Industrial

Figure 13.1 United States Energy Consumption in the 1990s

c. *Petroleum was the main source of fuel for transportation in the 1990s.*
d. *Nuclear power was a significant source of power for transportation in the 1990s.*
e. *Americans used no natural gas in the 1990s.*

3. *Identify the major concerns of environmentalists in the 1990s.*
4. *Explain the significance of the following statements:*
   a. *Improvements in air quality depend upon better automobile design.*
   b. *Natural gas is cleaner and more efficient than oil or coal.*
   c. *Increased use of recycled paper reduces the use of landfills.*
   d. *The end of the cold war has benefited environmental research.*

Health and Medical Technology

Research, funding, and technological development in the 1990s have focused upon AIDS, cancer, heart disease, and other global threats to human life. Advances were made in these and other areas critical to the quality of life.

At international AIDS conferences in the 1990s, the difficulties of achieving early detection of the HIV virus, which causes AIDS, were a major topic of discussion. The ability of the virus to remain hidden in the blood cells for long periods of time has increased the difficulty of treatment. Researchers have concentrated efforts to combat AIDS on the development of antibodies. Of the 18 such drugs produced to date, AZT, produced by the Wellcome company, a British firm, has received the most attention. AZT, however, appears to do little for patients who have the HIV virus but have not developed symptoms. For people with AIDS, AZT has provided definite benefits. Researchers have recently begun to focus upon instances of natural immunity to the HIV virus in the hope of duplicating the biochemical process in those without the immunity.

To combat the debilitating memory loss of Alzheimer's disease, scientists at Cytotherapeutics Inc. in Rhode Island have developed a miniature biotech factory that is inserted directly into the brain. No bigger than a grain of rice, it is a capsule filled with thousands of cells that produce a brain hormone called *nerve growth factor* (NGF). (The lack of NGF causes the disease.) The capsule is made from a special plastic membrane that has been engineered to shield its cells from attack by the body's immune system yet permit NGF to escape. Testing with rats and primates is in progress.

A team of British doctors discovered a useful acid called ALA. This natural compound sensitizes cancer cells to light for a few hours. Used with ALA, a low-powered laser can destroy cancers near the surface of the skin without leaving a patient sensitive to sunlight for weeks. Research is continuing to determine correct drug dosages and laser intensities.

Lung cancer kills about one million people a year. The cancer must be detected while still small, before it spreads. Canadian researchers have experimented with photosensitive drugs that make tumors glow under ultraviolet (UV) light. While the drugs do not destroy cancer cells, the Canadians have discovered that all cells have a pale red glow in the presence of UV light. Healthy cells also emit green light. To help detect the difference, a group of doctors started a company called Xillix to build LIFE (lung-imaging fluorescent endoscope) machines. These machines will soon be tested in a number of American hospitals.

Scientists and corporate executives have predicted that the 1990s will usher in a new era of genes as drugs. This statement was made after an American researcher developed a genetic treatment for cystic fibrosis, a disease that attacks the lungs. The treatment involves the use of an engineered gene to stimulate the lungs to make a protein to fight the disease.

Beyond killer diseases, advances in technology have also led to assistance for the disabled. For those with hearing problems, a new type of hearing aid that is the equivalent of a contact lens has been developed by Resound Corporation, a California firm. The device uses a tiny magnet, called Earlens, that is placed directly on the eardrum. Held in place by a drop of oil, it amplifies the movements of the eardrum that produce the sensation of sound. The result is better quality hearing. The eardrum magnet is activated by signals from a tiny receiver that can be worn on a necklace or pinned to an undergarment.

The development of virtual reality computer technology may help blind people use computers even when they cannot see the visual display. For some purposes, the monitor screen can be replaced by headphones giving a three-dimensional impression of the sounds in a room. British researchers are experimenting with the idea of using sound coming from a particular direction. Changing a menu into a sound requires changes to some basic program instructions. Research is still at an early stage. Another part of this European Union project is an attempt to develop a "sonic mouse." Sounds would indicate whether or not the user had clicked on the correct icon on the display. Another possibility is to use a speech synthesizer to read a menu aloud.

1. *Describe two advances in medical technology that may reduce the threat of deadly diseases.*
2. *Explain how a gene might be used as a drug to treat a deadly disease.*
3. *Interview a doctor or another type of medical professional to get her or his reaction to recent developments in health and medical technology.*

Transportation Technology

Advances in technology have made possible the Concorde, a supersonic airplane, which travels at speeds faster than the speed of sound; the hydrofoil boat, which skims the water on a pillow of air; the monorail train, a railroad that runs through a tunnel under the English Channel connecting Britain to the

European continent; and continuing improvements in the safety and comfort of automobiles and the roads upon which they move. Research in the 1990s has focused especially on faster and safer air and road travel.

Commercial airline manufacturers in the United States and Europe are working to develop longer range supersonic airplanes. The supersonic market is big enough for only one design. The National Aeronautics and Space Administration (NASA) has been spending much more, on an American design, than has Aérospatiale, a French firm working on a European model. Whether the supersonic airliner of the future is an American or European design, it will have a range of approximately 12,000 miles, twice the range of the Anglo-French Concorde, which went into commercial service in 1976. A future supersonic plane will carry up to 300 passengers, triple the number now possible on a supersonic flight. Yet fares are expected to be no more than 20 percent higher than for conventional subsonic travel. Airspeed will be the same as it is on the Concorde—up to two and a half times the speed of sound. Flying time between Los Angeles and Tokyo will be just over four hours. The trip from New York to London will take three and a quarter hours.

For environmental and other reasons, American and Japanese auto manufacturers have been attempting to develop a marketable electric car. In an unusual collaboration, Ford, General Motors, and Chrysler have been working on an electric battery that would serve the entire industry. Size and weight have been the main design problem. Lead-acid batteries require 100 times the weight and 30 times the space of conventional gasoline tanks. In Japan, Nissan Motors has been designing a nickel-cadmium battery that provides 50 percent more power, but at eight times the price. Others are working on nickel metal-hydride, zinc-air, and lithium-ion batteries. Some of those battery types are already used in computers, but they are not produced commercially in sizes suitable for automobiles.

Ford and Chrysler produce experimental electric-powered vans that are used mainly by public utility companies. American models have more power and longer range than the European Environmental Concept Car designed by Volvo. In 1996 General Motors announced the EV-1, a two-seat passenger car that would go on sale in the fall in some western U.S. states. The EV-1 was said to have a range of 70 miles in the city and 90 miles on the highway.

The Big Three American auto manufacturers have also been examining ways to reduce auto weight to improve fuel economy. General Motors, Ford, and Chrysler have sponsored joint research on aluminum, magnesium, and metal matrix composites. The use of such metals, along with more plastics, may make future cars lighter. Ford designed two concept cars that rely heavily on light metals. The Synthesis 2010 uses aluminum for every major component and is a half-ton lighter than a Mercury Sable. An aluminized Sable is 400 pounds lighter.

In pursuit of increased safety, Britain's Rover Company has attempted to adapt fighter aircraft technology to its automobiles. It has been testing a small radar device as a collision-warning system. The radar beam scans the road in front of an automobile to detect oncoming vehicles, animals, pedestrians, or debris. It emits a sound to warn the driver in time to prevent a collision. The European Union is funding development of this project.

"Smart" roads may prove to be the most effective way to make automobile travel safer and highways less congested. Smart roads depend upon sensors. The most basic is a wire strip across the road that works like a switch when a vehicle's wheels go over it. More sophisticated, and more durable, are magnetic induction loops buried in the road. The first use of sensors was to time and coordinate traffic lights. They can also count vehicles and determine the speed of the traffic.

This information can be given to drivers. On the Tomei Expressway in Japan, the volume and speed of traffic are electronically monitored to give drivers instant warnings about traffic jams and accidents. These are displayed on electronic signs, which also advise on other things, such as when highway service stations are crowded.

Such information can now be transmitted directly to cars. In Britain, the Trafficmaster system keeps an eye on highway congestion. Its warnings, together with the speed of traffic, appear on maps on small screens attached to the dashboards of those who subscribe to the system. Navigation systems like these could easily link up with traffic data to show drivers where to find an alternative route.

Sensing technology is already used for law enforcement in automatic speed traps. On the I-95 Interstate highway, between Pennsylvania and Delaware, trucks are also being checked to make sure they are not overloaded. Road sensors weigh the trucks automatically as they drive along.

In an effort to reduce accidents from speeding, British traffic authorities have been conducting another kind of experiment. Speeding drivers face instant recognition and identification on giant screens above the highway if they exceed a 50-mile-per-hour speed limit. The screens flash the license number of the car and its precise speed. Then they warn the driver to slow down.

When the Channel Tunnel between Britain and the European continent opened in 1994, it was hailed as a major advance in travel. Soon after, a consortium of entrepreneurs and engineers said it was trying to raise money to build a railroad tunnel beneath the Bering Strait that divides Alaska from Russia. The tunnel would be 60 to 80 miles long—longer than any other tunnel in the world. (The Channel Tunnel is 31 miles long.) The Bering Strait Tunnel & Railroad Group estimated the project would cost $40 billion. Will the project ever be built? No one knows, but its chances are probably better than a similar Bering Strait tunnel that was announced in 1905—and never built.

- *Describe one technological improvement in each of the following areas:*

  a. air travel
  b. automobile design
  c. road safety

Space Exploration

The age of space exploration began in 1957, when the Soviets launched *Sputnik,* an orbiting space satellite. Advances in satellite technology have resulted in improved television, radio, and telephone communications; more accurate weather forecasting; and important information about other planets. Voyager 2's trip past Neptune in 1989 was one of the most important exploration missions.

During the 1960s, scientists labored to place people in space. In 1969, two American astronauts landed on the moon. In the 1970s and 1980s, however, the emphasis was on orbiting space stations. In those large spacecraft, astronaut-scientists have been able to conduct experiments in a gravity-free environment. The United States also invested heavily in reusable space shuttles. Those smaller craft are a blend of space capsule and airplane and are designed for repeated voyages.

The exploration of the planet Mars has been a major objective in the 1990s. Previously, only the *Viking* Mars lander had visited the planet, in 1977. An American robot probe, *Mars Observer*, was designed to spend two to six years in Mars orbit. It was to map the planet in far greater detail than ever before. However, in 1993, the $1 billion probe failed to orbit Mars and was lost in space. The Russians also tried to reach Mars, losing two spacecraft in the process.

The National Aeronautics and Space Administration (NASA) made plans to place a vehicle named *Pathfinder* on the surface of Mars in 1997. *Pathfinder*'s landing was to be cushioned by a cocoon of air bags. The vehicle was to send out a tiny rover named *Sojourner* to navigate the Martian surface, taking pictures and scooping up soil. Ten or more seismic and weather stations and rovers could be deployed late in the decade to provide a global network of monitors called *Mars Environment Survey* (MESUR). A similar effort may be mounted by the European Space Agency. The spacecraft and the landers were all to be controlled from Earth.

These investigations of Mars are part of a new era of international coordination of space exploration. Cooperation among the European Space Agency, Russia, Japan, and the United States was made possible by the end of the cold war. Also, rising costs made a sharing of technologies attractive.

The planet Jupiter has been another space target. *Galileo*, an American spacecraft launched in cooperation with Germany, carried cameras that showed the spectacular effects of Jupiter's collision with a flurry of comet fragments in 1994. *Galileo* later went into orbit around Jupiter to study the dense clouds in Jupiter's atmosphere and the planet's many moons.

Another key project of the 1990s was the joint construction of an international space platform that will be larger than a football field. It will include seven laboratories to be used by Americans, Europeans, Russians, Japanese, and Canadians. Facilities will allow a crew to stay aboard permanently. Space shuttles will come and go from the earth's surface. In 1995, a U.S. space shuttle carrying seven astronauts docked with Russia's three-person *Mir* space station. It was the first joint docking of U.S. and Russian spacecraft since a one-time event in 1975. More dockings were planned as the two nations developed hardware and skills for constructing the space platform. The first unit of the international facility was set for launch in November 1997. Completion was planned for 2002.

The development of improved telescopes has been another advance of space exploration technology in the 1990s. The *Very Long Baseline Array* (VLBA) went into operation in 1993. It is the largest astronomical instrument ever built. The VLBA consists of ten dish-shaped radio antennas, each 82 feet in diameter, extending in a chain from Hawaii, across North America, to the Virgin Islands. All ten antennas are synchronized by the federally funded *National Radio Astronomy Observatory* in New Mexico. They are made to function as a single radio telescope of gigantic size. This gives the VLBA far sharper vision than that of any other Earth-based telescope. It will reveal the details of distant galaxies as they existed billions of years ago and will also serve as a powerful tool for measuring geological changes, and perhaps for predicting earthquakes, here on Earth. One of the VLBA's first discoveries was a dense mass, equivalent to 40 million Suns, at the center of a distant galaxy. Those who made the discovery said it was almost certainly a black hole—a collapsed star so dense that not even light could escape its gravity.

1. *Explain why space exploration plans in the 1990s include close cooperation among nations.*
2. *Complete each sentence:*
   a. *The era of space exploration began in 1957 when ____.*
   b. *Among the benefits gained from orbiting satellites have been ____.*
   c. *Space stations make it possible for scientists to ____.*
   d. *Two planets being explored in the 1990s are ____ and ____.*
   e. *A major international project of the late 1990s has been construction of ____.*
3. *Many people oppose funding for space exploration projects. They say that governments should focus on solving people's problems on Earth. Write a letter to the editor of your school newspaper in which you answer these critics by stating your views.*

Chapter 13 Review

A. *Write the letter of the correct response.*

1. *A consequence of the "plastic purse" revolution might be to use high-tech microchip cards to (a) replace cash for most*

daily purchasing (b) develop new accounting systems (c) create new uses for plastic.

2. *In 1995, the U.S. government ordered a supercomputer to help with the study of (a) whale migration patterns (b) atmospheric pollution (c) nuclear bomb explosions.*
3. *The term "interactive media" refers to (a) computers that talk to their users (b) integration of computer and telecommunications technologies (c) replacement of computers by more advanced televisions.*
4. *Among the advances in telecommunications technology in the 1990s have been (a) better cellular, digital, and satellite communications (b) shortwave radio transmission (c) the ability to teleport objects to satellites orbiting in space.*
5. *Besides distributing news, the purpose of a news tablet includes allowing people to (a) get information from distant libraries (b) cover news stories for local television stations (c) translate the news into various languages.*
6. *The term "sustainable development" refers to (a) logging and mining (b) economic development that preserves the environment (c) preserving endangered species.*
7. *A measure to reduce atmospheric pollution in the 1990s has been (a) reducing the rate of production of automobiles (b) promoting global use of natural gas as the sole energy source (c) improving automotive technology.*
8. *A major advance in medical technology has been (a) the use of genes as drugs to fight diseases such as cystic fibrosis (b) the discovery of a drug that can prevent AIDS (c) the elimination of all hearing disorders.*
9. *Smart roads use techniques such as electronic sensors, signs, and computerized cards to (a) identify drivers for security purposes (b) control pollution by checking on carbon emissions from vehicles (c) provide drivers with information about speed limits, congestion, and the availability of service stations.*
10. *A major space project in the years just ahead will be (a) constructing a large space laboratory for international use (b) landing astronauts on Jupiter (c) running shuttle flights to the moon.*

B. *Reread "The Expanding World of Telecommunications" on pages 264–267. Then answer the questions below.*

1. *What proposals have been made for global communications systems using satellites?*

2. *What sorts of new services might such a system provide?*
3. *How has telephone technology been improved outside the United States?*

C. *Reread "The Technology of Environmental Protection" on pages 268–272 and do the following:*

1. *Explain why the buildup of carbon dioxide in the atmosphere is an environmental problem.*
2. *Discuss the measures taken to reduce or prevent this problem.*

Unit III Review

A. *Study the list of nations below. Use information found in Unit III to complete the sentences that follow.*

Britain	*Russia*
Japan	*France*
Canada	*Sweden*
United States	*Austria*
Mexico	*Finland*

1. *A nation that was struggling to introduce free market practices in the 1990s was ____.*
2. *The nations that joined the European Union in 1995 were ____, ____, and ____.*
3. *A nation that experienced a drastic fall in the value of its currency in December, 1994, is ____.*
4. *An Asian nation that had a global trade surplus in the 1990s was ____.*
5. *The nations that signed the North American Free Trade Agreement are ____, ____, and ____.*
6. *Two longtime members of the European Union are ____ and ____.*

B. *Review Chapter 11 and do the following:*

1. *Describe the G-7 and how it operates.*
2. *State the changes brought to Europe by the Maastricht Treaty.*

3. *List arguments for and against NAFTA.*
4. *Tell why OPEC has trouble getting its members to agree on how much oil to produce.*

C. *Review Chapter 12 and answer the questions below.*

1. *List three developing nations that have had high rates of growth in recent years.*
2. *Explain why the economies of those nations are growing.*
3. *Tell what is meant by the term ''new economic order.''*
4. *Give pros and cons of the new economic order.*
5. *Explain how changes in global trade and investment have contributed to unemployment in Europe.*
6. *Identify the most dynamic Asian economies.*

D. *Use information from Unit III to write a brief essay on ONE of the following topics:*

European Economic Unity
Global Economic Development: The World Bank and the International Monetary Fund
The Computer Revolution

UNIT IV

BEYOND THE 20TH CENTURY

Consideration of global conditions beyond the year 2000 must be in the form of questions. For example: Will economics shape the 21st century, as two world wars and the cold war did the 20th century? What does the future hold for the impoverished nations of the Third World? Will the continued growth of technology lead to improvement in the quality of life? Will overpopulation and environmental destruction continue to endanger planet Earth?

There can be no certain answers to those questions. However, examination of current trends and projections can provide an interesting view of a possible future.

Chapter 14

The Political and Economic Future

By the 1990s, the United States was the world's sole military superpower. Yet Americans felt challenged by Japan's strong position in international markets. During this period, Europe established the world's largest trade bloc, the Middle East remained a vital source of fuel, and the developing nations of Asia and Latin America had the highest rates of economic growth. In Africa, however, poverty, drought, disease, starvation, and political upheaval served as barriers to economic growth.

For some historians, such trends indicate that economic issues will be the key to the 21st century. Status and power in the international community will depend upon a nation's productivity and ability to compete.

New Realities: Peace, Democracy, and Trade

The concentration on economics will be made possible by the achievement of global peace in the 21st century. Ending the threat of big-power nuclear war in the 1990s was a major step in this direction. Also, it is likely that, in the 21st century, there will be more democracies in the world than ever before. The democratic governments established in the 1990s will be in the majority in the Americas, Europe, and Asia. Historically, democratic nations do not make war on one another. Therefore, international conflicts should become a thing of the past in most areas of the globe. The armed forces of the democracies will be reduced to the minimum necessary for the defense of each nation or group of nations. The United States, Britain, and several other countries have already begun major reductions, preferring to depend on smaller, professional military forces.

Along with militarism, imperialism will also be curbed. Competition for foreign sources of raw materials, for example, will subside because fewer such materials will be needed for the manufacture of 21st-century products. Even oil will lose its strategic importance. Solar power and controlled nuclear fusion are expected to become the energy sources of the future. As the need for oil declines, the Arab states of the Middle East will become poorer and less stable.

In some regions, ultranationalists and petty dictators will continue to cause local wars and violent upheavals. The major powers, however, will be able to ignore them unless they seriously threaten their neighbors with aggression or genocide. When that happens, the United Nations will be able to take military and economic action or will authorize its member nations to do so, as was done in the Persian Gulf War. If the U.N. does not act, the United States and other nations that share its concern will have the capability to intervene. The willingness of the United States to play the role of "global cop" was indicated in the 1990s by American actions in the Persian Gulf, Somalia, and Bosnia.

We can expect cooperation with the U.N. to become the standard policy of all nations. Using the U.N.'s resources will be essential to solve such global problems as environmental destruction.

The United States will remain the dominant military superpower in a less heavily armed world. Although its forces will be smaller, high-tech weapons and a powerful nuclear arsenal will enable the U.S. to protect its friends, especially from dictators armed with nuclear weapons.

Competition among nations will be economic in nature. The weapons used will be growth rates, investments, trade blocs, imports, and exports. We can expect nationalism to be diminished by the steady growth of multinational trading blocs around the world.

The combined economic power of the European nations will increase dramatically in the 21st century. Despite the downturns and unemployment of the 1990s, the European Union may expand to 20 nations or more by the year 2000. Sometime in the 21st century, it appears likely that the Czech Republic,

Key to the Future?

Hungary, and Poland will be able to join the EU. Eventually, Ukraine, Russia, and most of Eastern Europe may have some form of associate membership in the EU.

1. *Explain why you AGREE or DISAGREE with the belief of some historians that the world in the 21st century will be shaped by economic issues.*
2. *State two reasons why the world might be more peaceful in the 21st century.*
3. *Complete the following sentences:*
   a. *The Arab states of the Middle East may become poorer and less stable because ____.*
   b. *European economic power will increase dramatically because ____.*

New Realities: East and West

It will be in the interest of the industrialized nations of the West to assist the emerging democracies of Eastern Europe to become stable and prosperous. As Western investments and technical assistance help to increase employment and the standard of living in the former Communist nations, East Europeans will be motivated to turn away from ultranationalism and ethnic violence. Economic benefits arising from association with the EU and from the formation of smaller regional free trade groups will dispel resentment of foreigners.

Nationalist or religious conflicts, such as those that ripped apart Bosnia-Herzegovina in the late 20th century, may continue to occur, but with less frequency. It must also be expected that countries like Bulgaria, Albania, and, possibly, Romania may not be able to successfully develop market economies or democratic governments. Reliance upon authoritarian leaders and government economic control may continue, as former Communists gain power under new political party names and slogans.

Among the republics of the former Soviet Union, the territorial and ethnic disputes that mushroomed in the 1990s may continue into the 21st century. Eventually, settlements may be agreed upon between Armenia and Azerbaijan, for example, over which nation controls which ethnic enclave, or between Russia and the people of Chechnya over how much autonomy should be given to that non-Russian region. Some historians regard the wars that raged in the Commonwealth of Independent States in the 1990s as the unavoidable upheavals of a period of political and economic transition. They believe that stability will come as the republics become more concerned with economic development and less involved in territorial disputes.

We can expect Russia to attempt to extend its influence over the smaller republics, especially in the areas of foreign policy and trade. That may cause competition with the United States, which began its own efforts to build up influence in the mineral-rich Transcaucasus (Georgia, Armenia, Azerbaijan) region. The administration of President Clinton assigned diplomats and security specialists to help resolve conflicts between the republics and ethnic or religious minorities that are seeking to break away.

In the Middle East, the success of the peace process under way in the 1990s may put an end to the Arab-Israeli conflict. Faced with increased threats to their security by the violence of militant Islamists, the moderate Arab governments may require more assistance from the United States. This will more likely be given if a peace with Israel is negotiated. Also, if predictions about the decline of oil as an energy source are accurate, then stronger commercial ties with Israel will be badly needed by the Arab nations in the 21st century.

1. *Describe the major changes likely to come to Eastern Europe after the year 2000.*
2. *Which statements are predictions made by historians about Europe and the Middle East in the 21st century?*
   a. *Ultranationalism will fade as economic cooperation improves standards of living.*
   b. *Bulgaria and Albania are the countries most likely to develop democracy and market economies.*
   c. *Russia and the United States will compete for influence in the Transcaucasus region.*
   d. *The Arab-Israeli conflict will grow worse.*
   e. *Oil will decline in importance as an energy source.*

New Realities: Japan, China, and Asia's "Four Tigers"

Economists expect rapid economic development and high growth rates to continue in Asia in the 21st century. Certain factors, however, may combine to temper Japan's economic growth.

The "samurai work ethic" of the Japanese may begin to weaken. New generations of workers may be unwilling to work the long hours of 20th-century corporate employees. Many have already begun to indicate a desire for more leisure time, larger homes, and a greater share of the wealth they create. The Japanese of the future may be unwilling to remain "poor people in a rich country," as some now call themselves. To respond to a desire for increased consumption of consumer goods at home, Japanese leaders will have to increase imports. That will lessen the disparity between Japan's exports and imports and reduce the nation's huge trade surpluses.

Competition for Japan is already building up in Asia. South Korea, Taiwan, Hong Kong, and Singapore—the Four Tigers—will be Japan's rivals, as well as its trading partners, in the 21st century. In the 1990s, they have had large deficits in their trade with Japan. In the future, however, they may be less willing to buy from a Japan that does not, in turn, buy a great deal from them. More importantly, those four nations may become alternative suppliers of manufactured goods to China and other Asian nations, thus cutting into Japan's markets.

Economists and historians are predicting the collapse of communism in China and North Korea after 2000. This will make possible the unification of Korea, which will then compete even more strongly with Japan; and the linkage of Taiwan's economic power with that of Hong Kong and China in a unified economic zone. Should this happen, the economic balance of power in Asia will be greatly changed in the 21st century.

If the United States reduces its military forces in the Pacific, as some Asians feared in the 1990s, China would become the strongest military power in the region. That would force Japan to change its constitution in order to permit it to rebuild its armed forces. Other Asian nations would continue the process of developing regional security arrangements to deal with aggression.

1. *Define the Japanese "samurai work ethic."*
2. *In what way are the "Four Tigers" a threat to Japan's economic dominance of Asia?*
3. *Suggest some major political and economic changes that may develop in Asia after 2000.*

New Realities: The Third World

The outlook for the world's poorest countries is not favorable. Although the U.N.'s effort to stabilize Angola may be successful, the misery caused by civil war, drought, disease, and famine in so many parts of Africa may prove to be beyond solution. Elsewhere, the picture is also grim. India, for example, will have a population of 1.4 billion people by 2025. Given the current state of its economy and the periodic disorder caused by religious conflict, it is unlikely that its output of goods and services will increase enough to eliminate that nation's poverty.

To achieve prosperity, a developing country must maintain a high level of economic growth for decades, while limiting increases in its population. Few of the poorer countries will be able to meet those requirements. By 2050, the world's population is expected to double, from 5.5 billion at present to 11 billion. During this period, global production of goods and services will have quadrupled. However, almost all of the population growth will take place in the less developed countries, while most of the increased output will occur in the industrial democracies.

In addition, developed countries are already buying less from the Third World and more from one another. In the 1990s, trading by Europe, North America, and the fast-growing economies of Asia accounted for 75 percent of global trade. And agreements between the largest industrial powers that have been lowering trade barriers have tended to favor industrial nations over developing ones. Continuation of such trends into the 21st century will result in growing prosperity for the richer countries while the poorer nations continue to struggle.

- *Explain why you AGREE or DISAGREE with the following statements:*

1. *The developed nations should grant special trading privileges to developing nations to help lift them out of poverty.*
2. *The problems of the developing nations will not be solved in the 21st century.*

Joining the Big Players?

New Realities: The United States

A number of factors will ensure that the United States will be one of the great powers of the 21st century. Its military strength, its 20 percent share of the world's gross domestic product, and its leadership in such high-tech fields as microprocessors and biotechnology make U.S. dominance likely. Furthermore, implementation of the North American Free Trade Agreement will increase the economic power of the U.S. and heighten its ability to compete with the European Union and Japan.

However, there is much to worry informed Americans. For the period 1985–95, the country's cumulative trade deficit amounted to more than $1 trillion. The national debt, in 1995, stood at almost $5 trillion. To pay its bills, the United States must reduce imports, invest more money in domestic economic growth, and greatly increase exports. Failure to do so will result in rising inflation, growing unemployment, and a loss of economic power.

Among America's greatest problems in the late 20th century have been faltering industries, too little investment, and a crisis in education. In the future, workers will need better education and more technological skills. Yet American schools have been called the least successful in the Western world. In addition, the U.S. has ranked relatively low in spending on nonmilitary research and development. Scientists and educators have warned that such factors may place U.S. science and engineering at a disadvantage in the 21st century.

It is entirely possible that Americans will address these problems successfully. The end of the cold war has made more resources available to do so. America's status as a world leader in the 21st century depends upon the finding of solutions.

1. *State the reasons why the status of the United States as a world leader in the 21st century might be jeopardized.*
2. *Complete the following sentences:*
   a. *The United States will remain a global power because of ____.*
   b. *Failure of the U.S. to deal with its trade deficit and national debt would ____.*
   c. *Implementation of the North American Free Trade Agreement will ____.*

Chapter 14 Review

A. *Write the letter of the correct response.*

1. *Historians have claimed that the 21st century will be shaped by (a) military conflicts (b) economic issues (c) competition for colonies.*
2. *After 2000, most countries in the Americas, Europe, and Asia will be governed (a) as democracies (b) by petty dictators (c) by totalitarian regimes.*
3. *The main energy sources of the future will most likely be (a) oil and other petroleum products (b) coal and hydroelectric power (c) solar power and controlled nuclear fusion.*
4. *In an era of general peace, the United States will remain the (a) sole economic superpower (b) sole military superpower (c) major source of technological knowledge.*
5. *The largest trading bloc of the early 21st century will be (a) the European Union (b) the North American Free Trade Agreement (c) the Chinese Economic Area.*
6. *In the Commonwealth of Independent States, there may be future competition for influence between (a) Russia and South Africa (b) Russia and the United States (c) the United States and Israel.*
7. *Historians have predicted the fall of communism, after 2000, in (a) China and North Korea (b) China and South Korea (c) Japan and North Korea.*
8. *In the early 21st century, Japan will face serious competition from (a) Singapore and Taiwan (b) India (c) North Korea.*
9. *A Third World nation for which a population of 1.4 billion people by 2025 has been predicted is (a) Mexico (b) the Philippines (c) India.*
10. *The future economic status of the United States may be threatened by a crisis in (a) the computer industry (b) education (c) medical research.*

B. *Use information in Chapter 14 to explain the following 21st-century newspaper headlines.*

ARAB NATIONS CUT PRICE OF OIL

JAPANESE WORKERS DEMAND CHANGE

EUROPEAN UNION REACHES OUT TO FORMER COMMUNIST NATIONS

AMERICAN WORKERS AND COLLEGE GRADUATES UNABLE TO COMPETE

Unit IV Review

A. *Select ONE of the themes listed below. Use information from Unit IV to write an essay that answers the following questions:*

- *What might happen in this area in the 21st century?*
- *What 20th-century events or developments indicate what the future might bring in this area?*

THEMES

1. *Economics shapes the 21st century*
2. *The growth of European economic power after 2000*
3. *Changed conditions in the Middle East*
4. *Economic patterns in Asia and the Third World*
5. *Challenges for the United States in the 21st century*

B. *Use information from Unit IV to define each of the following terms:*

1. *overpopulation*
2. *environmental destruction*
3. *global cop*
4. *multinational trading bloc*

INDEX